More than a century ago, one man with deep convictions and a country with benign ideals combined to create a place where black self-emancipation, black freedom, could flourish. The man was William King, a slaveowner and Presbyterian minister educated to the stern moralities of Edinburgh. The country was Canada and *Look to the North Star* is a vivid account of Buxton, the community in western Ontario which the Reverend Mr. King and his slaves founded in 1849 as a haven for black fugitives, both slave and free, in the harsh years before the Civil War.

William King strongly believed in the rights of the black man and his potential for full manhood in freedom; the history of Buxton stands as a confirmation and continuation of King's beliefs. The example of the village and its wide and varied achievements were finally admired by many (including Samuel Gridley Howe and Horace Greeley), but the early days were not easy. The idea of Buxton met opposition from residents of the region; King and his followers faced the same prejudice and racism we know today. The protection and support of Lord Elgin, then Governor-General of Canada, strengthened their courage and determination. Undaunted by irrational attacks, King and his supporters insisted on their legal rights, and the community was soon established as a stable and important economic force in the area. The fugitives made good use of their varied skills, and in Buxton rose the first brickworks and sawmill in the county. Because of King's talent as a teacher and his emphasis on the importance of education, Buxton's school was the best in the vicinity, and the settlement's white neighbors soon asked permission to send their children; the result was the first integrated public school in North America.

The men of Buxton were the first to demonstrate black political power in North America; time after time in the middle years of the nineteenth century their bloc voting assured the election of their member of Parliament. During the Civil War many of the men of Buxton returned to fight in the Union armies, and after the war many returned to the South to place their hard-won skills as doctors, teachers, ministers, and political leaders at the service of black communities. Congressman James Thomas Rapier, Dr. Anderson R. Abbott, and Thomas W. Stringer were Buxton men who served the ravaged South with tireless devotion. In their convictions and self-reliance the men of Buxton are the forerunners of SNCC, Julian Bond, and other leaders of the black community today.

Buxton in Canada today remains a community proud of the roles it has played in both American and Canadian life. Now a Canadian Historical Shrine, the settlement still rings its Liberty Bell, the bell which sounded on the safe arrival of every fugitive who sought the freedom of Buxton.

The author, Victor Ullman, is a former newspaperman who has devoted years to the research for this book, seeking out original source material in Louisiana, Ohio, Scotland, Ireland, and Canada. In addition to his writing for magazines and television, Mr. Ullman has been a member of the faculty of the University of Toledo. He is now at work on a biography of Martin Delany, a great figure in the black history of the United States.

☆

LOOK TO THE NORTH STAR

A Life of William King

☆

LOOK TO THE NORTH STAR

A Life of William King

BY VICTOR ULLMAN

BEACON PRESS : BOSTON

SAUNDERS OF TORONTO

Library of Congress catalog card number: 69–14606

Beacon Press books are published under the
auspices of the Unitarian Universalist Association

Published in Canada by Saunders of Toronto Limited
Printed in the United States of America

☆

To Frieda and Don, in loving memory

☆

CONTENTS

☆

ACKNOWLEDGMENTS

THIS ACCOUNT has been taken from literally thousands of letters, notes, reminiscences, documents both official and unofficial, and the memories of descendants of fugitive slaves in Canada. Much reliance has been placed on King's own attitudes, as revealed in his handwritten autobiography and diaries, and these have been quoted extensively. On the recorded facts of Canadian Negro history, any investigator would be helpless without the findings of such pioneers as Landon, Farrell, and Simpson.

Without doubt there will be continued investigation of Canadian Negro history because the field points essentially to a sharp contrast between countries. The history of the Negro in the United States is incomplete without study of the examples set by Canada.

Perhaps the greatest asset to such future study is in Ottawa, where the Canadian National Archives are under the direction of W. Kaye Lamb, Dominion Archivist. This institution sets a standard of interest and efficiency which could well be emulated by similar historical repositories in other countries. In it may be found, among other treasures, the

King papers, consisting of the original autobiography and much of King's correspondence with leaders of the Free Church of Scotland and with high British officials active in the African Aid Society. The collection also has many invaluable scraps of notes and speeches—many of the documents pertaining to King's own slaves.

All across Ontario there are documentary bits and pieces. In Montreal there are the Presbyterian College archives of the Canadian Church, gathered by patient work over the years by Dr. Neil G. Smith. In Toronto at the public library there is the Baldwin Room, presided over by Miss Edith Firth, with its remarkable collection of otherwise unavailable books and original letters.

In London, at the University of Western Ontario there is the "Treasure Room," most aptly named. This constantly growing repository in the university library is an outgrowth of the pioneer work dating to the beginning of this century initiated by Dr. Fred Landon, its retired head. No historical work on the Canadian Negro is possible without incurring obligation to Dr. Landon, whose enthusiasm and eagerness to assist have not abated in half a century. Such young researchers as Professor Donald Simpson and others have been encouraged to add their original contributions.

In Chatham, which was the capital of the fugitive slaves' havens, its brand new public library, directed by Miss Louise Schryver, has not only original documents but also an invaluable file of Canada West's old newspapers (chiefly on microfilm) as well as an ever-helpful and hospitable staff. Also in Chatham is the Chatham-Kent Museum, headed by Mrs. Wressell, with its various personal journals, correspondence, and the like left by early settlers.

At the University of Windsor, in Windsor, Ontario, may be found much of the story of the fugitive slaves whose first breath of free air was along those shores. Also to be found at this university are both the work and the presence of Dr. J. A. K. Farrell, whose fundamental study of the Negroes of Chatham is not only a remarkable contribution but most refreshing reading.

In Louisiana, where the original documents concerning King and the genesis of the Buxton settlement may be found, the archives are another treasure trove concerning the other side of the slavery coin. V. L. Bedsole, archivist of Louisiana State University, and his most knowledgeable staff are willing guides to a vast collection of ante-bellum material. In West Feliciana Parish, at St. Francisville, the energetic and delightful man-wife publishing team, the Robinsons, have files in the shop of their weekly newspaper *The Democrat* containing copies of the old Feliciana press dating to the first newspaper. In East Feliciana Parish, at the Courthouse in Clinton, is John Phares, a descendant of the family of King's first wife, who not only steers one through genealogical mazes, but right to the many original legal papers kept there.

Like Dr. Landon in Canada, Mrs. Dorothy Porter in the United States renders a distinct service to her country, and has done so for many years, by her dedication to the preservation of the materials of Negro history. There is no historian who is not in her debt, and it is because of her efforts that the Moorland and Spingarn collections at Howard University in Washington, D.C., are so invaluable.

I am personally indebted, in addition to all the above, to sprightly and energetic Beth Simmons of London, Ontario, who, while studying in London, England, found so much of the King material there and in Edinburgh, and found, in addition, children born to the original slave settlers at Buxton.

My greatest debt is, of course, to the wonderful friends in North Buxton itself, who searched their memories and attics for me over a number of years. Among all these friends I owe particular gratitude to Mr. and Mrs. Arthur Alexander, whose years of teaching generations of children in the Buxton School made them a ready mine of information; Dorothy Shreve, the efficient executive of the North Buxton historical group; Arlie and LaVerne Robbins and their son Matt, who all shared their knowledge of the village; Cleta Morris, the eager amanuensis of the proud Buxton history; Ira Shadd who always knows where to find everybody except the young members of his North Buxton Band; Lewis King (not a descendant), clerk of Raleigh Township, whose deep interest in the Reverend William King opened all his records; Lloyd Broadbent, directly descended from the earliest white settlers of the Talbot Road; and the many others who, like Earl Prince, showed me their family records.

The years have taken other friends in North Buxton, such as Mrs. Laura Garel, the last surviving fugitive slave; Flavius Shadd, one of the earliest born in the settlement; Harriet and Millard Hatchett, who spoke so lovingly of their fugitive slave parents, and sang so beautifully the hymns written by Harriet; and Bill Newby, the beloved cobbler who repaired children's sorrows as well as their shoes.

All across the United States are members of the King family whose generous sharing of their personal archives and information made possible so much. There are Mrs. Florence Kemmer, Maumee, Ohio; Mrs. C. W. Forest, Wichita, Kansas; Mrs. Jayne G. Hoffman, Sequim, Washington; and Miss Josephine Rupp of Kansas City, Missouri.

All of the above, and others unnamed, assisted over many years in placing before me the materials from which the account is taken. But without enthusiastic assistance in the search for information, endless deciphering of the handwriting on original material, and equally endless typing, this book might never have been completed. That assistance was given by my wife Louise.

—VICTOR ULLMAN

☆

LOOK TO THE NORTH STAR

A Life of William King

☆

PREFACE

I MET the darkskinned people of North Buxton for the first time on Labor Day, 1949. I watched the Homecoming Parade beside an elderly Negro lady from Ohio, not more than a hundred miles away.

"Why do we come to North Buxton? I guess it's to borrow a little peace of soul from these people. We go home better prepared to find solutions to the problems of our race," she said.

On my other side was a young Negro man who had just passed the Michigan bar examinations.

"I regain my self-respect when I visit with them," he said quietly. "They have pride."

Two weeks before, I had been in the tenements of Harlem. Two years before, I had been in the Delta cotton country of Mississippi. Thirteen years before, and during the intervening years, when I had been in a peonage stockade in Cross County, Arkansas, and in Tennessee, North Carolina, Georgia, Alabama, Louisiana—the South as well as the border states—I met Negroes. With the exception of a jail population in Meridian, Mississippi, and the stockade slaves in Arkansas, who found a bond of misery, I met suspicion, outright and surly antagonism, sometimes a deriding hatred.

Yet, in North Buxton, I forgot even my white skin at their dinner tables, in their churches, and on the ball field. I forgot their dark skins at parties, over a hamburg or a corn roast. Except in color, they bore no relationship to any of the Negroes I had ever met as a stranger and a white man, all of them "below the line," meaning the United States border, not the Mason-Dixon line. Why were they different?

I went back down the Center Road to St. Andrews Church and once more looked at the monument erected there that summer. I read the inscription again:

1949
In Memory of
REV. Wm. KING
who founded
BUXTON SETTLEMENT
1849
And Built
ST. ANDREWS CHURCH
1858

Who was William King? I did not know, and I was to learn that few historians even mention his name. Yet in North Buxton I had seen a more significant monument than the one before me. I had seen men, women, and children of all shades who held their heads high and, without saying a word, told me "I am your equal and you are mine."

Who was William King? A man who proclaimed self-emancipation for his Negroes fifteen years before Abraham Lincoln proclaimed their emancipation. A century later, William King's doctrine was successful and Abraham Lincoln's was not even approaching realization.

Later that Labor Day, 1949, I sat on a stool in Erwin Steel's hamburger, soda pop, and euchre center chatting with the tired and happy celebrants. There was a sudden silence and I heard it. A bell was tolling from down the Middle Road, from the steeple of St. Andrews Church. Erwin stood rigid, his brown face reverent.

"That's our Liberty Bell," he said. "It reminds us."

It reminds these Canadian Negroes of their forefathers who were slaves or so-called "free" Negroes who "followed the North Star" to a land where they too could share in democracy.

I am not an historian, but somebody must tell the story of William King. It begins with the pealing of another Liberty Bell.

☆

PART ONE: WILLIAM KING'S THREE AMERICAS

I : THE FIRST AMERICA

MONDAY, JUNE 11, 1833, was to be another bright, cloudless day, and young William King was awakened when the sun first sparkled on the broad reaches of the Delaware River.

A bell was pealing, now musically as its full volume was brought down to the waterfront by the light and shifting breeze, then as a distant echo.

From the deck of the brig *Dorothy* at anchor off Kaighin's Point William could see the mapled streets leading up the hill to a shining steeple. On this Monday morning, people were streaming up those streets, and carriages too. They were all heading toward the bell, the Liberty Bell in Independence Hall at Market and Second Streets.

The *Dorothy* had dropped anchor early on the Sabbath, and there was a Quaker quiet in the city. It had been a long day after the swift thirty-day passage from Londonderry on the *Dorothy* with Captain Durnys commanding, and with twenty-year-old William King as supercargo. William had his manifests ready and was eager to find the commission merchants and sell his cargo of potatoes.

Fortunately, the customs and health officials hurried aboard early that Monday morning. They quickly cleared the ship and its personnel for landing but informed William that he could not sell his family's potatoes that day. It was an American holiday. None of the commission merchants were open. William followed the officials ashore and up the hill.

There was a parade, and brighter than the sun were the resplendent uniforms of the Philadelphia fire companies. There were spit-and-polish soldiers in ceremonial continental blues, prancing horses and bedecked officers riding them, open carriages with somber-clad dignitaries. Bunting and flags—the latter with 24 stars now—drifted from the top stories and roofs of the houses and buildings.

Rivaling the call of the Liberty Bell were the blares of brass bands from Germantown and the rolls of military drums from Washington. Only by the shouts of the crowd could William tell who was passing and what was happening.

First there was the President of the United States, "Old Hickory," Andrew Jackson, the hero of New Orleans in 1815, of Florida in 1818, of the common man in the elections of 1828 and 1832, and—just three months before—the iron hand that stopped South Carolina from seceding.

Then came sundry officials and the parade-ground soldiers led by the commander of the Army, General Winfield Scott, "Old Fuss and Feathers," who was another hero of the War of 1812 and the Indian Wars.

The procession wound on, and the Liberty Bell still proclaimed triumph. Behind General Scott, their captor, rode two Indians, one in full chief's panoply and the other a medicine man. They were Chief Black Hawk and his prophet, White Cloud, who had surrendered to Scott just the year before at Fort Armstrong on Rock Island, Illinois. They were visible evidence to all Philadelphia that the last Indian confederacy in defense of their land was ended. Their presence in the parade signified that the westward flood of pioneers could now pass the prairies beyond the Mississippi in comparative safety. A maximum of whisky and a minimum of warfare had won through to the Pacific.

William King had landed in his first America at the height of its turbulent second revolution. What he had watched on his first day ashore was a triumphal celebration which had begun in Washington, continued in Baltimore, was to blaze for four days and four nights in Philadelphia and explode in New York. The Federalists were finished, defeated twice by the votes of the mechanics, the millworkers, the common folk who jostled William in the Philadelphia streets. Ten days before, on June 1, 1833, President Jackson had appointed as his third Secretary of the Treasury a young Philadelphia lawyer who was committed to breaking the stranglehold on the country's economy held by the Bank of the United States. A year before "Andy" Jackson had opened the West to land—so much land—land to be owned and tilled and kept forever by new Americans who had owned nothing but their labor.

The young man from Ulster County, Ireland, confessed later that he could not understand all this resounding display, much less appreciate its significance. To him the five-hour procession and the lengthy speeches, the people in their holiday dress and the bands in their ornate uniforms, were a demonstration of what he had heard about this raw and restless country back home. He could not know that he had arrived during a moment of climactic change in American history. Just two years before, Charles Carroll, the last surviving signer of the Declaration of Independence, had told another young newcomer to America, Alexis de Tocqueville, that "A mere Democracy is but a mob. The government of England is the only one that suits us. If we get along with ours, it's because each year we can push our innovators into the west." Two years later that statement was no longer valid.

The sonorous peal of the Liberty Bell on that bright June morning in Philadelphia was William King's introduction to three Americas—the commercialized East, the pioneering West, and the slave South. Each of William King's Americas was to be a preparation for his ultimate mission.

The young man was impressive in appearance. After a month at sea his leonine mop of thick black hair flowed from a broad forehead almost to his shoulders. His face was craggy, a strong jutting of nose and chin crowned by bushy eyebrows over large and steady eyes with coal black pupils. Just an inch under six feet, he was broad-shouldered and heavily muscled. His sisters described him as a boy always sure in stride and motions, a self-reliant and efficient youngster, and even at the age of twenty ready to assume leadership and to assert it most pragmatically.

William was ready and ripe for this raucous, rebellious kind of America. He was only two months away from the seething rebellion by the commoners of England and Scotland which resulted in Britain's first Reform Bill extending suffrage and eliminating some of the "Rotten Borough" representation in Parliament. With almost all of the other students of Glasgow University, he had marched the streets clad in "scarlet cloaks with wings instead of sleeves that hung from their shoulders, something like Grecian togas," as he reported. All through 1831 and most of 1832 William had joined the other students and professors in demonstrations and protest meetings, demanding support of Lord John Russell's reforms. His own professor in Greek, Sir Samuel Sandford, an Englishman who had been a gold medalist at Oxford, organized and chaired most of the Glasgow meetings, and William boasted that he attended them all.

When, in October 1831, the Crown quailed before the revolutionary temper of the commoners and the House of Lords accepted a mild suffrage reform, the students of Glasgow University celebrated the victory and continued their marches and meetings, beginning a new crusade. And that was how William became an abolitionist before he had ever spoken to a Negro.

Throughout the winter of 1832—in fact until he had graduated from the University with honors—William had continued to follow Sir Samuel Sandford to the streets and to the meetings. One series of debates on slavery lasted twelve consecutive nights, and William attended each one. Sir Samuel was chairman and preceded the speakers with a discourse on the history of slavery. Then the speakers began their marathon battle. In this historic series, the speaker for the West Indian planters against emancipation was Peter Bostwick. Speaking for the British Anti-Slavery Society was George Thompson, the leading English abolitionist orator of his day.

The debates influenced William beyond his merely taking to the streets with the other students. No doubt the speakers themselves failed to affect the thinking of this abolitionist Glasgow audience, but they at least started William in a course of study. He began to read the writings and speeches of the British emancipationists during the slave trade debates before 1807, and the later spokesmen such as William Wilberforce, Thomas Clarkson, and Sir Thomas Fowell Buxton.

He was in New York in September 1833 when the news came that Sir Thomas had at last been successful in Parliament with his annual emancipation bill. It had been signed by King William IV on August 18 and slavery was banished from the West Indies, the last of the British colonies to abolish it.

But Glasgow's seething rebellions had been only a maturing for young William, the tempering of convictions which he had held since the age of fourteen. Glasgow merely gave him that habit of protest which marked all of his life except the spiritual. It also gave him Greek, logic, mathematics, and a vast respect for teaching and teachers.

William was a precocious student, and he entered the senior form at Glasgow as a result of early preparation in the classics. Born on the family farm at Newton-Limavady, near Londonderry, on November 11, 1812, he was, at the age of six, entered in a common school run by a Roman Catholic scholar, a tyrannical disciplinarian but a most able classical pedagogue.

By the time he was thirteen William had absorbed all that the school could offer. His family had rented a larger farm, retaining the old one, at Calmuddy, where the tides from the Lough Foyle reached a mile and a half inland. There was no common school nearby, and William spent the next two years in farming, riding horses, and swimming, all the while reading history and biography. Here it was that William learned the land. His tutor was his brother John, who was a farmer by nature and choice. But the boy was planned for scholarship, and in 1826 he was enrolled in an academy near Coleraine, not far from Calmuddy. Once more William was fortunate in his headmasters. The Reverend Mr. James Bryce was a Presbyterian minister of the Secession branch, a Scotsman whose ancestors, like William's, had come to Ulster in the seventeenth century.

There was more to Mr. Bryce than his eminence as a classical pedagogue. That ability merely enabled William to be more readily admitted to the higher forms at Glasgow University. The greater influence that Mr. Bryce had upon his young student was as a minister, as a living example of the high morality William was to prize.

The old gentleman had firm convictions about his religion and his obligations as a minister, and for most of his forty years at Coleraine he was in conflict with his colleagues of the Presbyterian ministry. Because he considered the British government corrupt, Mr. Bryce refused to accept the government's bounty, the *Regnum Deium*, established by James I as a financial inducement to bring stable Presbyterianism into the wild Irish Catholic province of Ulster.

Not only did Bryce refuse the *Regnum Deium*, he castigated those Presbyterian ministers who accepted it—practically all such in Ulster. He spared no words in criticizing in merciless fashion his brethren of the cloth who took the British gold. At one stage he published a printed pamphlet, addressed to the ministry, which he based on the text, "They took the money and did as they were taught" (Matthew 28:15).

Such a man could not help but mold his students in his own image. During his second year at the academy William made an open profession of his faith in Christ and formally joined the Presbyterian church. At the same time he made his vow that one day he would become a minister in that church.

There was a necessity and a plan in William's education. The necessity arose from the same circumstances affecting many other Ulster families—lack of land. Most of them had been eager to purchase land in the "Ulster Plantations," and the Kings had obtained theirs at Newton-Limavady from a London company in about 1620. Apparently it was a large tract, but the original King had three sons among whom the land was divided. After three generations of such division, there was not enough land left to sustain the King family.

William's mother Elizabeth was a Scots Torrence whose family had settled in Londonderry at about the same time as the Kings. William Sr. and Elizabeth King had seven children, of whom William Jr. was the youngest. There were three boys: James was the oldest, born in 1792; John was born in 1796; the girls Elizabeth, Jane, Catherine, and Mary followed, and William was born in 1812.

James showed all of the aptitudes of a scholar and received a liberal education for a career in teaching, and John very early relieved their father of the responsibilities of the farm. But by 1824 the family had problems. While the Newton-Limavady land was highly productive and valuable (it was sold in 1833 for $120 an acre, a high price for that time), it was still too small to meet the family demands. There were dowries for three girls to consider and William's education as well.

Although the Kings had no capital for purchase of more land, John's reputation as a farmer and the family's long history of self-sufficiency allowed them to rent the large tract at Calmuddy. But it was not enough for John. While William was away at Glasgow University, John had fallen victim to the "land mania," as the younger brother called it. Throughout Ireland every corner and market town had placards posted by land companies in Canada and the United States which rivaled each other's extravagant claims about the fertility of vast stretches of virgin fields, conveniently surrounded by groves of precious woods awaiting the axe. On the maps decorating the placards and posters were numerous mushrooming towns and cities pleading for the produce of those fields and woods. Most of them were names coined by the land promoters of communities which never existed. However, where John was raising from thirty to forty bushels of wheat per acre—which was considered extremely good farming—the land companies offered double that return, plus all other crops, including silk.

Another consideration for the Kings by 1833 was the growth of the family. Elizabeth had married in 1826 and already had four children. Mary was married in 1827 and had three children. Then Catherine was married in 1828; two years later she moved to New Brunswick, Canada, and there had three children by 1833.

The parents were persuaded. The aim was to establish a homestead in Canada on which all the children and grandchildren could settle. That was entirely possible, the posters declared, because land was cheap, fruitful, and unlimited in the new world.

The decision to emigrate was made before William returned from Glasgow, his education completed except for his own plans to go on to divinity school. From the transatlantic sailing ships docking at Moville, on the Lough Foyle, with cargoes for Londonderry, John learned that the American potato crop was poor that year. On the other hand, the potato market on the Continent was diminishing as the plants spread through mid-Europe.

That year John had a remarkably good potato crop, in both quantity and quality. It was his thought and plan to charter the *Dorothy* and fill it with potatoes for Philadelphia. He decided to place young William in charge as supercargo, to sell the potatoes and hold the money for land purchases in Canada. Then, the family would sell out and meet in New York in September for the trip to Niagara.

It is difficult to determine why William, the youngest boy, was the choice. Why not James, the oldest, who was not married and was so much more mature? There is no doubt that the decision was made by John, to whom the father left all business matters. John's choice was not misplaced. Within four days, by June 15, 1833, the *Dorothy's* cargo of potatoes was sold to the Philadelphia merchants at prices higher than hoped for, and William had a letter of credit in his pocket for John when the family arrived in New York late in September.

It was more than sufficient to buy hundreds of acres at the advertised prices and to keep the King clan for a year until the new homestead sprouted its huge crops.

There was only one miscalculation in the whole emigration. It was almost October, and in Canada the winter set in early. There was no choice but to spend the cold months in New York and head for Niagara as soon as the ice in the waterways broke in the spring. And so they settled to wait.

All but William. On landing in Philadelphia, he had written to a classmate from Glasgow University, Bryce Hunter of Connecticut, who had gone directly from Glasgow to the Ohio country near Cleveland where he was both teaching and serving as a deputy sheriff. Bryce invited William to winter there with him. On October 1, 1833, William boarded one of the fine new Hudson River steamboats at the Battery, and headed for the gateway to the West, Albany.

☆

II : THE SECOND AMERICA

THERE WAS SOMETHING ELECTRIC in the American air and William could not help but respond to it. To him everything was excitingly new. He accepted it all uncritically.

Another twenty-year-old, Henry David Thoreau, at the Harvard College commencement in 1837 orated:

> The characteristic of our epoch is perfect freedom—freedom of thought and action. The indignant Greek, the oppressed Pole, the jealous American assert it. . . . Man thinks faster and freer than ever before. He, moreover, moves faster and freer. He is more restless, because he is more independent than ever. The winds and the waves are not enough for him; he must needs ransack the bowels of the earth, that he may make for himself a highway of iron over its surface. . . .

William took that highway. He reached it in Albany after a voyage up the Hudson of "unsurpassed beauty." He had once more been fortunate in the weather, and the Indian summer day was balmy and bright. An early frost, however, had already splashed the bluffs with riotous color all along the Hudson.

He spent no time in the busy Dutch town of Albany. He immediately boarded something else that was new, America's first and only railroad, the Mohawk and Hudson, and in one breathtaking hour had ridden the "highway of iron" the sixteen miles to Schenectady! He was drawn by that American mechanical marvel, the monstrous six-ton "DeWitt Clinton" locomotive.

The Erie Canal was in its heyday when William boarded his canal boat, to crowd into the five-foot bunks and the unalleviated stench of the crowded cabins while the boat crawled the 350 miles to Buffalo. Hauled by its span of horses, they advanced on Buffalo at a steady pace of two miles an hour.

At every relay stop and lock, for they were climbing six hundred feet to the surface of Lake Erie, the canal was lined with log huts and shacks housing the taverns, inns, and stores fattening on the mounting traffic that crowded the waterway to the West. The westbound freight was human—whole families of emigrants, farmers from the depleted East, speculators, merchants, and young men like William. This was a land rush to the Northwest Territory, and the fever of acquisition differed in no way from the later gold rush.

The eastbound traffic consisted chiefly of wheat, corn, and oats deep-laden in the boats, for the wilderness was retreating and the prairies were seeded. As the human flood increased—doubling within the decade of 1830–1840—so did the foodstuffs bound for the populous eastern seaboard.

It was a kaleidoscope of experience for William. Instead of the usual six days to Buffalo, it required eight because at Herkimer the canal broke and the repair took two days.

William was delighted. He had spent little time on the boat anyway. He continued lucky in weather and walked as much as he rode. He walked beside the horses and learned about the canal from the drivers. He made short sorties across bends, visiting with farmers and passers-by without fear of missing his canal boat. The two days gave him the first possible opportunity to obey John's orders to watch the land, to see how it was farmed. Did they use oxen, or horses? Would they be planting winter wheat, or was there just one wheat crop in this country? William trudged far from the canal to see. He was able to report that the New York land was "rich and in a high state of cultivation," and included high praise for the husbandry of the Dutch farmers there.

There were more unusual things to be learned along the

canal route. William's first introduction to the weird era of religious revolution, then in full flower on the canal shores, was on his own canal boat. The area through which he was passing in northern New York was sometimes called the "burnt-over district" because so many religious fires had flamed briefly but fiercely in its villages and valleys. These were not the pallid intellectual flickerings of Transcendentalism in Boston, nor the retreats of the religious communists whose settlements dotted all the New West. There were signs of rebellion against New England Puritanism, and against the rigidities of its creeds.

Here for the most part was a revival of primitive Christianity, and an outbreak of evangelism. A fellow passenger on the canal boat was an evangelist who was to bring communities throughout the United States to a frenzy within the next dozen years. This was William Miller, the Vermont Baptist whose sect was to be known as the Millerites. Just that year Miller had become a Baptist minister, but his message was sought in Methodist and Congregational churches as well, for he had developed into an eloquent revival preacher with a particular message. William listened to him at length and irreverently concluded that he "made considerable noise." He summed up Miller's message in a single sentence: "He believed that Christ would come on the 23rd of April, 1843, and reign personally on earth, and that the Saints who were dead would rise from their graves and reign with him."

William spent no time in either Buffalo or Cleveland. He reached the Ohio city, then of about three thousand population, by overnight steamer and walked the twenty miles to Northfield on the same day. He moved in with his classmate, rooming in the home of the Wallaces, who had come from Connecticut in the 1820's to found the Brandywine woolen mills.

Within a week there waited on William King a deputation of the trustees of Western Reserve College, which had been founded in 1826 about ten miles southeast of Northfield, in the village of Hudson. The institution was the beginning of Western Reserve University which later moved to Cleveland, but was then known as the "Western Yale" because so many of its early professors came from the divinity school in New Haven.

They had learned that a young graduate of Glasgow University had arrived and was unemployed. William was offered the chair of mathematics at Western Reserve College, an invitation he declined because he was committed to meet his family in Cleveland as soon as the ice was out of the Erie Canal.

In New York the Kings had learned that Canada was not only icebound for much of the year but also that buffalo still roamed the Niagara country and the bloodthirsty "aborigines" made settlement a matter of suicide. Of course, this was untrue. While Niagara and all of Upper Canada were sparsely settled, there were cities on the shores of both Lake Ontario and Lake Erie. The climate differed little from the southern shores of these lakes. Without question the Kings were duped by the propaganda of the American land speculators who "met the boats" and searched for emigrants with cash or even credit. The same fabulous posters praising the productivity of woods and swamps and the prosperity of nonexistent communities assailed the Kings in New York as they had in Ulster.

But that winter, William became a teacher anyway. Mr. Wallace, a trustee of the Northfield school district, begged William to teach the school for as long as he would be there. Mr. Wallace admitted that they could not pay William "anything like the salary" he deserved but only sixteen to twenty dollars a month and board, which was the going pay for teachers of public schools in the Western Reserve. William countered with an offer. He told Mr. Wallace that he would teach without remuneration if the students were young men and women only from 15 to 24 years of age, already possessing the rudiments. Another condition was that the term would end on April 1, 1834.

The Northfield trustees accepted gladly, and William's first school was opened with a capacity enrollment. It was a primitive log schoolhouse with a fireplace at one end taking four-foot logs. William quickly found that his students were the victims of very poor teaching. Their last teacher had not been able to carry them through a complete course in the fundamentals of grammar and arithmetic. After examining his students individually, William promised to accomplish at least this much, provided "they would apply themselves."

Soon after his school opened, William learned that there were still young men who could not attend. Their winter days were spent in timbering, both for the lumber crop and to build new homes. On condition that they would supply the tallow candles, he opened night classes too, and some of his day pupils simply stayed on. The classes were soon filled.

On April 10, William set out to explore land for his family. The winter in Northfield had convinced him that he would never again be free of the yearning to teach. He would be a teacher or a preacher, or preferably a combination of both. But first he would teach. Meanwhile he must find a homestead for his family.

The route that William set out for himself would practically outline the map of Ohio and run a bit westward into Indiana. He traveled a circuit due south to the Ohio River, westward to Cincinnati, northwest to Fort Wayne, Indiana, then northeast to the mouth of the Maumee River where Toledo now stands, and finally back to Cleveland. He used every existing means of locomotion, including his feet. He covered approximately one thousand miles by stage to Gallipolis on the Ohio River, by raft and then by steamer to Cincinnati, and finally north to the mouth of the Maumee River and Lake Erie by stage, horse, canal boat, canoe, and hiking.

William was not alone in his search for a homesite. He had joined the feverish land rush of the day and at Cincinnati became a member of a party heading for the government land office at Fort Wayne. There he was one among dozens of land-seekers, family men, and speculators who hungered for as much land as their cash or credit could purchase out of the vast Western Reserve. In Fort Wayne William heard rumors of a canal to be built between that village and Lake Erie, along the course of the Maumee. That sent him northward. He himself had carried the potatoes from Londonderry to Philadelphia. He had seen the produce-laden barges on the Erie Canal. If the future were to see water freight eastward to the Erie Canal and south to the Ohio and Mississippi rivers, a farmer would have two markets, and the most inexpensive means known to man of reaching them.

A few days later William was jubilant. He had found the ideal home at Fort Defiance on the Maumee, just sixty miles from Lake Erie, with three hundred acres, of which about twenty were cleared for planting. The King family could be self-sufficient by fall.

He continued searching the shores, while heading for Cleveland by canoe. At the village of Maumee he learned that land values were rising as a result of the influx of settlers. A few miles farther, almost at the mouth of the Maumee, he landed to look at a huge tract for sale, "a rough, broken farm which the owner would gladly have sold for $5,000." Had he bought the farm at Manhattan Landing, as it was then known, the King family might have become the richest in the Western Reserve. It was the site of the present city of Toledo.

The King family set out for Manhattan Landing the day after William's arrival in Cleveland. In the party were the father and mother, the brothers James, John, and William, and the sister Jane. They hired two wagons at Manhattan Landing and started for Fort Defiance, but they never reached William's choice.

John wanted to see more of the country nearer the mouth of the river, and they stopped to eat at a store and tavern on the edge of the Potawatomi Indian reservation operated by Peter Manor, famous half-breed of the Indian Wars. Peter told John about the Six Mile Woods west of the Maumee River, about twelve miles away. He not only provided horses but also guided John to the land.

The Six Mile Woods was six miles wide and twenty miles long with strips of oak openings at each border. In all that wilderness there were only four families at the time. The oak, walnut, and sycamore trees reached four feet in diameter, John told his family on his return, and there was scarcely any underbrush to clear. He had seen deer, turkey, and pheasants in herds and flights. A skilled hunter could get rich on wolf pelt bounties, for the government was paying seven dollars for each skin. Best of all, the Six Mile Woods was government land priced at $1.25 an acre. The potato money from Philadelphia was more than enough to buy outright a section of 640 acres.

As ever, John carried the day. He and William rode south to the government land office at Wooster, Ohio, and returned with full title to 640 acres just south of the town of Delta.

For William and the others, the work of pioneers began immediately. It required a full year, to the spring of 1835, before William felt that he could return to his own course. Their house was up; ten acres were cleared for planting. Catherine, her husband, John Donahue, and their three children were on the homestead. The other sisters were planning their own moves from Ulster County. There would be enough manpower to continue clearing the land, and the canal was actually begun. In addition, also under construction was the first railroad west of the Alleghenies, between the new settlement of Toledo and Adrian. The sailing boats were making the port of Maumee a more frequent stop, and so were the steamers to Toledo. The family's crops would have their multiple markets. John had been right about the land, as he usually was.

William wrote a few letters to classmates because "I was determined to teach a few years before I would study theology, to be no longer a burden to my family but to support myself and paddle my own canoe." In the fall of 1835 he received a reply from a classmate in Florence, Alabama, offering the princely sum of eight hundred dollars a year for teaching at an academy there. This was more than twice as much as he could hope for by teaching anywhere in the Western Reserve. It would bring him to divinity school so much faster. He accepted the post and promised his arrival in December.

To reach that distant southern point William borrowed $100 in Maumee, giving a twelve-month promissory note to repay $125. Why didn't he borrow it from his family? They had cash left. "I was determined to be no burden to the family but to be self-sustaining."

He left for the South two weeks after his twenty-third birthday.

☆

III : THE THIRD AMERICA

WHEN HE WENT SOUTH, William King entered a third America. For a few months in 1833, he had experienced the raucous commercial world of the Atlantic coast in the midst of its industrial incubation and social change.

The world of the pioneer in Ohio was still another America, one in which survival was the first aim, and self-sufficiency the reward for surviving.

But he still did not know the Negro.

In Philadelphia and New York, William had seen the "free" Negroes, but they were comparatively few in those populous cities. The census of 1830 shows fewer than three hundred Negroes in all of northern Ohio and only nineteen within a twenty-five-mile radius of the King homestead. There were 9,586 Negroes in the entire state, almost all of them concentrated in its southern sections along the Ohio River.

Although the Northwest Ordinance of 1787 declared that the territory was to be composed of free states, Ohio, at its first constitutional convention in 1802, missed becoming a slave state by a single vote. The first of Ohio's "Black Laws" was passed in 1804, and it required all Negroes to register for a certificate of freedom at a fee of twelve and a half cents for each name. In 1807, Negroes settling in Ohio were required to post bonds of $500 each and were not allowed to testify in any court case involving a white person. As late as 1831 Negroes, in addition, could not serve in the militia or on juries, nor attend any public schools, nor, of course, vote. Ohio, among all the so-called "free" states, was notorious for its suppressive legislation against Negroes.

The legal status of Negroes in Ohio during William's stay

in Six Mile Woods in no way resembled the kind of emancipation he had conceived while attending the historic debates at Glasgow. In his passionate partisanship, he had heeded only Thomas Fowell Buxton's side in the great parliamentary debates of 1827 with William's fellow Ulsterman, Prime Minister George Canning. Buxton demanded instant abolition and Canning a process of Christianization of the slaves.

In 1835, before going south, William had not seen a slave. As yet there was no emotional impact or involvement. He was still a theoretical abolitionist. He knew nothing of slavery.

He never reached Florence, Alabama. The weather dictated the young man's future. At Cincinnati he was informed that the Tennessee River, the only north-south route to his destination, was frozen. Even if there had been overland roads, they would have been buried in snow. He was snowbound in Cincinnati, where six inches fell in the next two days. William decided to go downriver toward New Orleans, "where I would have neither snow nor frost" and try to reach Florence from somewhere along the Mississippi. He booked passage immediately.

William's first experience with the institution of slavery was to begin when his steamer reached Cairo, Illinois, and it was to continue all the way down the Mississippi.

At every river port there were additions and embellishments to a fantastic tale that occupied the passengers throughout the trip. A certain John A. Murrell had organized a slave revolt in eight states, which was scheduled for the coming Christmas. The slaves were to rise in all of the major cities and towns during the bacchanal allowed them every Holy Season. All whites would be slaughtered, of course, but first the women would be raped.

The magnitude of the plot, which grew at every port,

did not impress William so much as the reactions to it. On board ship, his fellow passengers wore weapons, and there were armed men at every wharf. Except for members of the crew, there were no Negroes in evidence at any port. He saw hysteria on his steamer and grim preparedness ashore.

For the first time William realized that there was a "burden" for the whites in a slave country. It was a burden of fear, compounded with each slave insurrection. The slaveowners had not yet recovered from the worst slave revolt so far, the Nat Turner uprising in Virginia in 1831; and the Murrell plot threw them into a paroxysm of terror. This was something the emancipationists in Glasgow had not mentioned, and it was a revelation. The Black Code of Ohio was evolved for the protection of white property, but the Slave Code of the South had its genesis in the protection of white lives. William thought of this all the way to Natchez.

He went ashore there, with letters of introduction to two wealthy planters. He planned to see if the way to Florence was open and also to inquire about teaching opportunities in Natchez.

At the hotel there were still more rumors of arrests, shootings, and hangings. One story, later confirmed, was most discouraging to William. A young man from Massachusetts had arrived in Natchez in search of a teaching post. He was arrested by a Vigilance Committee because he could produce no proof that he was not one of Murrell's white confederates. "I observed after signing my name in the register several gentlemen went and looked at the register; at that time the planters were very suspicious of a stranger. Such was the state of sanity when I went South in December, 1835."

He himself was under the best of auspices. He had told the bartender in the hotel about his letters of introduction to Captain Jake Surget and Mr. Robert Dunbar. He could want for no better sponsors than these gentlemen. The captain (he had been a sea captain by virtue of marrying his skipper's widow) was the son of Pierre Surget, one of the original settlers of Natchez, and Robert was the son of the famous Scotsman, Sir William Dunbar, member of the American Philosophical Society, astronomer, scientist, and friend of Thomas Jefferson. Both are still revered names in Natchez.

He stayed at the hotel a few days, listening to the planters and their unceasing talk of the "conspiracy." A nice point of courtesy prevented his seeking out the captain and Mr. Dunbar with his letters of introduction. He felt that he would be demanding their hospitality. But no doubt he knew that the word would spread. Captain Surget learned of the young man in town with a letter to him, and he came to the hotel.

"When he read it he shook me heartily by the hand, welcomed me to that part of the country and with French politeness, invited me to go out and see him at his plantation."

William's introduction to slavery was indeed a strange one for an abolitionist. Strangest of all was the fact that he was so well received by the planters, because it was in Natchez that William set the pattern of his honesty. He wore no false colors. He made it clear that he was opposed to slavery. Throughout his life William King was to practice a scrupulous honesty in his private affairs. He was capable of duplicity, indeed was quite adroit at it while a conductor on the underground railroad. But about himself he was painfully honest.

When William went to Captain Surget's plantation, about three miles from Natchez, there began a round of southern hospitality which was to include many family mansions, where he met the leaders of Natchez society. When Robert Dunbar learned that he had recently arrived from Glasgow, William could not refuse to spend a few days on his plantation. He met the "Lord Byron" of Natchez, A. L. Bingaman, and the Fosters who owned beautiful Cottage Gardens, and the strange Judge Cameron who lived about thirty miles from

Natchez in a colony of Highlanders whose slaves spoke only Gaelic.

Each of the planters owned thousands of acres of cotton land and hundreds of slaves. And they all proudly showed William over their land, then in the midst of "last pickin's," the third cotton crop of the season. It was a society William had never known, where gracious living was a credo and all sins were committed discreetly. There was Natchez "On-the-Hill" and Natchez "Under-the-Hill." In the beautiful town "On-the-Hill" and its stately manors on the bluff, there were culture, huge libraries, exceptional music, serenely superficial society, and the vast wealth of the 1830's when the Black Belt trebled its cotton production and still could not keep up with the demands of the mills of England and New England.

Natchez "Under-the-Hill" was one of the havens of iniquity famous along the Mississippi. In its gambling, drinking, and whoring parlors the young blood of Natchez rubbed elbows and sometimes guns or knives with the wild rivermen, criminals, and fugitives from northern justice.

William found that there was no college or academy near Natchez in which he could teach. Jefferson Military College was six miles from town but had no opening for a classical scholar. The planters either had tutors for their children or sent them to England and France for education.

Once more, William was offered an opportunity. A group of planters invited him to open his own academy with their patronage. Here was additional testimony to the bearing and quiet confidence of this young man. The offer was made with full knowledge of William's views. It could be that the planters tolerated them because he had carried abolition from Scotland and not from Yankee-land. Whatever the motivation, it was another flattering offer refused by William.

"The country was in a disturbed state and I did not want to be entangled with any business that would confine me to the country. I wanted a situation in a College or Academy where I would have no responsibility but my class and could leave at the end of the term."

His new friends then told him that he would be likely to find teaching opportunities not far south over the Louisiana border, in Jackson, which was that state's seat of learning. He was told that there were both a college and an academy in Jackson, in addition to two female schools for the daughters of the planters.

William made a round of farewells and immediately set out for Bayou Sara, the river port for Jackson and all the rich Felicianas, East and West, which had been planted in cotton years before by the Spanish when they owned West Florida.

Characteristically, William did not delay in busy Bayou Sara. He rented a saddle horse and rode the twelve miles over the beautiful hills to Louisiana College, perched on one of the highest hills in Jackson. He arrived opportunely. There was a meeting of the college trustees then in progress.

Believing in direct action, William walked in and sat down. When the meeting had finished, he found the president of Louisiana College, Dr. Sherman, and presented his credentials from Glasgow University. Dr. Sherman then quizzed William in Greek and mathematics, and, satisfied with his qualifications, told William that he could have the first vacancy open if he were in the neighborhood; but there was no opening then.

One of the trustees, Colonel Solomon M. Brian, asked the young man's plans and was told that he would accept the first teaching opportunity offered.

Colonel Brian explained a situation that existed all through the South. There were no common or public schools. Louisiana College had had a preparatory school, but it had been neglected and was bound to close. The situation was so critical in education for college preparation that Louisiana College itself was down to a student body of fifty-five. It was a problem destined to grow more acute in the next few years, and William King was to be a key figure in its temporary solution.

When he had finished his explanation, Colonel Brian offered William the position of tutor to three families: his own, that of his father-in-law, Joseph Rogillio, and that of another of the Spaniard's sons-in-law, Thomas McKaeven. There would be eleven students—seven Rogillios and two each from the other families.

Either William was cautious or he was canny. He wanted to look the place over first and meet his potential students. At once he accompanied Colonel Brian on a tour and that night accepted the position at a salary of eight hundred dollars a year, with quarters, board, and use of a "horse to ride when I wanted."

William was happy, he notified his friend in Alabama. There was no need to travel north to Florence or south to New Orleans. His quarters were in the plantation mansion, and its table was managed by Mrs. Mary Brian, who had not only the warmth of her Spanish blood but its traditional cooking as well.

His schoolhouse was a neat frame building near the main house which had a yard filled with crepe myrtle, roses, and cape geraniums—some of them blossoming in the mild weather. And there were magnolias everywhere. Best of all, he was able to open the school on January 1, 1836, and lost not a single day from his course toward divinity school.

For two months William was happy, and then the character of the spirited teen-agers of the Felicianas nearly wrecked his school. The students were all cousins, but one of the Rogillios and one of the Brians had a feud of long standing. One was all Spanish and the other all Irish, and one afternoon the Rogillio boy whacked his cousin over the head with a porter bottle, nearly braining him.

For the next few days William taught only the McKaeven youngsters.

Then proud, touchy Joseph Rogillio, one of the oldest and wealthiest planters in the Felicianas, whose armored forefathers had settled West Florida, came to young William. He wanted to know what the teacher would do if he sent his hotheaded son back.

William's reply was forthright. First, he would determine whether or not the boy was guilty of hitting his cousin over the head with a porter bottle. If so, then he would thrash the boy and make him behave in the future. If the youngster did not behave, he would thrash him again.

Rogillio's reply was that his boy was not going to be treated the way he himself treated his slaves when they offended him. He would withdraw all seven of his children. And he did.

At this point, William made of Colonel Brian a lifelong friend. When the Colonel and McKaeven, worried that they would lose an able teacher, asked what his plans were, William's reply was, "I told them I would teach the year out as I had agreed, and that I would relinquish any claim to that part of the salary which the Spaniard was to pay."

This meant a delay in divinity school, but William felt that he was bound by a contract. There was no delay. Colonel Brian himself paid the Rogillio share on the proviso that William accept other students if they appeared.

He must have been an exceptional teacher. Or perhaps all the other planters were secretly happy that the arrogant Spaniard had been humbled by this youth who was no older than one of his sons. Or it might have been the way in which William made men out of Judge Thomas W. Scott's two boys.

These violent but typical scions of the time and place had been expelled, with others, from Louisiana College preparatory school. Their offense was to ape their elders. Two of their teachers were from New England—provocation enough, but it may have been more than that. The boys beat up the Yankees, teachers or not, and they were thrown out.

Judge Scott told William that he could do anything he wanted with his sons, but that they must be educated. Again William gave one of his characteristic "Let me look into the situation first" replies and called the boys in for a day of school. He kept them after school that night and talked their language to the sixteen- and eighteen-year-olds.

He would teach them if they made a promise to him. They would promise only two things: to stop being hoodlums and to study. He wanted only their words; without it, they could not return. They promised.

"They kept their word. They were with me two years and I had not two better boys in the school. They were diligent and obedient. They applied themselves to their books and made good progress."

Judge Scott was an influential planter. As a jurist too, and for many years state senator from East Feliciana, he was highly influential. The name of William King as an excellent teacher who could cope with boys who defied their own parents was spread through the Felicianas and southern Mississippi. In March 1836, William had four pupils. At the end of the year, he had forty.

"At the end of the first year I held an examination at which the planters attended who had their sons with me. They were so well pleased with the progress that they gave me an apartment, appointed three Trustees to look after the interests of the school, and raised my salary to one thousand dollars."

Now William was receiving more than four times the pay

he would have received in Ohio, and divinity school was that much closer. In addition, he received some of the fees, and could now afford a much-needed assistant.

He wrote to his brother James to come south.

☆

IV : THE WEB OF SLAVERY

FROM THE DAY he set foot ashore at Bayou Sara, William King was to make compromises with the society in which he found himself. For seven years, until he could concede no more to slaveholding institutions, each decision he made, every action he took—even his remarkable success as a teacher —were to thrust him into the very category he despised.

On January 10, 1841, he himself became a slaveowner. That was when he married Mary Mourning Phares.

The intervening years were an inexorable progression, much like the nightmare bringing the tortured dreamer to the cliff's edge. William was to learn that his conscience grew more painful with each compromise. The stumbling block of slavery for this young white man of 24, presentable in appearance and more than impressive in intellect, was an inability to hate either the slave land or the slaveowners.

The land itself, the Feliciana parishes, was fittingly named. The woods and hills, the fields and swamps along Bayou Sara and Thompson's Creek, were all richly fruitful with natural and cultivated life. The woods sang, for this was the Audubon country so lushly described by the great painter-naturalist's journals. Audubon had left the Felicianas just six years before, after he and Lucy, his ever-patient wife, had saved enough from teaching to go to Edinburgh and "see what I could do to hasten the publication of my drawings" which resulted in the *Birds of America*.

William was to follow exactly the same course. He too found beauty in the Felicianas, but he found something more: "I enjoyed those rides in the lovely nights that we had in Louisiana," he wrote. "In spring, the air was filled with the fragrance of the magnolia, honeysuckle and cape jessamine and the woods were vocal with the song of the mockingbird, the nightingale of the South. I would sit in my room at night and throw my window up and listen with delight to the varied notes of that wonderful bird. The birds were beautiful in their plumage and in their song, the breezes were fragrant and balmy, *but the land was cursed with slavery.*"

So were the people. There were six thousand white people in the Felicianas then, and seventeen thousand slaves. Most of the whites were "half-acre grubbers" on sandy hillsides, and some were merchants or cotton factors. Only a few hundred plantation families owned almost all of the seventeen thousand slaves, and they owned the fabulous wealth of the parishes as well. During the crop year of 1835–36 some of them received more than forty thousand dollars for the cotton alone, which was selling at seventeen and eighteen cents a pound. They were beginning to harvest the hardy "ribbon" sugar too. Corn, for both livestock and human consumption, as well as oats and other grains, grew well in the temperate hills. In the lowlands and swamps, fruits and berries were another money crop sought eagerly by the New Orleans market. The Louisiana assessment rolls of 1840 list the land value of the Felicianas as $9,000,000, second only to Orleans Parish, containing the Creole city.

By the nature of his position, William was allied with the holders of land and human property. He taught their children, for one thing, and within a year had so won the admiration of the parents that all doors were opened to him. Besides, theirs was a gracious and a cultured life, with gaiety and brightness, lavish food, and entertainment. There were beautiful girls and handsome young men, some of the latter fresh from their European grand tours. There were well-read men and women with whom to explore intellects.

Other than Dr. Buller, his own Presbyterian pastor, and one or two of the imported Yankee teachers at Louisiana College, William had no choice in his social and intellectual life. He gravitated to the slaveowners most naturally.

How could he hate them for owning slaves? Colonel Brian watched over him like a father, and Mary Brian fussed over him as though he were a thoughtless older son. He could not hate them, although they owned two hundred slaves and sometimes ordered whippings for them, and at other times, feasts.

How could he resist the enjoyment of gloriously stately Oakley near St. Francisville, where he watched Audubon's "beautiful Eliza" Pirrie, now the reigning beauty, as she swirled and glided in the dances of the day. He himself did not dance, but he could not scorn beauty; and soon he too thought little of the obsequious black man who offered him refreshments. Soon he did not even notice the black men and women who moved about the gracious halls of the many mansions he visited.

He was especially sought after in Jackson, because there Louisiana College drew parents to visit with their sons and then, apparently, to attend their separate balls and brawls.

"They would leave their plantations in care of an overseer, and they would come with their servants and equipage, living in high style and driving around the country in summer when the roads were good. At the closing of the College and schools in June for the summer vacation, the town was filled with the wealth and beauty and fashion of the state."

William King was sought after more and more as his importance to Louisiana education grew and was recognized. Every member of the Louisiana College board of trustees was his sponsor, and among them was John Phares, whose East Feliciana Parish plantation stretched to within a few miles of Jackson and was only slightly larger than his plantation across the river at Point Coupee. He sent his son, William Douglas, to King's school. Thus King met Mary Mourning Phares, a daughter by an earlier marriage. With that meeting, William King was even more a part of this extravagant world, for he fell in love with her.

William found himself in the position of hating slavery and respecting some slaveowners, horrified by the slave quarters he saw and entranced by the secluded "Big House," disapproving the cruelties of some planters and lauding the humanity of others.

All that saved William from surrender to the hashish of slavery was the hidden life of the Felicianas. At first, he only knew "Feliciana-on-the-Hill" but soon came to know its "Under-the-Hill" character. He came to know the excesses in all things—in gaiety, drinking, gambling, cruelty, and extravagance. He could deal with it among his students but not in their parents. They exchanged fortunes in bets on racing their horses at the St. Francisville Course, built at the same time as the Metaire Course in New Orleans. They financed construction of the second theater in Louisiana, and brought in the companies from New Orleans for a whirl of parties and performances. They drank and dueled in each other's homes and glens. The fathers traded dusky mistresses and their sons joyously combined in raping expeditions around the plantations' slave quarters.

From his own notes of horror, William King did not awaken to his own problems in relation to slavery until his third year in the Felicianas. He knew he was living a mockery of his principles when he realized that these families whose children he taught and whose hospitality he accepted lived a duality that was dedicated to the perpetuation of their black foundations. He was entertained by the Robert Percys, was genuinely fond of Emily and Bennett Barrow, admired Colonel Dupree's musical abilities, and approved of Dr. Ira Smith's strict guidance of his sons, who were William's students.

He would meet the men not only socially but during his

night rides, for often they challenged him. Robert Percy was captain of the 25-man vigilance committee established by the Parish Police Juries and "authorized to take and adopt means for the arrest and punishment in such manner as they deem necessary of all suspicious white men and slaves."

They were empowered to, and did, shoot slaves on sight. Bennett Barrow was known as a "whipping" planter. He lived high on his plantation nine miles from Jackson, was always in debt due to gambling, but was most meticulous in managing his plantation. That is why his work diary informs us that in one year he meted out 329 punishments to his slaves, 171 of them whippings. One entry notes whipping of all his house slaves because of general bad conduct and also because of his maxim, "Can't let a peach get ripe."

William was never to be a prude and generally agreed that man tended to reach heaven or hell in his own way. But he balked at hypocrisy such as expressed in *DeBow's Review*, the ante-bellum popular magazine of the South. An appraisal of East Feliciana ended with: "*Morality:*—the general tone of morals in this parish is, without affectation, far superior to many of the far-famed New England villages."

Whether or not the comparison was valid, the evaluation of sin is always a matter of degree. Thus, when William began his annual visits to New Orleans to report to the state legislature on his work, he was horrified, not so much by the "regular Saturnalia" between Christmas and January 8, which was the forerunner of today's commercialized Mardi Gras, but rather by the high state of organization of sin.

> The public and private morals were corrupt. They were more the laws of pleasure than the laws of God. Drinking, gambling, horse-racing and dancing were common on the Sabbath. Theatres were open and brothels were licensed and established by law. There appeared to be no restraint on the people. Everyone seemed to act like the children of Israel

when they had no king to do that which was right in their own eyes.

However, the only difference between the New Orleans and the Feliciana morality was that in the city all excesses were regulated by law, and in the "up-country" only by custom. For instance, the annual Christmas holidays granted the Negroes in New Orleans when they dressed as Dina and Sambia and freely paraded the streets, were duplicated in Bayou Sara and Jackson, as well as on the plantations. There was an economic basis for the slave orgies. This was a planting time. The seed for a human crop was best sown during the dancing, drinking, and high jinks of Christmas. The birth of Christ was somehow considered a proper time for the procreation of a new crop of slaves.

But the morals of this slave society did not concern William nearly so much as the hypocrisy of its religion. He might have compromised with the South "Under-the-Hill" and disregarded it, meanwhile enjoying the veneer of graceful rectitude of "On-the-Hill." But William was a devout and practicing Christian throughout his life. There could be no compromise with his religious conscience. It was clear to him quite early. "The South did not mix things sacred and profane. They drew a definite line between the Church and the world." The conflict was in separation of church and self.

This was the essence of William King's final rebellion against the South. If the church were not to be part of the world, where was the justification for its existence? Why was he, as yet not even a divinity student, teaching theology at Louisiana College? He was sponsored by his own pastor, Dr. Buller, as being qualified to teach the young men some of the tenets of Christianity, but what was the purpose if his students were to join their parents in profaning the Sabbath?

As for slavery and Christianity, by the time these conflicts and contradictions of the Third America began to gnaw at William, he was in the midst of a controversy reaching its height of passionate debate in the 1840's.

The problem as to whether Christianity and slavery are compatible resolved itself, for William, into the question: "Can I, in all sincerity, swallow the arguments of the ecclesiastical apologists of the South?"

Those arguments could be better understood if the same question were brought up to date. "Are Christianity and white supremacy compatible?" In William King's Americas, all whites, with the exception of a few Abolitionists, believed that such a question did not even exist. Negroes were not even a human species in the South, and in the North they were a nuisance disturbing both white conscience and economic ties with the South.

One religious argument assailing William in 1838 has persisted in relation to white supremacy. The standard in justification of slavery among Southern apologists at that time was the irrefutable fact that, had Negroes been allowed to remain in Africa, they would have remained heathens, no matter how many missionaries were to labor there. Prof. David Christy ("Cotton is King"), though a most unreliable statistician concerning William King's accomplishments in 1859, many years earlier summarized the rationalization by declaring that all the evangelical effort by all Christian churches had yielded only 151,433 converts to Christianity in Africa whereas in the slave states alone there were close to half a million black Christians.

This was a most potent assertion during William's stormy years of conflict in the South. It has persisted until comparatively recently too, for in 1943, James Truslow Adams asked "Would the 12,000,000 of Negroes in the United States today prefer that their ancestors had never been enslaved, and that they themselves, if alive, should at this moment be living as savages or barbarians in the African Jungle?"

A specious question? Of course, but not to be dismissed; for in 1838 it was important to William King because it represented the only thesis in favor of slavery that he could accept. If he were to become a minister, his concern would be the salvation of souls, not bodies. He was not yet the missionary he would become.

In that year, too, William King became involved in a little-known controversy that stirred up a frenetic storm among the people of the Felicianas and southern Mississippi, just a few miles away. William was part of it because he taught the children of a Methodist minister's congregation just over the state border in Amite County, Mississippi.

None could escape taking sides in the conflict that rose between Rev. William Winans and the famous Abolitionist Gerrit Smith of Peterboro, New York, one of the "Secret Six" sponsoring John Brown's raid on Harper's Ferry and for many years the financial angel of that incendiary Yankee sheet *The Liberator,* published by William Lloyd Garrison in Boston and banned from the mails in the South.

Mr. Winans, with all good intentions, had sought northern funds with which to build a new Protestant church in New Orleans, to care for its growing non-Catholic population. He added the name of Gerrit Smith to his list of philanthropists because that name appeared on a list of those who, in 1835, had contributed heavily to a theological seminary in Columbia, South Carolina. For this Gerrit Smith was lauded all through the South in one year and spat upon the next. He had undergone a conversion as a result of an incident in nearby Utica, New York, where a mob drove out an antislavery convention. Smith invited forty of them to his home, and both the convention and his conversion to Abolitionism took place simultaneously. Thereafter, his plenty was given to antislavery causes exclusively.

Mr. Winans did not know this until Gerrit Smith replied

by sending him a copy of *Zion's Watchman*, printing both the request for the money and the reply. This method of reply roused the Felicianas to a frenzy when Mr. Winans took both the antislavery newspaper and his own frothing answer to *The Louisianan*, which was printed in Jackson.

The anger of the Methodist preacher is understandable. What he took to be Smith's typical Yankee perfidy was compounded by the periodical the latter had used. *Zion's Watchman* was published in defiance of the Methodist Episcopal Church by the Abolitionist Le Roy Sunderland and a rebellious Methodist minister named Rev. Orange Scott. It was to be the major instrument in separating Methodism into Northern and Southern components in 1842. To Winans, it was anathema. Besides, Gerrit Smith was a Presbyterian.

For two columns of type, Gerrit Smith assailed slavery and vilified the Reverend Winans as a false Christian because he preached slavery as a Christian institution. For three columns of type, Winans poured vitriol on the decomposing minds of all Abolitionists, Yankees, and heathens such as Gerrit Smith. After all the abuse, each concluded with a promise of prayer in behalf of the other's soul, that they might find the true faith.

Every issue of *The Louisianan*, all sermons in all churches of all denominations, all public and private gatherings for weeks boiled with indignation against such a dirty Yankee trick, and the turmoil was reflected in William's classes.

He himself was perplexed, since he disagreed with both of the disputants. He himself had attended services in Mr. Winans' church and could not agree with Gerrit Smith's charges that the Methodist espoused heathen doctrine or intended to build himself a "heathen temple" in New Orleans. Winans was a sound Christian and New Orleans did need a new Protestant church.

On the other hand, Mr. Winans was in profound error too

when he falsely charged Smith and all Abolitionists with responsibility for a continuation of slavery. As a result of the lies and calumny spread by the Abolitionists, slaveowners had drawn back from their intention to voluntarily free their slaves, Winans said. William King knew full well that such intent never existed, but rather was a concocted reaction to all antislavery attacks. So long as cotton was needed, there would be no voluntary end of slavery.

Two weeks after the storm broke, William was a guest in the home of Colonel Brian. It was a party in honor of and in support of Winans. He recorded that he listened carefully and said nothing. By then, he was genuinely puzzled. He could agree with the purposes of both men, emancipation of the Negroes and construction of a church. Both were laudable objectives. But now that he knew slavery as an institution and a curse upon whites as well as Negroes, where did he himself stand? Was he still a Glasgow Abolitionist?

There was still another incident, a year later, that disturbed William profoundly. Dr. Buller surrendered to his own conscience. He could no longer live with slavery. He gave up his church, manumitted his slaves, arranged their transport to Liberia, and resigned from the faculty of Louisiana College. Dr. Buller returned to a New England ministry.

Had Dr. Buller announced his resignation a few weeks sooner, he might have changed the course of William's life. His farewell sermon was on the text: "What is a man profited if he gain the whole world and lose his soul, or what will a man give in exchange for his soul?"

Fifty years later William King was to recall that sermon as one of the most important messages in his lifetime. Its influence was to cause the desperation of the next three years until his escape from the South. Just a few weeks earlier he might have left with Dr. Buller, even though he had not saved enough money for divinity school. But that farewell Sabbath fell just before the week he was to open his own academy in Jackson and become a part of the Louisiana educational system. He had committed himself and was trapped by his own exceptional abilities as a teacher.

By 1840 William King was the key to continued higher education in all Louisiana. His academy had more students than Louisiana College itself and had outgrown Colonel Brian's little family schoolhouse.

Even if Louisiana College had been given sufficient funds for all purposes, it still was doomed to failure without a system of public education to supply qualified students. At no time in the twenty years of its existence did the College have more than a hundred undergraduates.

In the spring of 1840 Louisiana College had just 53 undergraduates, and King's preparatory department over 100 students. The shrinkage of the College was least among the boys who entered directly from his classes and that fact prompted his good friend Colonel Brian to take action. It is impossible to know whether the Colonel had planned to exert pressure on the Board of Trustees, or actually decided on his own to establish a new institution of higher education in anticipation of the end of the College. One objective is clear, however. He wanted William King in East Feliciana.

On May 27, 1840, Colonel Brian and his wife, Mary (Rogillio), signed over four acres of land to William and James King "for the consideration of the advantages already received and further expected from an academy being continued and kept up by the said William and James King or their successors. . . . Should the academy as above stated be discontinued by the said Kings or their successors" the land would revert to the original owners.

The new school was to be named "Woodland Academy,"

and total control over its policies was to remain with the King brothers. William did not agree to the plan without realization of its personal involvement.

> I saw the dangers to which I would be exposed from the world in the situation I was about to enter upon. There was the prospect of wealth and a gay and fashionable world with all its pleasures spread out before me, inducing the human heart to settle down in their midst and make this world my portion and to forget preparation for the next.

There never was a "Woodland Academy," except on the deed recorded in the East Feliciana courthouse. As soon as the Louisiana College Board of Trustees learned of the plan, they held emergency meetings. They knew that the College would not reopen that fall if King was not a part of it. They had seen, too, that the best-behaved and the best scholars came from the little school on the Brian plantation. More important, influential parents from all Louisiana, even from Orleans Parish, sent their boys to King rather than to the Louisiana College Grammar School. He had become politically important.

By unanimous vote, the Board offered King the position of Rector of the Louisiana College Preparatory Department. Characteristically, his reply was a request for time to engage in "due deliberation."

As usual, William's "due deliberation" was a thorough exploration of himself as well as the circumstances. He could be useful to mankind as a teacher, if only he could change the pattern of education at Louisiana College. And so he formulated certain conditions to present to the Board of Trustees before he would accept:

1. To rid the school of the odium of the past, it was to get a new name.

2. He was to have four teachers to assist him, and each was to be paid $1,000 a year by the State.

3. He himself was to retain the tuition fees as his salary and he personally was to have sole discretion on admission of deserving students unable to afford those fees.

Most important:

4. *The Board of Trustees was to rescind the regulation that "all boys above twelve years of age were to be treated as gentlemen" and he was to have the power to correct their misbehavior, holding himself "responsible to the Trustees for the use of that power."*

The reason for the last condition, which was revolutionary in that time and place, was the fact that those youngsters were not necessarily "gentlemen." They were preparing to live as their fathers did, and rejected all restraints. The head of Louisiana College, a political appointee, could not discipline them. As a result, college life there appears to have been a year-round Mardi Gras interrupted by occasional classes.

> One of the evils I had seen connected with the government of the Academy (Grammar School) was that the teachers had no power over the boys. When they misbehaved, the teacher cannot correct the boy and the boy set the teacher defiance. The result was the Southern boys, accustomed to command and impatient of restraint, rebelled and, as they could not be corrected they had to be expelled.

All of his conditions were accepted and the new school was named Mathews Academy in honor of the politically powerful Louisiana Chief of Justice who had just died. "So I was instituted as Rector of Mathews Academy with full power over both teachers and pupils."

The financial arrangement he had made, retention of tuition fees, was an assertion of his own self-confidence. He could have commanded a salary higher than his teachers. But

William was a canny young man. He leaves no record of the number of free students he admitted during the first year of Mathews Academy, but by the second year, when he went to New Orleans to report to the state legislature, he obtained its consent for state payment of tuition for four of his free students. By then he had over a hundred pupils and their tuition fees were twenty dollars for each "session" or semester. William was earning in the neighborhood of four thousand dollars a year, free and clear.

Within two months William had transformed the school into monastic conditions worthy of his own Jesuit classical teacher back in Newton-Limavady. The wonder is that the students remained.

They had been accustomed to "go out skylarking in the village and country and be out all night. Sometimes they would have company in their rooms with them feasting and drinking and having a good time generally and wholly neglecting their studies."

William was a spoilsport. He eliminated individual rooms and established a dormitory on the lower floor of the two-story building. At each end was a room for an unmarried teacher, and a lamp was kept burning all night so that bed checks could be made.

Bedtime was nine o'clock, when prayers were over. The boys rose at 6:00 A.M., had breakfast at 8:00 A.M., began classes at 9:00 A.M. Classes were broken for lunch, then continued to 6:00 P.M. dinner, and then the boys had supervised study from 7 to 9:00 P.M. This regimen was broken only for the Sabbath and two vacations, three weeks beginning December 20th and four weeks following the first Wednesday in June.

William himself was guilty of understatement when he issued the Academy announcement on December 2, 1841, after a year of experience.

> Particular attention is paid to the health and morals of the pupils. The government is strict, and at the same time parental, employing such discipline as may most effectually tend to call into action the best feelings of the scholar.

The discipline was not just strict; it was downright tyrannical. There was not another academy in the South like this, and at that time, Louisiana had seventy academies. Yet Mathews Academy, beginning with fifty students, had a capacity enrollment after the first session.

The success may have been due to the formula of placing the students "on their honor as gentlemen," but more likely it was a realization that this young headmaster, only a few years older than some of them, meant every word he said. King very soon set a new precedent in Louisiana education. He thrashed the sons of two prominent and wealthy planters and then took away all the boys' "toys," consisting of pistols, shotguns, rifles, bowie knives, daggers, and stilettos. Their replacement meant automatic dismissal, he told them. He had seen seven of his former pupils who entered Louisiana College "fall to a premature grave" in duels.

The immediate success of Mathews Academy and young William King's stature throughout the state both as an educator and disciplinarian gave him pride. But he never forgot that his full enrollment and the laudatory parents were binding him closer to slavery: outside his classroom "the land was cursed with slavery." And it was to come into his school too, solely because there was no alternative to becoming a slaveholder.

Mary Mourning Phares, William's wife, brought as part of her dowry two slaves, Amelia, her "Mammy," and Eliza, her childhood companion. They were more than her body servants. Amelia had nursed her and also raised her after the early death of Mary's mother. Eliza was her playmate, now grown as Mary was, but with all the attachment of sisters.

Under Louisiana law William owned Amelia and Eliza. They were as much "property" as a piece of land and the husband received title to all a bride's worldly goods upon their marriage. Perhaps William could have sent them back to the Phares plantation or sold them, but of course in reality he could do neither because he was in love with Mary.

She was just 21 when they were married, a diminutive, blond girl with a turned-up nose and curly hair. She was reserved in manner, perhaps withdrawn as a result of her mother's early death when she was seven years old. She was as frilly and dainty as Harriet Beecher Stowe's Nina, for she dressed no differently from the other wealthy Feliciana girls.

One thing was certain. Mary was totally in love with her husband and was fully prepared to change her luxurious life for the genteel poverty of a minister's wife.

Their wedding was the major social event of the holiday season. It took place on John Phares' East Feliciana plantation, just a few miles from Jackson, with all the lavish "fixings" of Southern hospitality and much more, because John Phares vastly admired his son-in-law. As a Trustee of Louisiana College, he knew intimately the value of William's work. Later, as its Treasurer, he was to rely heavily on the young man's abilities.

The wedding ceremony itself was incidental to the social occasion, for the festivities were enjoyed by hundreds who came from as far as New Orleans to the south and Natchez on the north. It was a guest list that combined the old Feliciana families with the highly placed and powerful in Louisiana and southern Mississippi. The Phares name, one of the oldest in the Felicianas, drew the elite, while William King's prominence as a teacher brought the powerful among the state's closed political society, some in gratitude for teaching their sons and others in appreciation of his key position in higher education. In five years this known Abolitionist (*not Yankee*) had created his own circle of slaveowning admirers.

Only James could attend from the King family. It was midwinter, and travel from Ohio was impossible for the elderly father and mother. The journey would have taken at least two weeks if it were possible to reach the Mississippi.

However, William had married a family too, one that he enjoyed immensely. His father-in-law, John Ebenezer Phares, was a friend as well. Apparently without education himself, Phares at first was awed by his new son-in-law and then was proud of him as he watched William being courted by the men of prestige and power in the state. When he realized the young man's rigid integrity, he named him co-executor of his estate in his last will.

Another Phares was John's brother David, with whom William had a great deal in common. Dr. David L. Phares was five years younger than William, and was the first graduate of any college in Louisiana to receive a Bachelor of Arts degree. Two years later, in 1839, he was awarded a medical degree and began scientific research in Mississippi's medicinal plants that won him fame. He was the founder of the Newton Female Institute in Wilkinson County, Mississippi, where he also had twelve hundred acres in cotton. He established Newton College there too, and the town's name was changed to Newtonia in its honor.

Since Dr. Phares was only about fifteen miles from Jackson, he and William saw each other often and they had a mutual goal. While William was working toward establishment of a common school system in Louisiana, Dr. Phares was making the same effort in Mississippi, and he was finally successful.

They too became fast friends, and with Mary's sisters and brothers, William had as full a family life as he could wish. It was another tie to the slave land. His affection for the Phares relatives was genuine and lasting, for he visited them in later years. His life was filled with rewarding work and challenges, with a group of friends and family of like interests, and a wife who worshiped him. It would have been easy for him to take the path of least resistance.

Divinity school? He could attend any he wished and have a church ready for him when he was ordained. If none was vacant, the Phares family would build one for him. Or, if he wished to remain an educator, he could choose a lifetime of useful work in the state, aided and encouraged by all the power from the Governor down.

But in November 1841, Mary gave birth to a boy, who was named Theophilus after the sixteenth century German divine and teacher, Magister Theophilus. While the child remained a baby, William thought little of the future when he would be a youth like the many in Mathews Academy, products of this slave country.

It was not until January 8, 1843, on his return from the annual report to the state legislature in New Orleans and his annual expression of disgust with the bacchanal there, that he grew desperate.

> There was black before me. My boy was now nearly two years old and I wished to remove him from the South before he was incapable of knowing between right and wrong. . . . To raise a family of boys under such corrupting influences was almost sure to corrupt their moral principles and ruin them for the life that now is and that which is to come. This danger I could not conceal from my wife who saw it as well as I did.

There was a festering scab on William's conscience before that, however. Despite all his principles and all his hatred of slavery he was forced to buy a slave on February 8,

1842. He bought, from Humphrey Taylor, at a price of one thousand dollars a "certain Negro boy named Talbert, aged about twenty (20), a slave for life and guaranteed to be free from all the vices and defects prescribed by law" as the deed reads.

Actually, William had no choice. For over a year he had fought against buying slaves as Dr. Buller had been forced to do. The circumstances were similar.

When he became Rector of Mathews Academy, William had fifty students to room, board, and teach. By the second semester he had over ninety. He had to have cooks, cleaning women, and groundskeepers to run the living quarters. "I resolved, if possible, to have nothing to do with the domestic institutions of the country and determined to hire the number of servants I might require." He found that a monumental task.

> After some trouble and difficulty I succeeded in hiring six, some were white and some were black. I had scarcely been in the institution a month when I missed several articles of clothing and finally a trunk full of valuable clothes were taken from one of the rooms. Suspicion rested on my own servants. I appointed a man to watch their movements who soon found out that a white servant in my employment was the guilty person. I had him arrested and the stolen articles were found in his possession. He was tried, found guilty and sentenced to the penitentiary for twelve months. I hired another white man whom I had to dismiss for drunkenness and immorality. My cook died of drunkenness at the end of the first year.

This was the situation when William was approached by Talbert. Humphrey Taylor was a good master, Talbert told him, but he had heard of William's problems and saw in belonging to William a chance to learn to read and write and improve himself. Of course, Talbert had the wisdom of slaves, too, and he knew that any man who refused to buy black men spelled a master who might eventually make freedom possible. William was impressed by the young Negro and tried to hire his services from Taylor, but was refused. However, Taylor offered to sell the slave, pointing out that Talbert had been a house servant, and therefore could run the domestic side of the school. William surrendered and Talbert, a slave, was put in authority over the whites and blacks he was able to hire. William never regretted the services of Talbert, only the sin of purchasing him. Even the relief from the worry over the servant problem added to his guilt.

When he returned from New Orleans in January 1843, William was desperate. He talked it over with Mary and she agreed that it was time to break away from slavery. They now had the money for divinity school and Theophilus was old enough to travel.

The opportunity came almost at once. William himself was committed to finish out the school year and had over 100 students. But he could be free in June. His brother James could take over the Academy.

Then he was approached by Colonel Brian and his father-in-law, who had been deputized by the Louisiana College Trustees to persuade William to help save the College. The situation was a farcical one. The semester was about to begin and Dr. Lacy, the president, had three professors on his staff who were being paid $2,000 a year. The Louisiana College student enrollment totalled exactly three. The Louisiana legislature would never appropriate funds for Louisiana College or any other institution with such an imbalance. It would mean the end of the College.

However, they had a plan. If William would allow the Mathews Academy to become a part of Louisiana College and its over-capacity enrollment were counted, the legislature would keep the College alive. They were authorized to offer

William a salary of fifteen hundred dollars as well as retention of all his tuition fees, and no lessening of his authority over his preparatory students.

This, of course, was an outright fraud and William refused it flatly. He also offered his resignation, effective at once, and told them he would leave for divinity school as soon as possible.

His resignation was refused and John Phares called in his brother David to help persuade William. The argument was that the Louisiana College only required time. The Trustees themselves would recruit students from among their friends. With an enrollment of over one hundred and William King's name, Louisiana College could survive. They needed only a semester in which to work.

But the telling argument was offered by John Phares. Did William propose to pack up Mary and Theophilus tomorrow and go off to divinity school with them? What if he were not admitted? Wouldn't it be wiser and kinder to his wife and child first to gain admission to a divinity school, find a place for them to live, and then come for them? Or did he propose to leave them for years?

Of course the wisdom of that argument won out. William lent his name to a futile effort to salvage Louisiana College. Two years later it was sold to the Methodists and became Centenary College.

Meanwhile, William began preparations for departure after the Mathews Academy semester was over in June. James was entirely willing and eager to take over the school. So long as he himself did not own slaves, he was happy in Louisiana. He could live with slavery, though his brother could not. This was proved out quite soon when James married a landed widow, Mrs. Martha Sims-Douglas. She brought James a rich plantation and seventeen slaves who were promptly manumitted and sent to Liberia. He was to remain at Louisiana

College until it expired, was elected mayor of Jackson, and finally was governor of the new lunatic asylum there until his death in 1879. He accepted the system of slavery, though he would not own slaves. William refused to accept the system, but soon bought more slaves.

It was John Phares' logic again. One of the Rogillios who owned 240 acres abutting the Phares plantation on Thompson's Creek was anxious to sell out. William had visited there. It would be a good home for Mary and Theophilus while he was away, as well as an excellent investment. John Phares promised that he would see that the land was profitable and that the crops were sold. When William had found a home for his family and decided he did not want the land, Phares himself would either sell it or buy it.

There was only one drawback. With the land went two female slaves, Fanny and Mollie, with their eight-year-old children, Sarah and Peter. Perhaps it did not take William long to rationalize that. He had already purchased Talbert. When he became a minister he would free them all. On October 17, 1843, he bought the land and slaves for $2,300 and moved in.

He was to buy another slave, through John Phares as agent, in December 1843, just before his departure, because Talbert alone could not be expected to farm the 240 acres. And so a "certain Negro man named Jacob, about twenty-two years of age," was bought for $625. William now owned eight slaves, including Mary's dowry.

He had swung a full cycle since Glasgow University. He was 31 years old, a family man, a man of property, a responsible man with cash saved during the seven years—and a slaveowner with an unrelenting hatred of slavery. Yet he was going to seek admission to a branch of a church militantly opposed to slavery, a branch then in the process of rebellion against its established hierarchy.

William intended to go to Edinburgh and apply for admission to the College of the Free Church of Scotland, which was even then in the midst of "The Disruption." On May 23, 1843, just six months before, Dr. Thomas W. Chalmers had led his Presbyterian ministers out of the Established Church in defiance of a Parliamentary edict, and was creating a new church with a simple formula of returning religion to the congregations. Thomas Babington, Lord Macaulay, was to rise in the House of Lords and proclaim his admiration:

> Four hundred and seventy ministers resigned their stipends, quitted their manses, and went forth committing themselves, their wives, their children, to the care of Providence. Their congregations followed them by thousands, and listened eagerly to the Word of Life in tents, in barns, or on those hills and moors where the stubborn Presbyterians of a former generation had prayed and sung their psalms in defiance of the boot of Lauderdale and the sword of Dundee. The rich gave largely of their riches. The poor contributed with the spirit of her who put her two mites into the treasury at Jerusalem. Meanwhile, in all the churches of large towns, of whole counties, the established clergy were preaching to empty benches.

William King chose this spiritual storm center as the site for fulfillment of his vow that one day he would be a minister of the Presbyterian Church. That choice revealed the missionary zeal that was to possess him all the rest of his life.

In mid-December 1843, he boarded a cotton ship in New Orleans for Liverpool and Edinburgh.

☆

PART TWO: PULPIT AND NORTH STAR

V : THY WILL BE DONE

BY THE FIRST WEEK in January 1844, William King was one of 300 divinity students drawn from all over the world to the New College of the Free Church of Scotland. The lodestone was Dr. Chalmers. The leader of the Disruption was not only moderator of the Free Church Assembly, president of the New College, professor of divinity there, director of the West Port Mission, fund raiser for the hundreds of new churches, spokesman against hostile political and ecclesiastical authorities, but he also seldom failed to preach on Sabbath.

For all of his three years in Edinburgh, William was to be in Dr. Chalmers' thrall, as a student, a protégé, and a friend. He met the founder of the Free Church on his second day in Edinburgh, and thereafter was to pattern his life and beliefs after that man's rare combination of unswerving faith and administrative practicality.

Of course, William was an exceptional student. By then, at the age of 31, the habits of learning had been reinforced by teaching. And he was privileged to be among the original twenty-four pioneers who put into practice Dr. Chalmers' "City of God" in the mission of West Port.

This was a section of Edinburgh quite similar to the poverty ghettos of any country in any age. Slums like West Port have been the subject of sociological study *ad nauseam,* and some of the theories have even concluded that such slums would not exist if there weren't a profit in them. In all of England and Scotland that profit was in cheap labor. Conditions in the slums in the 1840's were further aggravated by the potato famines of that decade. The Irish, faced with a choice of starvation at home or starvation abroad, flooded Scotland as well as most other countries of the world.

There was a strange similarity apparent to William between the whites of West Port and the black slaves of Louisiana. Both represented degrees of servitude which resulted in moral, physical, and mental dissolution. The crimes and carnality expressing their degeneration were exactly the same. There was only one essential difference in their conditions. In West Port the whites were expendable because there was an over-supply of labor. In East Feliciana the blacks were property and, as such, required at least sufficient care to maintain their value in labor. For the first time, William was able to understand the violent accusations of the planters in the pro-slavery argument that slaves in Louisiana were better off than mill children in Lawrence, Massachusetts, because they ate better. It was true. In West Port, as in Louisiana, he was to learn that the evidence of degradation was no proof that among certain classes and colors there existed an innate predilection for bestiality. This mission disproved it, as his own mission was to disprove it.

For the divinity student, the West Port Mission was a far greater inspiration than any of his theology classes. He adopted, for the rest of his life, Dr. Chalmers' concept of a "City of God," an ecclesiastical approach to the "inner-city" problems of the poor with which we are familiar today. Only the ingredients differ. Dr. Chalmers believed that the motivation for self-elevation lay in a Deity who was as concerned with the most miserable dweller of the Edinburgh slums as with the nobles and ladies who attended the Established Church from which he had broken. In his very first sermon in Glasgow, he called on the congregation in the Tron to "Dismiss then, my brethren, all your scholastic conceptions of the Deity, and keep by that warm and affecting view of Him that we have in the Bible."

A second ingredient for a "City of God"—and to this William King subscribed most fervently—was that Christianity and education were interchangeable and became Christian education. The content of such educational effort was not confined to the Sabbath School. It embraced patterns of living as well. The famous Scots geologist and essayist Hugh Miller attended services in the West Port Mission on August 3, 1845. Dr. Chalmers preached; but, as William King proudly reports, on that Sabbath he was allowed to deliver the opening prayer. Miller wrote a lengthy account of those services:

> The rude tannery loft was, we found, a true church after all—a place in which the poor had the gospel preached to them. We saw, too,—for its *dress,* like that of so many of the congregation which it sheltered, has impressed upon it the stamp of week-day labor,—that it was something more than a church. There were book-shelves ranged along the wall, bearing an array of somewhat tattered books, with a vast number of boys' slates, and a few calculating frames. The old tannery loft was not only a church, but also the school, of the locality; we were informed, too, that it was occasionally a lecture room and that the preacher had delivered in it, only a few evenings before, a lecture on savings banks. He intimated at the close of the singularly impressive service, that on the following Wednesday the school was to be examined; and invited all to attend. . . .

In Dr. Chalmers' faith in the "City of God" William was given his inspiration, and in the actual work of the West Port Mission he was given his pattern. He became Superintendent of the Sabbath School, being unable to teach regularly due to his own classes; but his experience with the wild young scions of Louisiana planters was to be put to practical use. This was in connection with the night school for older boys.

Keeping order was a problem. "The boys had been allowed to grow up without any restraint or moral training. They did not know the name of Jesus, only to swear by Him. In School they were up to all manner of mischief."

And so William, during the first year of the night school, initiated a most unorthodox method of pedagogy. He had the lights (gas) turned off for a few minutes each night, and the boys pitched into each other in a glorious free-for-all. When the lights were turned back on, they settled down to study.

In April 1844, William went to Liverpool. He was a happy man. When he returned to Edinburgh that fall, he would have his family with him and could show them off to his host of friends.

Both Mary and Theophilus would be taken out of slave country, never to return. They would be in the free air of Edinburgh for at least the next two years, and after that he would be a minister in the Free Church. He would free his slaves, and at last his conscience would be free as well. The future was clear and satisfying.

There had been no difficulty in obtaining permission from Dr. Chalmers to leave after the end of the session at New College, so long as he would be back for the new session. By then they were close friends. Mrs. Chalmers had seen to it that Mary and Theophilus had a home to come to. She had approved his choice of a house only a mile and a half from their own, at No. 1 Lord Russell Place. It was not large, but no houses in Edinburgh were, except the manors of the wealthy. Mrs. Chalmers had taken over the responsibility of seeing that the house was ready for Mary when they returned. It was a wonderful prospect for Mary, too. In Mrs. Chalmers she would have a mother and a confidante. There was nothing to mar William's joy as he hurried to the Liverpool docks. But the packet *Patrick Henry* had a capacity load of passengers and he would have to wait a week for the next ship. That was not for him. He was too eager to reach Louisiana.

Once again William showed his resourcefulness. He waited in the agent's office on the dock until the Captain came ashore. They were to sail in the morning. No, there were no cancellations by passengers. No, he had a full crew. He only lacked a second mate.

William had crossed the Atlantic twice, the first time with Capt. Durnys as supercargo, and he had occupied some of his time learning a few of the rudiments of navigation, such as using the quadrant. He had the mathematics to calculate longitude and latitude. On his second trip, from New Orleans to Liverpool, he had been too seasick to care.

He must have been exceptionally persuasive. "I bought me a red shirt and a Sou'wester and shipped as Second Mate on the good ship *Patrick Henry* for New York. . . ."

William stayed in Louisiana only long enough to visit with the family and check up on the affairs of his land and slaves; then, with Mary and Theophilus, he started up the Mississippi. He had little time if he was to return to Edinburgh for the beginning of the session at New College. The quickest way would have been by ship from New Orleans, but William was a husband and a father. His own family had never met his wife and son. His mother had died, but his father was still alive and in the Six Mile Woods with the hugely grown family, John's and his sisters'.

Then began a series of tragedies. At Detroit Theophilus took sick, and he died on the canal boat alongside the Maumee River. They carried him to Delta in a coffin and there he was buried in the King family plot.

Mary was ill when they left for Liverpool, but seemed to recover by the time they were in Edinburgh. She was well enough to join with William in the work at West Port Mission, and on September 11, 1845, gave birth to a daughter. Mary was extremely slow in recovering, and it was not until November 2 that she was able to attend the great event—the baptism of their child by Dr. Chalmers—right in their own church, the West Port Mission. She was named Johanna Elizabeth Chalmers King, for Mary's father, William's mother, and the Scots divine.

Mary was sick that same night. She suffered from a persistent cough and lassitude, which were complicated by extreme depression when news came from Louisiana that her father had died suddenly. The leading physician in Edinburgh, Sir James Simpson, diagnosed the illness as "lingering consumption." Mary died on February 25, 1846, and again Dr. Chalmers officiated. All of the students and the faculty of the New College attended the rites in Leith Cemetery.

They all returned to the very same graveside a few months later, where Dr. Chalmers conducted funeral services for little Johanna, who died on May 9, 1846, of a "brain inflammation."

"After the death of my child, the last of my family, I was now left alone."

A man's grief cannot be explored but his faith is revealed in his works. A man of lesser faith than William King would have been shaken from it by such losses—a wife and two children in less than two years. At the least he would have pleaded, "My God, why hast Thou forsaken me?"

There is no evidence at all, in his daily work in Edinburgh and later, in his sermons, letters, or diaries, of what would have been an understandable bitterness. His actions demonstrate quite the reverse—a closer communion with his Maker, and a greater dedication to the needs of his fellow man.

It may be because he was so close to Dr. Chalmers during his time of trouble. He acknowledged that Dr. and Mrs. Chalmers saw to it that he was not alone. Throughout Mary's illness, Dr. Chalmers "was constant in his attentions, often visiting my wife upon her death bed, talking kindly to her with regard to her spiritual state. . . . The kindness which I received from him on that trying occasion will never be forgotten. His sympathy and kind words were a great comfort to me in that painful bereavement."

Dr. Chalmers also kept William busy in West Port and walked home with him after their weekly committee meetings there. He saw to it that William was at his home often, where Mrs. Chalmers "did the honors of the table." William was a constant guest at the leisurely Wednesday morning breakfasts when Dr. Chalmers would entertain as many as fifty or sixty distinguished guests. It was at such breakfasts that William met Dr. Lyman Beecher, father of Harriet Beecher Stowe. There he met the world's theological leaders such as Dr. Frederick Monod, the French Huguenot, and Dr. Jean Henri Merle D'Aubigne, historian of the Reformation in Europe. Again, on St. Patrick's Day William joined the other Irish students in a huge dinner for Dr. Chalmers, for that was his birthday.

Slavery was to haunt William in Edinburgh too. Just as he had become involved in the institution, so he was to become a victim of one of its conflicts.

It was September 1845, and William was attending an Abolition meeting in Queen Street Hall with Rev. William

Cunningham, a leader in the Free Church, one of his professors, and a friend. Mr. Cunningham had spent that summer in the United States, raising money for the Free Church of Scotland. He had been highly successful in his tour, ranging from Boston south to Virginia; and some of the funds were to build the new West Port Church.

On the platform were the most articulate Abolitionists of the day, including George Thompson of the British Anti-Slavery Society, and James N. Buffum and Henry C. Wright of the American Abolitionists. But the excited, overflow audience had come to hear one of the greatest Americans of any color, Frederick Douglass. The fugitive slave commanded the attention of all the British Isles during the two years he spent there.

The audience in Queen Street Hall knew that this black man before them was an escaped slave and that he had left the United States with the help of the Abolitionists immediately after publication of his scathing "Narration of Frederick Douglass," the story of his slavery and escape. He was put aboard the S.S. *Cambria* because his friends in the American Anti-Slavery Society feared the slave catchers would extend themselves to find him. Since 1841 Frederick Douglass had developed into the most effective antislavery orator in the country. He stood and spoke as a living example of the black man's potential in freedom, a proud, self-taught, compassionate man who was owned by Thomas Auld of Maryland. Not for another year was he able to return to the war on slavery in the United States, not until a Quakeress, Miss Ellen Richardson, had raised 150 pounds in England to buy his freedom.

In his autobiography Douglass relates the crisis in Edinburgh in detail. The question agitating the Free Church and all Scotland was a most puzzling one. If the Free Church was opposed to slavery, should it accept money from slaveowners with which to build churches and schools? It was the reverse side of the Smith-Winans conflict so familiar to William King. Douglass declares that the debate had the people "deeply moved."

That the people of Scotland were "deeply moved" by the question is an understatement. Even Arthur's Seat was painted with the legend "Send back the money!" William reports that "Placards were put up everywhere in the City crying 'send back the money!' Children on the streets, when they saw a Free Church member they would cry to him 'send back the money!' "

It was in this atmosphere that William King heard Frederick Douglass lash out at a hypocrite who would preach the gospel while a slaveowner, and against the Free Church for admitting a divinity student who was a slaveowner.

> The delegation from the United States had by some means learned that I was a slaveowner and was studying in the Free Church for a minister. . . . I was not named but the students all knew that I came from a slave state and that my wife was the daughter of a planter. . . . I told Dr. Cunningham my position and said that I would go on the platform and explain my position but he advised me to say nothing about it.

The cancerous fact of slavery allowed both Frederick Douglass and William King to be right, the first in his charges and the second in his helplessness. The institution itself fostered conflict between honest men.

William and Mary did own eight slaves at the time of the meeting. It was legally impossible for him to set them free without a special act of the Louisiana legislature for each case, because each one was under thirty years of age. That age limit was set under a law of 1807, and there was only one exception—when a slave of any age saved the life of his master or any member of his master's family. In 1827 this law was liberalized a bit by allowing the manumission of a slave under the age of thirty through vote of three-fourths of a Parish Police Jury, providing the slave was born in Louisiana. This required first a petition to the Police Jury and then an appearance before it. Then, in 1830, there was another complication. Any manumitted slave was required to leave the state, and the law required the owner to post a bond of one thousand dollars for each slave to assure his departure within thirty days. In 1842, the state legislature also forbade freedom for any slave—statu liber—at a specified time in the future requested by the master.

William had examined the laws well. He also knew that no East Feliciana Police Jury had ever manumitted a slave under thirty years of age, only a handful much older who had become burdens to their masters. He had only one course in freeing them, to bring them himself into a free state and give them their manumission papers.

At the time of the meeting in Queen's Hall, that was physically impossible. Johanna was just born and Mary was ill. William could go to Louisiana and bring out only his own slaves, not Mary's dowry. When Mary died, he could not even then free all his slaves because the Louisiana law made Johanna her mother's heir to such property. On that basis William's sister-in-law filed suit to determine whether he could inherit any slaves at all, including those left by John Phares to his daughter in his will. Nor could the will be probated until William returned to Louisiana. Phares had named him co-executor.

William's legal complications and sheer inability to go to Louisiana could not be explained publicly either. The Slave Code was written to protect those who wished to keep their slaves, not free them, and no Parish Police Jury would honor his intentions. Dr. Cunningham's advice to William to keep quiet while being lashed by Frederick Douglass was his only possible course.

Yet Frederick Douglass was entirely justified in making his accusations. The only circumstances known were that a slaveowner was studying for the ministry in a church that accepted tainted slave money. That could not be refuted. But the whole incident was only symptomatic of the relationship of all churches to slavery. Of course the Free Church accepted slave profits. All over the United States, in the Abolitionist headquarters of Boston as well as in the South, churches were built with slave profits, from ornate cathedrals to trim New England Gothics.

In the British Parliament during William's years in Edinburgh, there was continuous debate on two issues which were to affect not only his future but events in North America. One was the economic about-face taken by Great Britain in establishment of free trade, and the other was slavery on the North American continent. One fed upon the other.

The students of the Free Church followed the parliamentary debates on both the slave trade and the tariffs avidly. *The Edinburgh Witness* faithfully and at length reported the speeches and comments of Edinburgh's own M.P. and idolized spokesman of the Opposition, Thomas Babington Macaulay. Macaulay's remarkable powers of satiric expression were never more effectively used than during the Peel administration of the 1840's. At New College the divinity students studied his speeches as well as the Scriptures; but William was the only one among them with a slavery background and experience. And when, on February 26, 1845, Lord Macaulay slashed open and exposed the hypocrisy of the British Prime Minister in proposing prohibitive tariffs on Brazilian sugar because it was raised by slave labor, William King was the authority to testify to the truth of the indictment. He could cite personal experience to endorse each charge. There were many. Macaulay declared:

> The United States, it is said, have slavery; but they have no slave trade. I deny that assertion. I say that the sugar and cotton of the United States are the fruits not only of slavery, but of the slave trade. And I say further that, if there be on the surface of this earth a country which, before God and man, is more accountable than any other for the misery and degradation of the African race, that country is not Brazil, the produce of which the Right Honourable Baronet excludes, but the United States, the produce of which he proposes to admit on more favourable terms than ever. . . .

This scathing evaluation, coming from an Englishman who had not lived with slavery as William had, who was not entangled in it as William was, made a difficult time for the divinity student. Sometimes he wavered. Was he right in keeping his own slaves in bondage until he could bring them out of Egypt himself? Shouldn't he give up or postpone his theological studies until he had freed them? He was continuing slavery for eight human beings by following his own ambitions. The question assailed him often, and each time he brought it to Dr. Chalmers, at his home or on their walks back from the West Port Mission.

Each time, Dr. Chalmers reminded him of the Free Church Assembly decision that slaveowning was sinful only if the master did not set his slaves free as soon as the opportunity presented itself. He agreed with Macaulay entirely and pointed out that if, like William, all masters planned to free their slaves within their lifetime or at least, on death, within a generation slavery would disappear.

This was adequate to quiet William's conscience, but perhaps more potent was another argument advanced by Macaulay which bared the heart of his own problem. He could arrange to ship his eight slaves to Liberia after freeing them. But wouldn't that be similar to returning the Irish refugees to starvation in Ireland from the West Port Mission? They would be lost to Christianity then, and be subject to spiritual as well as physical starvation. There was another alternative, the Free States of the North. But William knew them too well. His people would have no true freedom, nor would its semblance be secure due to the Black Laws. They would remain in ignorance and always under the threats of the slave catchers or encroaching political power of the slave expansion. One of Macaulay's points in the February 1845 speech reached the ears of his troubled conscience. What were his slaves to do when set free?

> There is another point to which I must advert. . . . I mean the antipathy of colour. Where this antipathy exists in a high degree, it is difficult to conceive how the white masters and the black labourers can ever be mingled together, as the lords and villeins in many parts of the Old World have been, in one free community. Now this antipathy is notoriously much stronger in the United States than it is in the Brazils. In the Brazils the free people of colour are numerous. They are not excluded from honourable callings. You may find them among the merchants, physicians, lawyers; many of them bear arms; some have been admitted to holy orders. Whoever knows what dignity, what sanctity, the Church of Rome ascribes to the person of a priest, will at once perceive the important consequences which follow from this last circumstance. It is by no means unusual to see a white penitent kneeling before the spiritual tribunal of a negro, confessing his sins to a negro, receiving absolution from a negro. It is by no means unusual to see a negro dispensing the Eucharist to a circle of whites. I need not tell the House what emotions of amazement and rage such a spectacle would excite in Georgia or South Carolina. Fully admitting, therefore, as I

> do, that Brazilian slavery is a horrible evil, I yet must say that, if I were called upon to declare whether I think the chances of the African race on the whole better in Brazil or in the United States, I should at once answer that they are better in Brazil. I think it is not improbable that in eighty or a hundred years the black population of Brazil may be free and happy. I see no reasonable prospect of such a change in the United States.

Macaulay was prophetic. The "antipathy of colour" was and is the essential difference between North and South America. As for the slave trade from Africa, William had known even the quoted prices for slaves shipped via Havana. To claim that the United States had abolished the slave trade was an outright lie. Nor would it disappear so long as the domestically raised crop of slaves was insufficient to supply the need in the South.

The Abolitionists themselves took slave profits, as William well knew. Thousands of antislavery tracts were printed as a result of contributions from New England and New York which derived from slave smuggling.

William himself had seen the coffles of slaves from the east, and he had seen the New Orleans slave market selling freshly smuggled slaves from Cuba or Mexico.

Yet the United States had declared the African slave trade illegal three weeks before the British took similar action. President Thomas Jefferson signed the bill abolishing slave imports from Africa on March 2, 1807, to be totally effective on January 1, 1808. Like the 14th Amendment, however, it had no enforcement features and was disregarded.

The major route into the Black Belt for smuggled slaves was through Florida. In 1853, a veteran of some fifteen years as factor of a smuggling station there, Richard Drake, was to say, "this business of smuggling Bozal negroes into the United

States. It is growing more profitable every year, and if you should hang all the Yankee merchants engaged in it, hundreds would fill their places."

The years in Edinburgh were, for William, a period of confusion and doubt in regard to emancipation. He had come a full cycle since the Glasgow University marches and meetings had demanded "Set the slaves free NOW." Then he had derided those like George Canning who warned Parliament that the slave must first be taught to be free or else the Briton "finds too late that he has only created a more than mortal power of doing mischief, and himself recoils from the monster of his own creation."

William asked himself: Was there no further obligation than freedom for his own slaves?

He knew them, as he knew the exceptions among the slaves in the Felicianas. How could he turn them loose in the white man's society such as Ohio, so unprepared to meet the most rudimentary problems of their positions in that society? He had seen them, the "free" Negroes there, and knew that they were defenseless.

Liberia? It was a mockery to send them into a foreign land and back to Africa while the slave trade replaced them tenfold daily in the cotton and sugar fields. Slavery had degraded them below even a capacity to function in a primitive civilization as well as the natives.

Like many countries had done before his time and since then, William was trying to determine the extent of his obligation to the Negroes, and his conclusion was that mere manumission was not enough. If slavery were ever to be ended in the minds and motives of a people, even after freedom, more than emancipation was needed. He would see that his slaves had their own "City of God." This determination was made before he left Edinburgh.

William completed his studies and was licensed by the Edinburgh Presbytery. He had, with five others, specifically requested foreign mission work, in Canada, and on July 17, 1846, was appointed by the Colonial Committee of the Free Church of Scotland as its first missionary there.

> The meeting appointed and hereby appoint the Rev. William King as missionary to Canada for a period not exceeding three years, but instead of nominating him to any particular charge they preferred that he should be under the direction of the Presbytery of Toronto. They resolved that Thirty Pounds should be voted for his outfit and necessary expenses in this country and a farther sum of Twenty Pounds for his traveling expenses. Also the usual sum of Ten Pounds for Books, etc. That he should be prepared to sail for America during the month of August and remain there for three years at least and that he should not remove beyond the bounds of the Synod of Canada during that time except with the consent of the Committee, & so long as he remained without being placed over any particular congregation as their permanent pastor that he should receive the usual allowance of One Hundred Pounds per annum, payable half-yearly (the first half year's salary being payable in advance), which however would cease either at the termination of three years or on his being appointed Minister of a particular charge.
>
> Extracted by I. A. Balfour, Sec'y.

It was now Reverend William King. He was now nearly 34 years old. It had taken twenty years since he first determined to become a minister in the Presbyterian Church. The Sabbath following his appointment he preached at West Port at last, before Dr. Chalmers, and then set sail from Liverpool. Now he could set his slaves free and dedicate himself to a "City of God."

☆

VI : BREAKING THE WEB

WHILE HIS APPOINTMENT directed him to proceed to Canada in August 1846, the Reverend Mr. King obtained permission to go to Louisiana first in order to settle his personal affairs. He did not explain to the Colonial Committee what those "affairs" were, feeling certain that he only needed to pick up his own slaves and take them to Canada with him. Apparently only his friends in the Free Church knew his situation, Dr. Chalmers, Dr. Cunningham, and Dr. Candlish.

He now owned fourteen slaves. A copy of John Phares' will sent to him as co-executor listed Mary as inheriting Ben, Emeline, Robin, Ise (Isaiah), and Old Stephen as well as a share of the residue of the slaves in the estate, which was to bring him Harriet.

> I could now see the dispensation which appeared so dark and mysterious to me at the time I lost my whole family, that it was preparing the way for me to manumit the slaves that were coming to me by inheritance.

That was literally true. Had Johanna lived, her father would have been unable to free the inherited slaves. Now, however, William inherited from his daughter and could take those slaves to Canada too.

He was in for complete disillusionment. When he reached Jackson, William found himself in a family, financial, and legal morass. John Phares had been married three times and there had been children by each wife. Only Mary's brother and sister, William Douglas Phares and Martha Brame, had reached their majority. Three children by the second wife were minors, and there were also the widow, Frances Emmaline, and her baby daughter, Clara.

The estate consisted of approximately one thousand acres in two plantations, valued at twenty-five thousand dollars. In addition, after all bequests there were 38 slaves remaining to be divided among all the heirs. But even that was further complicated by a clause in the will preventing liquidation of the East Feliciana plantation for ten years. John Phares had considerately wished his widow and child to have a home for at least that long. Therefore, the slaves on that plantation could not be distributed for another nine years.

In addition, there were livestock, cash due from factors for cotton and sugar, a complex mass of promissory notes to and from other planters to be balanced against each other. Finally, the inevitable family quarrel broke out. Martha Brame protested William King's right to inherit at all, based on the fact that Johanna had been born abroad, not in Louisiana. This placed William in an anomalous legal position because he was also co-executor of the will. His title to the slaves and any residue after bequests would always be in question.

There were many meetings of the family without further action than appointing trustees for the minors. Finally, on October 21, there was a meeting at which William requested that Dr. David Phares be appointed interim executor until the question of William's own right of inheritance was decided in the Parish Police Jury. Without such a decision, there would always be a cloud on his title, nor could the estate be distributed.

It was also agreed to sell the Pointe Coupee land and transfer the slaves to Dr. Phares' keeping. Thus there would be funds available to keep the East Feliciana plantation in operation. This agreement was legally recorded and the optimistic estimate was made that the estate could be distributed within a year.

Meanwhile, William had his own problems, as a slave- and landowner. He was informed by various merchants and cotton factors that he owed a total of $1,100 for supplies and advances to his own plantation during the 1845–46 crop years. During 1844, with John Phares' supervision, the 240 acres had paid its way. But, in the succeeding year, Phares first was ill and then died late in 1845, then boll weevils hit the cotton hard and the crops were small. Cotton was down to seven and eight cents a pound. But even with such bad times, Phares might have saved William's interests. What happened in those distant years happens today among Negro sharecroppers who exist in a form of peonage. They are at the not-too-tender mercies of the whites with whom they trade, and some are inevitably enslaved by debt.

By then both Talbert and Jacob could read but dared not reveal it. They could figure a little, but were forced to accept the arithmetic of others. Credit had been extended to them because every merchant and cotton factor knew that he could seize both the slaves and the land if their bills were not paid. If William were to believe Talbert, and he did, those bills still could not be challenged in any court in Louisiana because no Negro could testify against a white man.

Slavery still had him in its tentacles. William was now a minister of the church and could not sell his slaves, worth between five and six thousand dollars at that time, even if he possessed a convenient conscience. He would be barred from the ministry if the Presbyterian Church authorities learned of such a sale. He took the only decisive action he could to pay the debt.

"I moved all my servants to Dr. Phares'. . . . I ordered my horses, corn, household furniture and land to be sold and the debt to be paid."

He could wait no longer and left for Canada, arriving in Toronto on November 16, 1846, having celebrated his thirty-fourth birthday with the ever-increasing King family in Delta, Ohio.

Once more William King demonstrated his capacity for enduring friendships. He registered at the Wellington Hotel in Toronto, and the following morning there was a knock at his door. It was Dr. Robert Burns, the revered leader in the Canadian Presbyterian Church who was to adopt this new missionary much as Dr. Chalmers had adopted him, as a protégé and an ever-lasting friend.

Dr. Burns was being courteous in calling on William. He notified him that his books and clothing had arrived from Edinburgh, and invited him to stay at the Burns' home until he received his assignment from the Toronto Presbytery. Meanwhile, he also put the Rev. Mr. King to work.

On the very next Sabbath, King preached in Knox Church, Hamilton, to be invited back the following Sunday. His reception by various congregations was so laudatory that the Toronto Presbytery utilized him as a guest minister throughout Canada West. He was not given a permanent mission assignment until he himself created the Buxton Mission two years later.

As a result, William received an invaluable indoctrination into the problems of the future province of Ontario. He met many familiar concerns there, for Canada West was in the same stage of development he had found in the Western Reserve more than a decade before. The land-hungry immigrants, chiefly Scots and Irish, were pushing westward toward the Thames River outlet into Lake St. Clair and to Owen Sound on Lake Huron. There, forested Crown and Clergy Reserves were to be had at low prices, like the government land the Kings had bought in Ohio. The new settlers were pioneers, and William knew them well. He himself had experienced all of their difficulties.

Perhaps that is why his sermons were received so well wherever he preached. He could laugh with them and lament with them because he too had raised blisters on his hands, had been trapped in the mud of the crude roads, had gloried in the first crop from virgin land. William King was well able to translate the Scriptures into their everyday terms. Besides, he knew these people, both the Scots and the Irish, for he had been raised among them.

It was during this period of indoctrination that William King came to realize his own mission. His superiors assigned him to preach at the new St. Andrews Presbyterian Church in Chatham, then a sprawling village along the Thames River and McGregor's Creek. It was a typical pioneer settlement in which the taverns were the centers of political and social activities, and "drink or fight" was the prevailing attitude. But Chatham was far from typical in one respect. Its population of approximately twelve hundred within the township was one-third Negro in 1846.

There were good reasons for this concentration. While Windsor and Amherstburg on Lake Erie were points of refuge for escaping slaves from the South or from the "Free" North, Chatham was the burgeoning commercial center for all the newly settled "up-country" of Kent County. It was the terminus of the rude wilderness Talbot Road cut from the east, and had water transport to all the lakes through the Thames River.

There was work here for the fugitive Negroes, many of whom had brought with them plantation skills urgently needed in Chatham. The first ironworker there was a Negro, as was the first stonemason. Many of them had navigated the Ohio and the Mississippi, and were skilled in poling the barges up or down the Thames. In contrast, neither the Scots nor the Irish immigrants had had much opportunity to learn skills in the old country. The former tended to the land, and the latter to all the unskilled work of any new settlement.

Another reason for the Negro concentration was the Dawn Settlement some thirty miles north, near Dresden, where the Rev. Josiah Henson (Uncle Tom) had settled and the Dawn Institute for ". . . Education, Mental, Moral and Physical of the Coloured Inhabitants of Canada not excluding white persons and Indians" had been founded four years before by British Abolitionists. It was known as the British-American Institute and taught Negroes crafts and trades urgently needed in Canada, and particularly in Chatham.

William King preached at Dawn, at Colchester, at Amherstburg—wherever Negroes had gathered. In these settlements too he was highly successful as a preacher. Once more it was because he knew these people. He owned some of them. They were forever on his mind and conscience as he waited out the year until he could return to Louisiana for his slaves. It was in these Negro settlements that he formulated his plan, both for his own slaves and for all Negro fugitives. It was his first exposure to these groups that matured his own thinking in regard to "The Slavery of Ignorance."

After preaching before them, two congregations offered him permanent pastorates, and King was forced to refuse both. For one thing, he could accept no ministry so long as he was a slaveowner; and by then he had determined his sphere of missionary activity. However, dominating all his future was the liberation of his slaves. He could not plan, could not promise, could not pursue any given course until he himself was free.

In March 1847, William made a decision. He could no longer delay the work he wished to do. He appeared before the Toronto Presbytery and explained his situation. "The news fell like a bombshell on the members of the Presbytery."

He also offered his resignation because he intended to return to Louisiana and find some way out of slavery.

> I did not know what might befall me and should anything happen to prevent me from carrying out my intention the Free Church would suffer no reproach on my account for I was no longer a member of that Church.

He was given a hearing on March 28 and the following was the decision of the Presbytery:

> Mr. William King, missionary, appeared in the Presbytery; after lengthened conference with him the following resolution was unanimously adopted: That, while the deportment of Mr. King during the time he has been within the bounds of the Presbytery and his services as a missionary have been entirely satisfactory, yet in respect to certain relations in which Mr. King stands as brought out in the report of the Committee and the conference with him, and not known as he admits to any member or Presbytery of the Free Church at the time of his leaving Scotland, the Presbytery cannot while these relations continue employ him as a Probationer or missionary. . . .

Was William King being dishonest with the Colonial Committee and the Toronto Presbytery in waiting so long before informing them that he could not free his slaves as yet?

It is difficult to know the answer. It should be remembered that he had fully expected to free his slaves before entering his duties in Canada. It should also be remembered that his one dominating worry was that word would reach Louisiana of his intention to set them free. He knew the Black Laws and the power of the planters there. Neither the Colonial Committee nor the Toronto Presbytery could realize that mere word of his intention would decide the East Feliciana Police Jury against his inheritance in the legal suit brought by Martha Brame.

On April 6, after the hearing, William poured his heart out in a letter to Dr. Cunningham, explaining the situation he was in. He asked his friend to consult with Dr. Candlish about it and advise him. But, he added:

> I also wish, if you think it necessary to lay the subject of this communication before the [Colonial] Committee, to keep it private. I do not want it to be made public till I have liberated my slaves. To make it public now would embarrass me in my operation and perhaps, frustrate my design altogether.

Again and again, in his letters, William expresses this fear.

Far from feeling that he was under a cloud, however, William quite characteristically seized the opportunities to present his plan for the future. He had the whole Toronto Presbytery before him at the hearing on March 28. What if his status was on trial? The important question was the future of the Negroes in Canada, and he pursued that question aggressively.

> I also laid before the Presbytery the destitution of the coloured race in Canada, urging on them the necessity of doing something for their spiritual wants, and offering to preach to them. The Presbytery entertained the proposition favourably, but could do nothing at present for want of men and means.

Nor did King neglect the chance to recruit support for his plan in Edinburgh. In his lengthy letter to Dr. Cunningham he appended:

> If permitted to return to Scotland, I would lay before the Committee the cause of the coloured people of Canada and should the Free Church deem it necessary to establish a mission among them, I could easily raise the funds necessary to erect a station from those who feel so much sympathy for the slave. In Canada they are perfectly acceptable and many of them worse off (spiritually) than the slaves in the U.S.

William King was never conscious of being on trial for owning slaves. He felt that he was on trial to prove his conviction that a "City of God" was possible among them. And William was a tenacious man.

During the first week in May, while waiting in Toronto for a reply from Edinburgh, William's hands were untied. He received a letter from Frances Emmaline Phares bearing the glorious tidings that the East Feliciana Police Jury had ruled in his favor. She suggested that he hurry south because the affairs of the estate could now be wound up in all respects except the Feliciana plantation. Meanwhile, the other heirs wished a partial distribution.

William set out for the South. He planned to stop for only a day in Ohio to see his father and family at Delta, then continue down the Maumee Canal.

Once more he was to be frustrated. He found another letter at Delta. Dr. Phares wrote to warn William that a yellow fever epidemic was already raging throughout the South and it would be unsafe to expose himself to it until the October frosts had ended the scourge. During his years away, William would have lost whatever immunity he had acquired and would be particularly susceptible. This meant a postponement of some five months, wasted months of idleness because he could not return to his mission. He had no appointment.

William proceeded to make his own appointment as a missionary. He founded the first Presbyterian Church in Ohio north of the Maumee River. From 1834 when he had settled his family in the Six Mile Woods until his return and forced stay in 1847, there had not even been a Presbyterian preacher circuit-riding the area.

A few other Presbyterian families had settled in Delta and around the Six Mile Woods, and John King had established his home as a Sabbath Center. With the large King family, it became an unguided congregation. Sabbath was both a social occasion and a day for reading the Bible as well as such religious works as Clark's *Commentary on the Scriptures.*

When William arrived in May 1847 his proud father asked him to conduct full services, and he preached. Soon the family barn began to fill up each Sunday, and John King canvassed the neighbors on the score of financial help in building a church. He accumulated a sufficient subscription list, and after a summer of growing attendance it was decided that a church and affiliation was necessary. William borrowed a horse and took the subscription list approximately 50 miles southeast to the nearest Presbytery in Findlay, Ohio.

The Presbytery promised a mission station in Delta which would also serve the surrounding area, and William returned to help organize the First Presbyterian Church of Delta. The missionary, Rev. Crabb, was to arrive within a few weeks, and by late October William was ready to leave.

In Louisiana, William was to find a curious situation. The Phares family had made plans for the young widower, most logical plans, and Frances Emmaline, then thirty years old, had accepted them as ideal. She and William would be married. They would combine the East Feliciana land, stock, and slaves left her by John Phares with the adjoining 240 acres, stock, and slaves owned by William, and be wealthy. If William insisted upon being a minister, he would have a choice of churches. In fact, the family could build him a new one. It was all so suitable.

It was also touch-and-go for William and Frances Emmaline. They were together a great deal that winter, since William was now restored as active executor and Frances Emmaline was executrix.

In March 1848, William himself did sell the Pointe Coupee property to a neighboring planter, but without the slaves. These had been sent to join his own on Dr. Phares' plantation. Apparently the sale climaxed a series of frightening experiences.

The fright came from the circumstances of their stay in the Pointe Coupee homestead, not the dangers experienced in reaching there with Frances Emmaline and her baby. Those were bad enough. They had set out in the family carriage, as executor and executrix, from Jackson to cross the river to the plantation on the west bank, at Blind River. But the rains were heavy, the driver lost the road, the Mississippi was in flood, and they almost drove over a crumbling cliff into Thompson's Creek where it feeds into the river. Darkness fell, mosquitoes clouded thicker than the skies, and, when they reached the ferry landing, the ferryman refused to venture onto the swollen river with the carriage and horses. Finally, William bribed him to take them across in a skiff. The treacherous ferryman left them on a sandbank thrown up by the river and refused to hear William when he shouted for him to come back. There was no choice but to wade through the water and the swamp. Frances Emmaline was brave through it all, even though she lost her slippers and silk stockings. They dragged themselves to the Big House at eleven o'clock that Friday night, William with the added burden of the baby.

But that hazardous experience was nothing compared with the clear warning bell William received that weekend from Frances Emmaline and others. The planter buying the Phares land asked William to preach that Sunday in a schoolhouse on the bank of the Mississippi, since there was neither preacher nor church in the vicinity. He readily agreed. Slaves carried word to the surrounding plantations and there was a goodly congregation.

> After the sermon, I stopped and conversed with the people who had assembled to hear me. I found many of them young men from the North who had received a liberal education and had come South to better their worldly circumstances. Many of them would marry with wives and settle down as planters, and whatever their views may have been before they came, they soon became, when they married and settled there, the strong supporters of slavery. Such was the corrupting influence the system had on the minds of young men.

With Frances Emmaline around his neck, small wonder that William reported that "I hastened to wind up the affairs of both plantations."

He did manage to escape from Frances Emmaline for the next few weeks with a valid excuse. Whenever and wherever asked, he had traveled to most of the churches in the Felicianas for long weekends and Sabbath preaching. Now he had an invitation from New Orleans and hurried off.

By mid-April he was ready to shock the Phares family. While the land and other property distribution would not take place for some time, the slaves were distributed. William waived all further inheritance.

> I received the number coming to me by my wife, and put them with my own on Dr. Phares' plantation. Up to this time I had said nothing to any of the family what I intended to do with mine. I had not hired them out. I had sold my plantation and was not purchasing another. It was generally believed that I would marry the young widow and settle down on a plantation. However, I was soon forced to divulge the secret.

William does not relate how Frances Emmaline took the shock. But planters offered him nine thousand dollars for his slaves. Dr. Phares offered to hire them for nine hundred dollars a year. He had suspected William's intention since the latter had not prepared land for planting that spring. William hastened to get his bills of sale for the slaves and then called them before him, in Dr. Phares' presence:

> I told them that in two weeks I was going to leave for Canada and would take them with me. The journey was long and I wished them to be ready by that time. They seemed not to understand what was meant by going to Canada. Most of them thought it was some new plantation I had purchased and was going to take them to it. I then explained to them that Canada was a free country, that there were no slaves there, and that when we reached that country I would give them their freedom and place them on farms where they would have to support themselves by their own industry. Until I was ready to start, they would have a holiday to visit their friends and to prepare for the journey. . . . The good news seemed to have little effect upon them. They had come to consider that slavery was their normal condition. They did not know what freedom meant. They thought that to be free was to be like their master, to go idle and have a good time.

William had planned to start for New Orleans the next day and book passage on a steamer, picking up his slaves at Bayou Sara on May 5, but he was delayed by Harriet. She had not known that she was to be separated from her four-year-old son Solomon. "The woman was so distracted about leaving her child that I bought it." He had barely enough money left to get them all to Canada but paid $150 for Solomon.

By this he had compounded his sins. Again he had bought human flesh, but now he was a minister of the church. In later years, he was accused of this too, and could never deny it. It did happen. As far as William was concerned, however, the breakup of a family, a mother and child, was a greater sin, and he described the bill of sale for Solomon as "a curious document in its way. He is warranted to me to be a slave for life although I was going to set him free in a few weeks." Slavery festered a number of differing moralities.

William went on to New Orleans still not knowing whether his mission would be successful. By then, word had spread through the Felicianas plantations that this seemingly sane man, who had taught so many of them in Mathews Academy, was actually taking his slaves to Canada where they would be certain to be free. If he had manumitted them for Liberia that was acceptable. But some of the planters had lost their slaves to the North Star. All of them resented the talk in the slave quarters about the fifteen slaves who were going to an unknown plantation called "Canada" to enjoy something called "Freedom." Such talk made the slaves restless, and, like Bennett Barrow, the planters believed that thinking by slaves led to trouble. "Can't let a peach get ripe."

In spite of these questions and doubts, William realized the obligation before him. While in New Orleans, trying to make arrangements for the northbound steamer, he decided the future with a letter to the Colonial Committee of the Free Church on April 22, and addressed to the Clerk, Mr. Balfour:

> I have been successful in my mysion to the U. States and have finished my business last month. In two days I leave this city for Canada . . . with fifteen servants that I have manumitted. I have still a duty to perform toward them, and that is to provide them with a home. I will not be able to labour in the services of the Colonial Committee when I return and therefore decline having my appointment renewed.

Then William returned to his search for a steamer, and his worries whether, actually, he would ever be freed completely from slavery. Would the planters let him take his people?

But William had placed his faith in Dr. Phares. This

good friend had given his word that William's slaves would be ready at midday May 5, on the wharf at Bayou Sara with whatever belongings they were taking. "I had confidence in him that he would act honorably with me."

They were there on the dock at Bayou Sara. Dr. Phares was with them as well as his overseer. None of the throng of planters would dare cause trouble for Dr. Phares, and at the rail of the steamer, William knew that his mission would be completed. There was no incident.

When the captain rang the bell and the steamer started upriver, William saw to it that his Negroes were bedded down on the foredeck and then went to his cabin to give his thanks to God.

The fifteen hundred miles to Cincinnati were without incident, but there was intense curiosity among the white passengers. William allowed his slaves the freedom of the boat, as far as it was allowed to Negroes, and when they stopped at the piles of fuel wood, the Captain was happy to let them help load it. One planter warned William that he was giving his slaves too much freedom, that they would run away. A white minister lectured William on the old Southern comfort that the slaves would be better off on a plantation where their spiritual life could be sponsored, rather than to live in heathenish freedom.

When they reached Cincinnati, William called all of his slaves together and told them they were free, that he had manumission papers for each of them, and they had the right to go their own way. They had that choice, or that of going north with him to his family's farm in Delta, and then on to Canada when he had found land for them.

None of them asked for their manumission papers. Old Stephen spoke up for them and asked "Massa" King to take them wherever he was going.

But there was trouble. The regular packet on the canal

to Toledo was refused to the Negroes. Also, the well-meaning and justifiably suspicious Abolitionists in Cincinnati (whose Underground Railroad activities were made famous by Levi Coffin) warned his Negroes that many a planter and slave dealer had reached their city with promises of freedom, only to sell them piecemeal to slave states at higher prices.

Old Stephen reported the conversation to William. He said that they asked where the group was going and Stephen replied that they did not know, were going wherever the master was going. That was when the Abolitionists warned Stephen that they might be sold to a slave state and the Negro laughed. His master wouldn't have brought them fifteen hundred miles for that purpose when there was a thriving slave market right in New Orleans.

But William's slaves were worried when he finally arranged for a barge to take them north on the canal while he himself planned to take the packet. They begged him not to leave them, and so he shared a tiny cabin with the captain and his crew while the Negroes were bedded in the hold.

On that canal boat William King preached before his first mixed congregation. Each of the three nights the boat was stopped at sundown for services, and the crew attended with the Negroes. This was in Ohio before the Black Laws were relaxed. He could have been fined a thousand dollars for such an act.

There was another mixed congregation in the King family barn one mile south of Delta, Ohio, that Sunday. After regular services, William held special prayer services in thanksgiving.

His slaves were safe, despite the Black Laws. They were not yet free because they had not crossed the "line." But the King men would protect them from slave stealers, having had a good deal of experience in such activities. The King farm by then was the area's Underground Railroad station on the overland route to the woods that bordered the Detroit River and Lake St. Clair, across from Canada West.

They were safe but still not freed from the "Slavery of Ignorance," or the slavery of economic dependence. To make a start in liberating them from ignorance, William arranged with John for their instruction with all the King children, in reading and writing.

Then, with his own mind free, William set out to liberate them economically. He started for Canada to find them land—land that they themselves could own, could buy, and not merely receive as a gift.

William set out for Canada with little money but an indomitable self-assurance. He would be back for his slaves very soon. He would find land quickly. He had written to the Toronto Presbytery that, although his private mission was about to be accomplished, he could not undertake a church mission until his slaves owned land and were self-sufficient. He did not know how this would sit with the Presbytery, but he was convinced that mere emancipation was a lofty act without substance. He sought *self-emancipation* for his slaves.

☆

VII : "KING OF THE DARKIES"

WILLIAM KING returned to Toronto to find himself a hero. The news of his role as Moses had preceded him to the "Promised Land," and it was to aid him against all opposition.

First the New Orleans newspapers had printed the story, taken from the captain of the steamer on which they had traveled north. In the system of "exchanges" by which newspapers filled their columns in those days, the New Orleans stories had undergone a transition on their way north. The successive rewritings had changed William from a misguided Abolitionist in the South to an exemplary Christian in New York, an heroic liberator in Boston, and a man of sheer good judgment for his choice through all of Canada.

In Toronto he was hailed by the leaders of the Canadian Presbyterian Church. Its Synod was in session there in June 1848, and William received a "warm reception." Instead of opposition to his ideas, he was given a most enthusiastic welcome, was asked to present his plan, and the Synod voted on it within twenty-four hours.

Always ready to seize an opportunity, King pressed his advantage. He sought refuge not only for his own slaves; he asked for a pattern embracing all Negroes entering Canada in the future, whether fugitive slaves or those escaping from the Black Laws of the North. His formula was simple:

> I believed that these persons who had escaped from slavery, when placed in favorable circumstances, were able and willing to support themselves and to become respectable members of society. And to accomplish this I believed it was necessary to provide them with homes where the parents could support themselves by their own industry and their children with the blessings of a Christian education. Three

things were necessary for that end: land, to place the families upon; a church where they could assemble on Sabbath and hear the gospel; and a day school where the children could receive a good Christian education.

Action by the Presbyterian Synod took on a breathless pace. In response to the "King Memorial" setting forth "the plan that I propose for improving the coloured race settled amongst us" which was delivered to the Synod on June 21, 1848, a committee to consider it was immediately appointed. Its recommendations were made the following day.

Actually, King had proposed a most modest beginning. He suggested the purchase of 200 acres of Crown or Clergy Reserves at a cost approximating $3,000, including buildings. "I am of the opinion that 6,000 persons can be found in Canada who would contribute fifty cents each toward the improvement of the coloured race." The growth of the settlement would, he believed, surround this nucleus, for in it would be the church and the school.

In his Memorial, King continued to voice an intent that was to be the larger goal he would seek year after year—attacking slavery at its heart, which was Africa itself. His plan for the Canadian "City of God" was never changed, merely expanded beyond his own initial dreams, and his concept of ending the slave traffic was also to expand.

> The inducements which such an institution would hold out to actual settlers, located, as it would be, in the midst of fertile lands that could be obtained on reasonable terms, the school affording sound religious instruction for the children, we might confidently expect in a few years to have a large and flourishing settlement. Our line of operations would soon be extended, and imitated by other demoninations, until the whole coloured race would be gradually absorbed into the rural districts and brought under the influence of religious instruction. A band of coloured preachers would at length be

WILLIAM KING

raised to carry the gospel into the heart of Africa where the white missionary has never yet penetrated. It is a duty we owe to Africa for the multiple wrongs we have inflicted on her.

The Synod considered this a worthwhile objective but far in the future. They concerned themselves with the practical aspects of the proposal and made the following decision:

> That the Synod as a spiritual body cannot originate or conduct any scheme of settlement for the coloured population, but that they think favorably of Mr. King's proposal and are ready to appoint a committee to cooperate with him in bringing the object before the public, with the view of an Association being formed for the purpose of obtaining subscriptions to the object and they recommend that Mr. King and the committee shall communicate with Hon. James H. Price, the Commissioner of Crown lands, on the subject of a settlement on one of the Crown locations in the West. They also resolve to bring the matter before the Colonial Committee of the Free Church of Scotland with the view of Mr. King's appointment by them as a missionary to the coloured people in the Province.

A committee of seventeen was named, six of them ministers, including King, and the balance either elders in the Presbyterian Church of Canada or prominent in their communities. The committee "members at or near London were constituted an advisory sub-committee for Mr. King. . . ."

On the face of it, the Synod's action would appear to be an evasion, but their practical political wisdom soon became clear. Had the Church alone undertaken the mission its base would have been narrowed to the Presbyterians only, and inevitably to the New England and New York State Abolitionists, for financial support.

As a result of such farsighted planning, the King mission became the first all-Canadian project for Negro welfare in

Canada's history. The composition of the initial committee was a broad one, including many of the clergy, among them Dr. Robert Burns, Moderator of the Presbyterian Assembly, Dr. Michael Willis, head of Knox College, and Rev. Alexander Gale of Knox Church. But there was a wholesome leavening of the clergy with merchants and others prominent in political affairs, which included the highly respected John Redpath, wealthy merchant of Montreal, Judge Skeffington Connor, James Scott Howard, and Nathan Gatchell, all men of affairs and politically powerful. All geographical areas were covered by the committee's representation: Montreal, Toronto, London, Hamilton, and even Quebec City, though this was nineteen years before the Confederation.

The political wisdom of the Synod was quickly proved. With John Redpath of Montreal and James Gibb of Quebec City, William King quickly obtained an audience with the Governor-General of Canada, James Bruce, Earl of Elgin, who was to be rewarded with a baronetcy for his remarkable accomplishments in the North American provinces.

Lord Elgin gave the committee a full hearing, and then the support of his government. They went from him directly to the Commissioner of Crown Land, James H. Price, who supplied King with maps of fertile, timbered Crown and Clergy lands in Essex, Kent, and Hamilton Counties to the west. Commissioner Price also pledged his assistance and, at a most crucial time, was to save the entire plan by keeping that pledge.

All of this had transpired within a couple of months. In that time William King also received his appointment as a missionary from the Colonial Committee of the Free Church, as well as plaudits for having carried out his personal mission. The Synod then appointed him to find a site, and to form the "Association" which was to establish the settlement.

All of King's past equipped him for the dual task. He had

farmed in Ulster, had cleared lands and farmed in Ohio, had supervised 240 acres in Louisiana. He had worked in the West Port Mission practically from its inception, and knew every administrative problem he would meet.

And he knew the Negro. No white man in Canada knew his people so intimately. No Negro in Canada was as ideally equipped by education and experience. It is true that King created his own mission, but that mission also made the man a positive force in the future of the Canadian Negro and fugitive slaves from the United States.

Within weeks he was to acquire the name he bore for the rest of his life. He was "King of the Darkies," so dubbed by the students at the University of Toronto. It was a term of tolerant affection, the kind often bestowed upon a zealot whose beliefs cannot be challenged, but whose single-mindedness is somewhat trying. Wherever he preached, and he preached wherever he was asked, his sermon concerned the Negro in Canada. No matter what the text of his sermon, it was to be an appeal for aid to the self-emancipation of the Negro.

King began his search for land before the snows that fall. He visited some of the Crown tracts with Crown Commissioner Price on a tour of the west as far as Chatham. Some of the areas he was visiting for the second time. His return to the Negro settlements at Dresden, Sandwich, Chatham, and smaller groupings confirmed his fears that the lack of any one of his three components, land, religion, and education, was fatal.

He was to find one component or another lacking in all of the Negro concentrations on the land that he visited. But, early in the new year, 1849, he set out, once more with Crown Commissioner Price, to follow the Lake Erie shore toward the village of Chatham on the Thames River.

Commissioner Price's maps showed a Clergy Reserve

tract in the township of Raleigh, in Kent County, of about nine thousand acres. It lay between the tiny settlements of East Tilbury and Chatham. Its northern border was the meandering Thames River on its way to Lake St. Clair, and its southern border was Lake Erie itself. Approximately one hundred miles to the east, by the roads of those days, was the populous town of London, and fifty miles to the west were Windsor and old Detroit, across the river. Best of all, the old Talbot Road was practically completed by 1849, and as wilderness roads go, it was mostly passable all the way from London to Windsor. Markets were accessible by road or water.

King borrowed a horse and, while the ground was frozen, was able to explore the entire tract. It was almost entirely virgin forest. The few settlers along the Talbot Road were white families, and they held only one hundred acres deep on both sides.

One reason they had not penetrated deeper into the forest was because the tract was deficient in natural drainage. Much of it became swamp in the spring rains, and one large section, later named Duck Pond Swamp, was a year-round morass. In such terrain, planting would be late and harvesting never certain. No roads could be built even if tillable land were cleared. Water discouraged the early settlers.

At the very time King was exploring the tract, a meeting of the Kent County Agricultural Society adopted a resolution asking the government to "take immediate steps to drain and settle the Crown lands on the plains." The Society took note of the "great hardships and difficulties under which many of the inhabitants of Raleigh labor in traveling to mills and markets across the Raleigh Plains, which is for the greater part of the year covered with water. . . ."

But King had seen a good deal of water rush a mile and a half inland from Lough Foyle during the equinoctial tides and cover his brother's farm fields at Calmuddy. They left behind them rich deposits of topsoil and annually enriched the King farm. In Louisiana, right on his own land, he had seen Thompson's Creek back up from the Mississippi and deposit topsoil. Down in the lowlands below Baton Rouge he had also seen the levees and the drainage into the bayous, man-made ditches assuring a fruitful balance between soil and moisture. Water was an asset, properly utilized, King knew.

He also knew that his brother John would be wealthy if he had had such a valuable money crop in the thick standing timber, with waterways to transport it to market. It was "one unbroken forest" with ash, oak, hickory, elm, and walnut. Some of the oaks were four feet in diameter, and reached upward eighty to ninety feet.

Again, King knew from his own year of clearing the forest in Ohio, that wood could be the first money crop for any settler, and if the timber could not be sold or transported, the pearl ash made from it could. Once before he had made a choice of land, at Fort Defiance, because it was cleared, and his brother John had proved wiser. Timber was an asset, not a nuisance.

His decision made, King left Commissioner Price and hurried back to Toronto. There his committee approved his choice of the site and immediately assigned him his second task, the formation of an organization to finance and control the future of the new settlement. The purpose of the organization was solely to assure the purchase and availability of the land to the fugitives, and its responsibility was never exerted beyond that point.

Within two weeks after approval of the Raleigh Township site by his committee, King had ready a prospectus for the new organization which he titled:

Prospectus of a Scheme for the Social and Moral Improvement of the Coloured People of Canada

The Committee having taken into consideration the peculiar circumstances in which the coloured people came into the Province and the debasing influence exerted by slavery on their character, and having held extensive correspondence with gentlemen in various parts of the Province and of different religious denominations who are known to have an interest in this matter, have come to the conclusion, that it is highly important to the successful operation of a Christian mission among this class of people, that a tract of land be purchased and a settlement formed in a suitable locality, consisting entirely of coloured persons, placed under a careful and judicious supervision; they are also of [the] opinion that a tract of unoccupied land containing about 9,000 acres lying in the township of Raleigh in the western district presents greater advantages as regards soil, climate, and nearness to market, and adaptation to the physical constitution and habits of the coloured race, than any other that has come within our view.

The Committee after a careful examination of the whole subject have resolved to submit to the Christian public, a proposal to form an Association, under such a name as may be afterwards agreed upon, for purchasing the tract of land above referred to in order that it may be opened for settlement by people of colour and to solicit for this purpose the aid of all who are desirous to promote the improvement of the long neglected and deeply injured race. The sum necessary to effect this purchase is about $4,000; it is proposed to raise this sum in shares of ten pounds each, one tenth of the subscription to be paid in hand and the remainder in nine equal annual instalments with interest so far as it may be necessary that the stock may be paid out but it is probable that not more than four instalments will be required; as soon as the stock is subscribed, it is proposed to call the stockholders together in order to appoint officers for the Association and to make arrangements for the immediate settlement of the lands.

The entire management as to the terms of settlement and the financial concerns of the Association will continue in the hands of the stockholders, and be administered by those whom they may appoint. The only conditions which the Committee propose are that the lands shall be exclusively reserved for coloured settlers and sold to them on the lowest terms which will remunerate the stockholders for their expenditure. As the object of this effort is one of pure benevolence undertaken solely with the view of improving the social and religious condition of the coloured people in Canada, we confidently expect and earnestly solicit the sympathy and aid of the Christian community in behalf of it.

(signatures) Michael Willis, D.D.
Chairman of the Committee

Revd. Alexander Gale
Secretary of the Committee

We whose names are subscribed having carefully considered the above scheme, prepared by the Presbyterian Church, for the religious improvement of the coloured people of Canada, fully approve of its object and earnestly recommend it to the countenance and support of the Christian public.

John Piraf, Minister — Enoch Wood, Minister
R. B. Sullivan, Judge — J. S. Howard, Treasurer
W. E. Thompson — James Dougall, Windsor
James Piper, Minister — John Redpath, Montreal

Within two months all the stock required was sold and a meeting of the stockholders named themselves the Elgin Association and elected their first officers. The first president was Judge Skeffington Connor. Dr. Willis and Dr. Burns were vice presidents. John Scott Howard remained treasurer and Nathan Gatchell, secretary.

William King was named the Managing Director, and his advisory committee in Chatham was retained, though with young Archibald McKellar as its chairman. That was the beginning of a lifelong friendship and fraternal dedication.

King was ready to found his "City of God" in the spring of 1849 but he was to fight every step of the way. The only organized and sustained anti-Negro action in Canadian history began in Chatham that summer.

Canada had a proud tradition as the first portion of the British Empire to abolish slavery—in 1793. However, that does not imply that the traditional antipathy toward color was abolished too. It existed in Canada in 1849 and it was an import with the immigrants from abroad, particularly among those who competed with Negroes for the available job opportunities. Canada West was so close to the U.S. border that the anti-Negro attitudes which had caused riots in most of the Northern cities crossed the "Line" with every American newspaper and visitor. A few sporadic incidents of violence had been recorded as early as 1826, separate schools existed for Negroes and whites (though the U.S. had only a handful of public schools for Negroes), and the social ostracism of the Negroes was as severe in the larger Canadian cities as it was in Boston, New York, or Philadelphia. A by-product of insecurity is white supremacy, and Canada was as much afflicted as her neighbor. William King was well aware of that when he wrote to a fellow minister on July 15, 1849, that ". . . the prejudice which exists against the Coloured Man in the Northern States has followed him even into this free country and operates against his moral improvement."

The difference between Canada and the United States lay in the governmental levels, although the color antipathy was the same. In the United States no Congress nor President would dare violate the color code by any such statement as that made by Sir John Colborne in 1829, when he was visited by a Cincinnati Negro delegation seeking refuge for a thousand Negroes who had been driven from that city by three days and three nights of bloody riots:

> Tell the republicans on your side of the line that we royalists do not know men by their colour. Should you come to us *you will be entitled to all the privileges of the rest of His Majesty's subjects.*

If those "privileges" were wanting in some respects, their deficiencies were shared equally by white and black. Time and again, through all of Canada's history, the legal equality of Negroes and whites has been proved in the courts, and at the ballot box.

It seems strange that this fact in Canada's history should be so little known today, and so seldom mentioned. Such equal protection by the law and by law enforcement bodies dates from Canada's very first Parliament in 1793, when Governor General Simcoe included legal guarantees in his bill for emancipation of Canada's slaves. It was no more than Thaddeus Stevens had pleaded for on the floor of the House, on January 3, 1867, when he sought Negro suffrage.

> But, it will be said, as it has been said, "This is Negro equality!" about which so much is said by knaves, and some of which is believed by men who are not fools. It means, as understood by honest Republicans, just this much and no more; every man, no matter what his race or color; every earthly being who has an immortal soul, has an equal right to justice, honesty and fair play with every other man; and the law should secure him those rights. The same law which condemns or acquits an African should condemn or acquit a white man. . . .

In a democracy the assertion seems indisputable, but

generation after generation in the United States have looked the other way while Canada has continued its proud tradition. The United States has had hosts of racist leaders, but Canada has had only one. Because that single instance of organized anti-Negro prejudice to assume the proportions of a popular movement is peculiar in Canadian history, and because it was fomented as a result of the founding of the Buxton Settlement, the phenomenon deserves exploration.

Edwin Larwill, the Chatham tinsmith who was to be King's personal opponent for fifteen years, was a displaced demagogue. If he had had any of the social graces, he would have been the prototype of a deep-South governor of yesterday and today, elected and re-elected to the extent that he adhered to the color line.

Larwill had settled in Chatham in 1841. He opened his shop on King Street that year. He was also a most articulate man and a clever local politician, with his own organization called the "Free and Easy Club," a tavern society. His first activity in public life was in 1842 when he was elected a school commissioner for Raleigh Township. He was elected to the Western District Council, chiefly because he was the last editor of the *Chatham Journal*, a weekly newspaper, and made it a personal conservative sheet, which expired soon after the 1844 elections. Larwill then went to Parliament, but in the Annexationist troubles of 1849 he made the mistake of opposing Lord Elgin and proposing that the provincial capital be moved to Quebec City, an abomination to the people of Canada West. As a result, he was defeated for Parliament in 1851, by George Brown, editor of the *Toronto Globe*, who ran on the Reform platform while Larwill remained a Tory. However, in 1854 he was to win over Archibald McKellar, on an anti-Negro platform, for the seat in Parliament.

Long before King's arrival, Larwill had noted the influx

of Negroes into the growing village of Chatham, and organized opposition to school aid for them. However, with the exception of Dawn Institute near Dresden, there were few Negro settlers on the land.

That was not true of the area to the east, where the full settlement of the land predated the Chatham area by twenty years. There had been no Chatham until late in the 1830's. It had been called The Forks, for the joining of the Thames River and McGregor's Creek, a tributary named after the settler who built the first grist mill at that point. The Indians had not left the lands that were to become Chatham Township until 1827, and there were fewer than half a dozen white families in the entire area then.

There is an interesting historical sidelight on the ways of the Larwills of the world. One of his favorite themes was the glorification of the hardy pioneers who settled this raw wilderness. One of those pioneers was a United Empire Loyalist named William Alexander Everett who reached The Forks in 1796, a refugee from republicanism. His nephew in Boston became quite prominent as President of Harvard University, Secretary of State under Fillmore, Lincoln's Ambassador to London, and the speaker who then so overshadowed Lincoln's Gettysburg address.

In extolling the virtues of the Everett family as examples of white supremacy, Larwill probably did not know that in 1848 President Edward Everett had replied to the students of Harvard University who were protesting the admission of a Negro to the student body:

> If this boy passes the examinations, he will be admitted, and if the white students choose to withdraw, all the income of the college will be devoted to his education.

In that same year Larwill was a delegate to the existent

governing body, the Western District Council. The meeting was held in Colchester, on Lake Erie, due south of Windsor; and Larwill prepared another of his resolutions, this one denying suffrage to all Negroes. It was adopted, and reads in part:

> The increased immigration of foreign Negroes into this part of the Province is truly alarming. We cannot omit mentioning some of the facts for the corroboration of what we have stated. The Negroes, who form at least one-third of the inhabitants of the Township of Colchester, attended the township meeting for the election of parish and township officers and insisted upon their right to vote, which was denied them by every individual white man at the meeting. . . .

Larwill was to utilize the Western District Council again in March of 1849, after the battle had been joined; and in October of the same year, with resolutions to the Provincial Parliament which were substantially the same in character—only more vituperative—he asked that the Elgin Association be forbidden its settlement. He was to issue several petitions and resolutions, through his positions as a Raleigh Township Councilor, school commissioner, and member of the Provincial Parliament.

The first inkling of Larwill's operations was given to King right after the Elgin Association was announced, and by an unidentified white man. King had returned to Chatham from Toronto to arrange for the necessary survey of the tract. He was riding down King Street on horseback when the stranger stopped him and warned him not to remain in the village after dark. He said Mr. King's life was in danger.

> I had visited the township of Raleigh before purchasing the land and preached two Sabbaths in Chatham. I was very

popular but when it was known that I intended to settle a colony of coloured persons in the township, my popularity fell rapidly.

Wild rumors had been spread. One was that he intended bringing in an entire shipload of slaves from the United States instead of his 15 Negroes. As he continued down King Street that day, he noticed that men he knew now gave him the "cold shoulder."

It was then he learned that Edwin Larwill had organized his petition campaign, and that a memorial had been sent to the Presbyterian Synod with over a hundred signatures, among them some of the more prominent Chatham residents.

The Petition revealed that the Chatham Municipal Council had asked Parliament to prevent the settlement, and the Synod was urged to withdraw its sponsorship or ". . . the responsibility of every consequence resulting from the Settlement, if made, will devolve upon you."

It is a fascinating document. The first signature is Larwill's, and the sentiments are his, too:

> The Negro is a distinct species of the Human Family and, in the opinion of your Memorialists is far inferior to that of the European. Let each link in the great Scale of existence have its place. Amalgamation is as disgusting to the Eye, as it is immoral in its tendencies and all good men will discountenance it.

Larwill warned that if Rev. King's plans were consummated, the direst of evils would result, such as the depreciation of property and the departure from the country of "hundreds of old and respected settlers," familiar arguments today. It is interesting to note that Larwill's predictions, which he regarded as evils, matched exactly the purposes of the Elgin Settlement:

> Your Memorialists would observe farther that if such a Colony should flourish in Raleigh, under your protection, the consequences would be still more lamentable to the Province. Other religious and Philanthropic societies would adopt a similar course and other Townships and other Districts would be crowded with Negroes. . . .

It will be recalled that this was King's fervent hope in his initial "Plan."

But still further horrors are pointed out:

> Would not offices of trust, honor and emoluments ultimately fall to their share? Imagine our Legislative Hall studded and our principal Departments managed by these Ebony men. It would be impossible to keep them out of the smaller elective offices. Black Councillors, School Trustees, Path-masters, etc. The Pinions of our Institutions would be destroyed!

Five days later, on a Wednesday night, Larwill received his first knowledge of the kind of opponent he was challenging. King did not leave Chatham. He did not run back to Toronto to mend his fences. He decided that the battleground was right in Chatham.

After receiving his warning from the stranger on King Street, he sought out Archie McKellar and arranged for the use of the recently built Presbyterian Church on Wellington Street for a meeting at eight o'clock in the evening of the following Wednesday. Word was sent out through the village and surrounding country.

The church was filled a half hour before the meeting and Archie McKellar served as chairman. King spoke for about three quarters of an hour, explaining the purpose, size, and planned self-sufficiency of the new colony. He declared his belief in the colored people as assets, not burdens, to any community when given an opportunity. Then he invited any who wished to speak to take the pulpit.

Nobody came forward and the meeting ended in an orderly manner. William was staying overnight with McKellar, and it was only when they had reached the latter's house that he learned that he was to be guarded wherever he went in Chatham or in the woods. Among the Negroes in the mixed audience that night had been twelve armed men, and they had guarded both King and McKellar until the house door was shut on both of them. Thereafter, King seldom saw his bodyguards, but they were always there.

He left for the tract the following morning and completed the purchase of his own land, on the Middle Road almost in the center of the nine thousand acres. He bought one hundred acres from William White, one of the earliest settlers, who had come to the Middle Road in 1825 and by 1848 had much of it cleared. The records do not show the amount of down payment, but the Whites gave William a mortgage for two hundred dollars which was not discharged until five years later.

There were two reasons for King's purchase. First, he was white and therefore not eligible to purchase Elgin Association lands, and secondly, his fifteen slaves in Ohio were his responsibility until they had their own land. But there may have been a further purpose. The White farm was so central that it would be an ideal site for a church, as well as a home and parsonage. St. Andrew's Church was built on King's original tract, and has been there ever since.

King started for Toronto a few days later, and when he boarded the stage, found Sheriff John Waddell Jr. also bound for Toronto. He was bearing a petition to the Governor and to Crown Commissioner Price against the settlement and in the same language as the petition to the Synod. This memorial had 376 signatures of white residents of Chatham, headed by Larwill's. In addition, the Sheriff showed King a "requisition" requiring him to call a public meeting for August 18. In addition, he warned King that there was a letter circulating in Chatham which threatened his life if he persisted in settling the Raleigh tract with Negroes, and that Larwill was organizing a vigilante group.

Later events proved the Sheriff's warning concerning the vigilantes well founded, but the threatening letter has never been substantiated. However, King dismissed the well-meant warnings and told the Sheriff he too would attend the meeting.

While King was away, Larwill continued to agitate, and he had the Chatham newspaper of the day to help. The *Chatham Chronicle* of August 14 addressed an appeal to the prominent members of the Elgin Association, and it summarized the opposition arguments:

> This Association must be fully aware that a strong current of public feeling has set in and is still increasing against locating the coloured people in the heart of the prosperous and thickly-settled township of Raleigh, or of any other township similarly circumstanced. That such a prejudice does exist on the part of the white settlers toward coloured people is an undeniable fact. We believe it to be wrong but its existence is undoubted, nevertheless. We ask, therefore, if it is expedient or politic for any self-constituted body of men, such as the Elgin or any other Association to excite the feelings of one class of the community by the unpopular manner in which they are about to exercise their sympathies toward another. . . . Let lands be purchased in some isolated place, where no immediate intercourse can exist between the two races, and the contention and animosity which we are afraid will occur between both if they are sent here, will have no ground of existence. We hope this Association will reflect on its proceedings and pay a proper attention to the remonstrances and petitions of the influential settlers of this township.

The reasonable tone of the editorial is belied by the statement that Raleigh Township was thickly settled, and that its residents had joined the protest. Neither was true. Recorded titles show no more than half a dozen settlers in the Elgin tract, and none of their names appear on the petitions. It was the Larwill faction of Chatham that was protesting. The signatures on the petitions represented about 21 percent of the adult white population. This was an organized minority speaking for a majority.

William King's courage on the afternoon of August 18 went far in dividing the Larwill forces. He had transacted Elgin Association business in Toronto and started back for Chatham by lake steamer for Windsor. He arrived there on the evening of the 17th, in plenty of time to take the *Brothers*, the Thames River steamer for Chatham. But that ship was not sailing. It had developed engine trouble.

The meeting was scheduled for two in the afternoon of the following day and King was fifty miles from Chatham by the shortest roads. (There were no railroads yet.) He rented a horse and buggy and drove all night, reaching McKellar's home in the morning.

There he found ominous preparations being made for the meeting. Trouble was expected. The village was tense, and rumors were that all the lakeshore settlers from Raleigh were coming in to stop the settlement—by violence if necessary.

He found George Young, the Magistrate of Quarter Sessions from Harwich, at McKellar's where he was swearing in twelve special constables to keep the peace. The magistrate, at that time the chief judicial officer of the county government, was opposed to the settlement but agreed that King had a right to be at the meeting, though he warned him it would not be wise.

By noon the village of Chatham was filled with settlers from various parts of the western districts of Kent County.

George Young

North Buxton (Ontario) Museum

King Street was never that crowded except on the Queen's Birthday holiday, or at militia events.

There was no town hall in those days, and the meeting was to be held in a large barn in the rear of the Royal Exchange Hotel. By two o'clock the barn was packed and the men were pressing in from the outside. The meeting was called to order promptly with the reading of the public petition requesting it, and Magistrate Young, as the chief county officer present, was its chairman.

King assumed the offensive immediately. He was the first to speak, and asked the chairman to state the purpose of the meeting. Young hesitated a moment, and then said frankly that its sole purpose was to prevent the purchase of land in Raleigh Township by the colored people.

King's next question was whether or not the Negro had the legal right to buy a home in Raleigh and the answer was in the affirmative. In that case, King replied, the meeting was an illegal one since it was called to perform an illegal act and its proceedings would be without validity. The crowd's protest drowned out King's voice for a moment, but he went on to warn Magistrate Young that people were excited and, if there were any disturbance resulting from the meeting, he, the magistrate, must be held responsible.

After that, nobody could be heard. Those outside, given the tenor of King's questioning, demanded a voice and a hearing. Finally, before they became unruly, the audience inside and out unified in one shouted demand to adjourn the meeting to the front of the Royal Exchange Hotel. Everyone could hear the speakers there if they were on the hotel balcony, one floor up.

This was done and the assembled speakers, including Larwill, who had not yet been heard, all went to the balcony. King went with them, but at first was refused the right to speak. But Archibald McKellar was there too.

> Mr. McKellar was the only man in Chatham then who had the moral courage to stand beside me while I was advocating the right of a coloured man to purchase a home in the township of Raleigh.

With McKellar's insistence that King be heard came the authoritative demand for fair play from Dr. A. R. Robertson, who also demanded the right to disagree with King after he had finished speaking. The chairman granted the stubborn preacher ten minutes.

But the crowd refused to hear. They shouted and hooted and were becoming a mob. But they silenced when Larwill stepped forward—to tell them that King had no right there. He was a Yankee, and had no right to speak.

This unleashed a storm from the men milling below, and it was fortunate for King that they could not climb the balcony.

It was then that William King began to win the admiration, if not the agreement, of the men of Chatham. They respected a fighter. While they hooted and jeered, King stepped closer to the rail and folded his arms. He was motionless and stared at them stonily, his head held high and his face without expression.

To the crowd he represented a menace, as explained by Larwill. Nearly four hundred of them had signed the petitions. They were highly organized by Larwill, whom they knew well, who was a great man for a drink, a joke, and an election campaign. This Yankee was a stranger. But one by one they fell silent. Not even Larwill's henchmen in the crowd could keep up the chorus of boos. They fell silent before that silent, indomitable figure who stood there and made no attempt to speak. They were ashamed.

When the crowd had finally subsided to mutters and an occasional yell, King seized his chance. He knew these men.

KING STREET WEST—CHATHAM, 1860
The balcony of the Royal Exchange Hotel may be seen at the left.

F. H. Brown Historical Collection

He was one of them. He too was from Ulster, the inheritor of Scots traditions, and he also knew the Irish who had escaped to this land from the potato famines. He bellowed out suddenly:

"I have come two hundred miles to attend this meeting and you cannot put me down. Besides, I am from Londonderry and Londonderry never did surrender."

Now, who among these Scotsmen and Irishmen could fail to respond to such a call? They cheered and laughed and then were quiet while King told them briefly the objectives of the Elgin Association. He predicted that the improvement of the "wild lands" would add to the tax revenue and wealth of the township and county; he declared flatly that the settlement would increase, not depreciate the values of land around it. Nor did he fail to tell them that he had been born a British subject and had marched for the Reform Bill, that he was a ratepayer in Raleigh Township and had every right to vote.

The crowd was shocked when the next speaker, Walter McCrae, one of Larwill's cronies and later to be Mayor of Chatham, raised the horror of "amalgamation," of mixing of the races which, he said, was a "necessary and hideous attendant" of such settlements. But he was not anti-Negro or opposed to "freedom" for them. "Let the slaves of the United States be free, but let it be in their own country; let us not countenance their further introduction among us, in a word, let the people of the United States bear the burthen of their own sins."

The meeting proceeded to its purpose, a resolution to be submitted to the Provincial Parliament forbidding the settlement and the establishment of a "Committee of Vigilance" to get together the petitions and present them to Parliament at its next session; further, to spy out the movements of Rev. William King and make them public through the newspapers, leaflets, and meetings. The Vigilance Committee was also to approach the township officials of Raleigh, Harwich, Chatham, and Dresden for township funds to be expended by the Committee on postage, printing, stationery, and other expenses. The Vigilance Committee was formed and the co-sponsors were Edwin Larwill and Dr. Robertson.

King was one of the last to leave the balcony. He had wanted to hear and evaluate all of it. When he did leave, side by side with Archie McKellar, the men who had cursed him before now opened a respectful path.

King accomplished a great deal by his speech, though he failed to prevent the purpose of the meeting. Thereafter when he rode into Chatham, men saluted him with respect, though continuing to oppose him. Many minds were changed later as some of those who had signed the petitions came to him one by one to ask him to strike their names from them. In that crowd too were a few who turned from Larwill and were to help the settlement with warnings before each move planned by the anti-Negro organization. His speech from the balcony of the Royal Exchange Hotel on August 18, 1849, won for King respectful attention throughout the Province, for the story of how he faced down the mob was quickly spread. It won him new white friends in the cities, and among the Negroes of the Province he became a collective responsibility. They became his eyes and ears and guardians wherever he went.

Tired though he was, after the all-night travel, King left Chatham immediately for Toronto, where he accomplished a more audacious coup than in any of his future Underground Railroad exploits. Before Larwill could even get the petitions printed or organize any of his patrols to spy on King, the land was bought.

The whole transaction probably was highly illegal. The Elgin Association itself could not legally exist until it was incorporated by an Act of Parliament, which was not to take place until a year later, on August 10, 1850, when the Buxton Settlement already was an accomplished fact.

Yet William King, Judge Skeffington Connor, and Charles Berczy, postmaster of Toronto, took the funds raised by sale of the Elgin Association shares and made a down payment on four thousand three hundred acres in Raleigh Township at the Clergy Reserve price of $2.50 an acre. They assumed the title of "Trustees" of the nonexistent corporation.

More illegal was the fact that Crown Land Commissioner Price, with Lord Elgin's approval, accepted the money and registered the sale. He completed the transaction even before the land had been surveyed, a very definite requirement for Crown and Clergy land sales to protect the titles of those who were given location tickets on purchase.

It is only possible to conjecture as to the willingness of the Crown's representatives to cut legal corners in helping King get the land. One reason may have been the fact that Lord Elgin had been appointed Governor General of Canada in 1847 from a similar post in Jamaica, a Crown colony, where he had had the unhappy task of overseeing the adjustment of the island to full emancipation of its slaves under the Act of 1833 which became fully effective in 1840. He could appreciate the validity of King's repeated arguments that the Negroes must be provided the means for self-emancipation.

Another influencing factor was political. Just that spring, in April, mobs in Montreal had pelted the Governor General with stones and rotten eggs. The mob went on to burn the Parliament buildings, which was one reason the tiny lumber village of Bytown was renamed Ottawa and later made the permanent capital of Canada. The riots in Montreal between April 25 and April 30, 1849, were inspired by the Tory opposition to the reform government and to Lord Elgin's rule, which Canadian historians have termed "The Great Administration" due to the many constitutional advances made. The mercantile groups provoking the riots and the members of the "Annexation to the U.S. Manifesto Society" that year were the same, and King's opposition came from their western branch. Larwill and his group were proclaimed Tories and annexationists.

King recognized a certain kinship.

> Both Lord Elgin, after whom the Society was called, and myself were at that time very unpopular. His Lordship had the Parliament House burned over his head and he was driven from Montreal and his carriage rotten-egged by a howling mob. My life was threatened if I attempted to settle a colony of coloured persons in Raleigh.

But the legality of the sale very soon became moot because Larwill did not get his petitions ready until October 8, and by then, in spite of the Vigilance Committee terrorism, the tract was surveyed and the parcel boundaries approved by the Crown Commissioner. By the time the news of the land purchase reached Chatham, the Negroes too had organized, and the months to follow were uneasy ones. On two occasions there could have been bloodshed. The first one was avoided by a fortunate illness.

King had hired a prominent surveyor in Chatham named Parr, not knowing that the surveyor was a Larwill man. He arranged for Parr to meet him and the government land agent, Dr. Hugh McMullin of Sandwich, on a certain day at a certain point on the Middle Road, and the outer boundaries of the tract would be quickly settled. Parr was to travel from Chatham, and King, with McMullin, from Sandwich.

Parr informed the Vigilance Committee, and a gang was recruited, all armed, to keep the appointment and throw the whole party off the land. What they did not know and King was not to learn until much later, was that a large group of Chatham Negroes, from whom no secrets could be kept, all decided to go hunting in Raleigh Township on that day.

Larwill, Parr, and his gang spent the day in the woods, not knowing they were surrounded; and they spent it drinking and boasting of their treatment of King the moment he showed up.

He never showed up. McMullin had taken to his sickbed the day before.

> Had I come that day, there probably would have been bloodshed. But I was providentially saved from it by the sickness of the agent. The coloured people were determined to fight if I should be attacked. A collision with the people at that time would in all probability have proved fatal to our cause. I had to counsel them to be patient and suffer rather than fight.

Eight days later McMullin was recovered, and King sent word to Parr to meet them the following day. He knew nothing of the party that had been raised for him by Parr's treachery. This time, however, the Vigilance Committee did not believe the surveyor, though the Negroes went hunting again. They may actually have hunted some because none of Larwill's gang appeared and the boundary lines were run that day. And that night King was told about Parr and fired him. He found a surveyor from another town who quickly completed division of the tract into 50-acre parcels. Now the land could be settled, and Larwill had been defeated to that important extent—though there were to be many more battles fought. The Negroes continued to guard King.

The conflict with Larwill, meanwhile, had also entered the political and publicity arenas; and King revealed that he could trade words with the best of the orators and letter writers. In addition to his own abilities, King had a tremendous assist in placing Larwill on the defensive in the person of George Brown, the young Scotsman whose *Toronto Globe*, in only a few years, had become a powerful voice in Canada West.

Brown's joyously unrestrained journalistic touch is evident in the report of the Chatham meeting carried in the *Globe* on August 25 as a letter signed "Quid." Brown was in the habit of adorning his reports, and his work was always recognizable by his Tory political adversaries.

His bias is quickly apparent. King is identified as a "Steady friend of the blacks," but his company on that balcony was another matter. Magistrate Young was dismissed as a man who was habitually wrong; Dr. Robertson "a learned chirurgeon" not too skilful in using the Bible to condemn the Negroes. Larwill gave a "tinkering" speech meaning that it sounded much like his mallet on his tin, with "elegant phraseology and rounded periods."

But the town of Chatham itself came in for some choice words:

> Three things struck me as peculiarly deserving of reprobation, viz: the gross partiality displayed by the Chairman, the intemperance of the speakers and the behaviour of the crowd. Among the latter drunkenness abounded and obscene language and shocking oaths were bandied from mouth to mouth.

On September 13, the *Toronto Globe* carried another and lengthy letter signed by 106 prominent residents of the Western District, among them three Justices of the Peace, McKellar, Thomas Williams, and George Jacobs. This was an open letter condemning the Larwill faction and addressed to the "President and Directors of the Elgin Association." It assured them that the purposes of the Elgin Association had the approval of the signatories, and "we think it right to inform you that a large and respectable portion of the inhabitants of the District offer no opposition, and take no part in such illegal proceedings."

However, on the home front, in Chatham and Kent County, the *Chatham Chronicle* became the Larwill organ, and its report of the August 18 meeting reflected little of that meeting's character. But it did report verbatim the resolutions and the lengthy "*Appeal to Canadians*" which was distributed to all the Canadian press. This is a remarkable document, at one time expressing pride in Canada's abolition of slavery and, in the next sentence:

> Nature, however, has divided the great family into distinct species for good and wise purposes, and it is no less our interest, than it is our duty, to follow her dictates and obey her Laws. . . . With what a feeling of horror would the people of any of the old settled Townships of the eastern portions of this province, look upon a measure which had for its avowed object the effect of introducing several hundreds of Africans into the very heart of their neighborhood, their families interspersing themselves among them, upon every vacant lot of land, their children mingling in their schools, and all claiming to be admitted not only to political, but to social privileges? And, when we reflect too, that many of them must, from necessity, be the very worst specimens of their neglected race; the fugitives from justice; how much more revolting must the scheme appear!

The *Chronicle* did print King's letter of objection to the report on the August 18 meeting three weeks later and appended the explanation:

> As regards the above, we can only say that the report of the proceedings of the meeting alluded to, was handed to us for publication in the *Chronicle,* which we inserted without either note or comment, and do not, therefore, consider ourselves responsible for any error which may have been committed in taking down Mr. King's expressions.

And this was followed, in the very next issue, with a letter nearly two columns long from "One who was present at the meeting." This unrestrained personal attack on King accuses him and the Elgin Association of being formed ". . . for purely selfish and speculative purposes—calculated to enrich its members at the expense of the labor of the colored man, and that benevolence and philanthropy are mere cloaks to conceal its real intention."

It is difficult to determine whether or not Larwill wrote all of the letters. He signs his name to only one, in which he called McKellar a liar concerning the open letter in the *Toronto Globe*. He also wrote to Lord Elgin a request (that was quoted in the *Chronicle*) that no land be sold to the Elgin Association until the Western District Council met on October 6. Of course, Lord Elgin hadn't waited, but Larwill did not know that then. The deed was not recorded until October 22nd.

Larwill was on the defensive and must have been desperate, because he then did something he knew would have to see the light of day in public print. The Western District Council on October 8, 1849, obediently adopted his resolution addressed to Parliament. But Larwill added a most explosive addendum never acted on by the Council. Without the authority of this elected group, Larwill simply adopted the Ohio Black Laws. He advocated that:

1. All Negroes be barred from public office and public schools.
2. They be forced to pay a poll tax though "also, to ascertain whether it would be politic to allow them the right of suffrage."
3. They be required to post bond to remain in Canada as free citizens.

There was a good deal more from Larwill's own initiative, including the familiar warnings on amalgamation, race riots, and a public burden. All of it helped to alienate Larwill more and more from even his own supporters and committed anti-Negro Canadians.

While the debate degenerated into the press and reached the Larwill level, King dropped it and went to work on the structure of his mission. The land was there, paid for by the Elgin Association, even though Parliament had not yet acted on its incorporation. The path toward a church and a school was clear, for the Presbyterian Church of Canada had made his plan a part of its structure. The name chosen by King was accepted. The Buxton Mission was named in honor of Sir Thomas Fowell Buxton who, sixteen years earlier, had so thrilled young William King by finally getting an emancipation act through the British Parliament.

All the planning and pleading were at an end by November 1849. King set to work building his "City of God" in the forests and swamps.

☆

PART THREE: BUILDING A "CITY OF GOD"

VIII : ECONOMIC INDEPENDENCE

THE BUILDING YEARS began on November 28, 1849, when William King arrived in Raleigh Township with his fifteen slaves. It would have been fitting for his people to have been the first Negro fugitives to reach their haven, but they were not. King had received too much attention from the Canadian newspapers as a result of Larwill's attacks. The plan for the Elgin Association settlement was known throughout Canada.

Camped in King's barn and waiting for him were Isaac Riley, his wife, and four children. They had escaped from their master in Missouri and made their way to St. Catharines just a few months before news of the Elgin Association was made public. Isaac, who could read, had seen a copy of King's prospectus and thus learned that the settlement would have a church and a school. He had trekked the three hundred miles to Sandwich where he requested a location ticket for 100 acres closest to the proposed school.

Now King had twenty-one Negroes to settle, and, within weeks, more began to stream in. To the head of each family William explained the conditions set down for settlement at Buxton, and there was no deviation from his regulations.

There can be no denial that they were William King's own conditions, and he was criticized later for being dictatorial in his regulations. He was.

For instance, land could only be purchased. It could not be rented or sharecropped until the purchaser had paid for it fully and received unencumbered title. Only then would he have the full right to use his land as he saw fit.

Land could be sold only to Negroes by the Elgin Association. If resold before the expiration of ten years after the down payment had been made, it must be transferred to Negroes only, whether or not it had been paid for completely.

This would appear to be outright segregation as well as a form of indentureship. Each family was to be colored and each was to be tied to the land for ten years. There could be and were no exceptions. It might seem contradictory and arbitrary on the part of a man who, only a few years later, was to join Archie McKellar in a fight against the Larwill forces and their insistence on segregated schools in Chatham.

The two other components of King's plan must be taken into consideration before judging those conditions, however. Religion and education were interchangeable, for the Bible must be read to serve the first, without which he believed no achievement of moral values would be possible. Nor could there be a degree of self-sufficiency without at least the fundamentals of an education. Ten years were a short enough period to accomplish this. King knew that few of the fugitives who would come to him knew more of Christianity than that it was a belief incorporating slavery as a divine institution. He had heard the preachers in the slave quarters. Almost none of the fugitives would be able to read, let alone write.

The regulation assuring an all-Negro settlement for at least ten years was included to protect the settlers from the whites—from either their possible preying on the innocent fugitives, or their becoming a "foreign" element in the community. The whites had never been slaves, and certainly there were no Canadians who would submit to his paternal guardianship for the ten years he had set to establish patterns in his "City of God."

That paternalism extended even further than preserving the homogeneity of the community. King set up minimum housing standards which were part of the purchase agreement.

The entire tract of nine thousand acres was surveyed into fifty-acre lots, the minimum purchase allowed; King had decided that that was a minimum for support of a family. There were four lots on each two-hundred-acre "concession," a term applied to subdivisions of Crown lands; and each lot faced a concession line along which a road was to be built.

The housing regulations required that homes must be set back no less than thirty-three feet from the road. Each homestead was required to have a picket fence and a garden in front of it. The garden could be any kind of house garden, *but it must include flowers.*

The log cabin itself had minimum standards. A front "gallery" was a requirement, extending all across the side facing the concession road. The houses were to be no less than twenty-four feet wide and eighteen feet deep and the roof no less than twelve feet high. Each house was to be divided into no less than four rooms.

These were minimum standards. Building above or beyond them was a choice of the settler, but his agreement was not to build less. The specifications were as complete a departure from slave quarters as King could realistically expect from the unskilled labor he anticipated would settle the land. The one-room shanties and barracoons of the South, in which families crowded together without a hope of privacy, were forbidden. In all the history of Buxton there was only one exception allowed to these architectural minima. That was

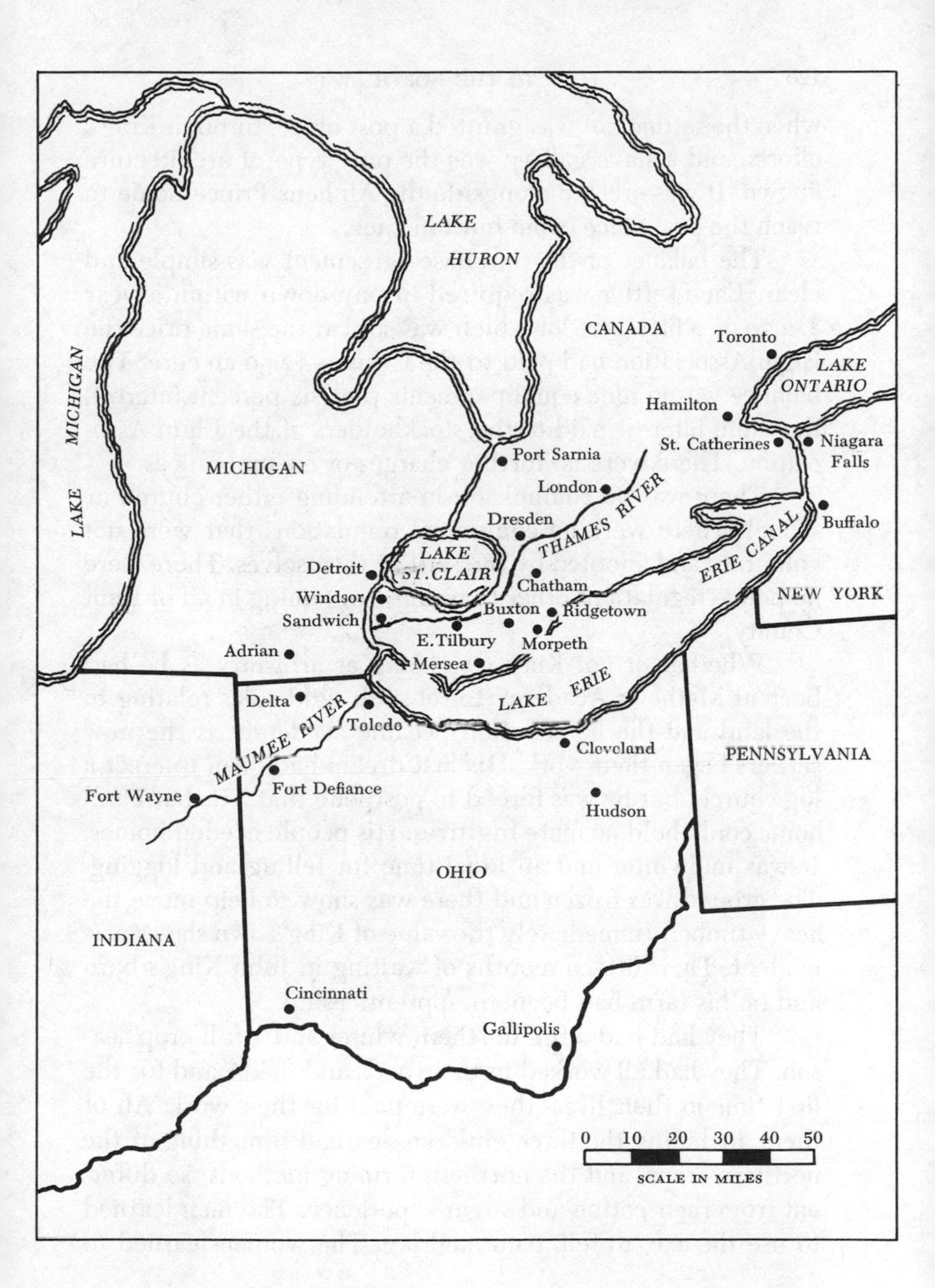
LAKE HURON
CANADA
Toronto
LAKE ONTARIO
Hamilton
St. Catherines
Niagara Falls
LAKE MICHIGAN
MICHIGAN
Port Sarnia
London
THAMES RIVER
Dresden
ERIE CANAL
Buffalo
LAKE ST. CLAIR
Detroit
Chatham
Windsor
Buxton
Ridgetown
Sandwich
NEW YORK
E. Tilbury
Morpeth
Adrian
Mersea
LAKE ERIE
Delta
MAUMEE RIVER
Toledo
Cleveland
PENNSYLVANIA
Fort Defiance
Fort Wayne
Hudson
OHIO
INDIANA
Cincinnati
Gallipolis
0 10 20 30 40 50
SCALE IN MILES

when the settlement was granted a post office, through King's efforts, and a slave gallery was the only type of architecture known. It was erected alongside the Alpheus Prince home to reach the post office cabin built in back.

The balance of the purchase agreement was simple and clear. Each settler was required to pay down within a year $12.50 on a fifty-acre lot which was sold at the same price the Elgin Association had paid to the Crown—$2.50 an acre. The balance was in nine equal payments plus six percent interest, the same interest paid to the stockholders of the Elgin Association. There were no further charges or encumbrances.

There was no compulsion in attending either church or school. There were no communal regulations that were not voluntary and adopted by the settlers themselves. There were no police regulations other than those obtaining in all of Kent County.

Whether or not King was being as arbitrary as he had been at Mathews Academy to set such rigid rules relating to the land and the homes soon became academic as the new settlers began their work. His first dream had been to erect a log church, but he was forced to postpone that. His barn and home could hold no more fugitives. His people needed homes. It was midwinter and an ideal time for felling and logging. The ground was frozen and there was snow to help move the heavy timber. Immediately the value of King's own slaves was evident. Their fifteen months of waiting in John King's barn and on his farm had been an apprenticeship.

They had had a full northern winter and a full crop season. They had all worked in the woods and fields, and for the first time in their lives, they were paid for their work. All of them, including the three children, learned something of the northern crops, and the northern farming methods, so different from their cotton and sugar experience. The men learned to use the axe, to fell, trim, and log. The women learned to preserve the fruits and vegetables against the winter. All of them had gone to school.

On the King homestead in Ohio at that time there had been at least two dozen of his nieces and nephews, sons and daughters of his brother John and his sisters Catherine and Mary. There were volunteers aplenty among the Kings, Donahues, and Kanes to carry on continued classes in reading and writing.

Their Sabbath services had been held in the big barn, and they learned new hymns. As their reading progressed they could take turns reading the Gospel instead of depending only on Talbert. All except five-year-old Solomon could read by the time "Massa" King came for them, and even he could recite some of the prayers. The two nine-year-olds, Sarah and Peter, could read and were learning to write, as well as all of the adults.

Their period of indoctrination into the farming ways of the North and Christian education was to prove invaluable in the early years of the Buxton Settlement. They set a pattern of industry and avid desire for learning and religion which was exactly the example King required. They were the nucleus establishing the character of the colony for all the fugitives who were to arrive in Buxton.

The men in King's own group immediately showed the worth of their Ohio experience. They formed the core of a "cabin raising" crew of twelve to fourteen men who, with a yoke of oxen, could raise a log cabin in a day. He first worked with them individually, and one day announced that they would begin work at 7:00 A.M. and have a cabin ready for roofing by 7:00 P.M. They did.

> The wood was all standing. I divided the party into four divisions; two to cut down the logs to proper length; one to haul them in; four to take the corners to saddle the logs down and five to remain on the ground to assist in rolling the

> logs up on the building. I ordered all hands to clear off the foundation, and lay down four oak logs for the foundation eighteen by twenty-four. I took my axe and showed how the saddle was to be cut at the corners. In two hours the foundation was laid and slabs hewn on one side and laid on it and by seven in the evening the whole body of the log cabin was up, eighteen by twenty-four—twelve feet high and ready for the roof.

"They soon became acquainted with the work," and King could depend on them to meet every housing crisis. There was one aspect of both the "raisin'" and the "clearin'" bees in Buxton that violated every practice in Canada West and, for that matter, in most pioneer settlements. "The coloured people had their chopping bees, and their logging and raising bees, all without liquor." This was almost unheard-of around Chatham.

The next urgency was in clearing the land for first planting. They had only a few months in which to clear enough on each lot to provide the family with eating crops first and seed crops later. This too was organized as a team project, with the women and children helping to burn the timber and stumps. But again the example and inspiration was given by King. Robin Phares recalled those times before his death in 1898.

> We were just like wild deer in the woods and didn't know how to take care of ourselves. Mr. King had to teach us and do everything for us . . . One by one those that escaped came dropping in and we were all busy as bees, chopping, burning, boiling, singing and talking. When we grew tired of the cold and hard work, Mr. King would jump upon a stump and swing his axe around, calling out "Hurrah boys" and set us laughing over some nonsense. . . . Those were days of hardship but they were happy days, and we were frolicsome as kittens. What I cannot forget is that Mr.

King was an educated man and a gentleman, accustomed in the South to the finest and best of everything and plenty of servants, and that he would bend the shoulder and bear the burden and go through mud and water night and day. . . .

Within twelve months more than a dent was made. There were forty-five families living in Buxton who had taken up two thousand five hundred acres of land within the Elgin Association tract. In addition, twelve Negro families had purchased improved farms bordering the settlement. A total of 230 acres of land was cleared and in crops. 192 acres were in corn and other grains, 24 in wheat and 12 in tobacco.

In August, 1852, there were seventy-five families in the Buxton Settlement and its population was about four hundred. An additional twenty-five families had located in the immediate vicinity. There were 350 acres cleared for planting. New crops were hemp and maple sugar. In addition, a start had been made in livestock, milk cows, sheep, and hogs.

By its fifth anniversary, in 1854, several of the farms had been paid for. The full ten years allowed had not been necessary. The first brick cottage had been built and there were several frame homes, eight of them beyond the minimum standards originally set. Families: 150; acres cleared: 726; corn, 334 acres; wheat, 95; oats, 48; mixed crops, 100. In livestock the settlement had 150 cattle, 38 horses, 25 sheep, 700 hogs.

One of the most reliable reports on the Buxton Settlement was made five years after its founding by Benjamin Drew who visited most of the Negro settlements in Canada in 1854. He wrote:

> The settlers at Buxton are characterized by a manly, independent air and manner. Most of them came into the Province stripped of everything but life. They have purchased homes for themselves, paid the price demanded by the government, erected their own buildings and supported

their own families by their own industry, receiving no aid whatsoever from any benevolent society but carefully excluding donations of any kind from coming into the settlement.

Mr. Drew's last statement was not entirely correct. A few months after the first settlers arrived members of the American Anti-Slavery Society in Boston heard of the new settlement, due to the wide publicity given it in the *Liberator* by Larwill's opposition, and sent a few boxes of clothing to King. As was his practice, he called a meeting of the people.

He told them of the gift and the problem it created. They could send it back but that would insult well-intentioned friends as well as discourage their aid to fugitives who had just crossed the line and needed everything. But, he explained, Buxton was to be self-supporting, was to show "that coloured men, when placed in favorable circumstances, could support themselves and their families as well as the white settlers." He advised them not to depend on others since "to do so would destroy their self-respect and independence."

They voted to accept the clothing and authorized King to inform the world that the Buxton settlers would support themselves and were "determined to show the world that they only wanted a fair field and no favor."

This was the only gift other than for religious or educational use ever accepted by Buxton Negroes. It was the only Negro colony in Canada ever to attain and maintain such self-sufficiency. William King inculcated and guarded that independence fiercely. Benjamin Drew saw his plan.

> Mr. King, having full faith in the natural powers, capacity and capability of the African race, is practically working out his belief by placing the refugees in circumstances where they may learn self-reliance and maintain a perfect independence of aid, trusting, under God, in their own right arm.

One reason many of the community could pay off for their land was the Canadian railroad's reaching Canada West in the early 1850's. The demand for labor was so great that a man could nearly earn his annual instalment for fifty acres of land with a couple months' work. The railroads were paying $10 a month and keep to all who could lift a shovel or a pick axe. There was so much need for labor that Negroes and Irish worked side by side in greatest companionship. They were not competing for jobs.

But this bonanza worried King. He feared that the impoverished fugitives would leap at the opportunity for immediate money and leave the land that was to have been their salvation. Sabbath after Sabbath he warned them that the lure of the railroad money, at the expense of their land, would be a poor bargain in the long run. By 1855, after the completion of the Great Western to Windsor, he was able to report to the Elgin Association stockholders that "the coloured population have manifested a more fixed determination to raise from the soil what will support themselves and their families, without going abroad to work a part of the year for money to purchase the necessaries and comforts of life. . . ."

There was another reason for this determination. The settlers were beginning to harvest their richest crop—timber. It was estimated that in oak alone the Elgin tract had a stand valued at $57,000. For maple, hickory, and other hardwoods the estimate was $70,000. But timber had value only when it went to market, as logs or lumber. There was no equipment large enough to haul the logs and no sawmill to produce the lumber. Without roads, neither could reach either the Thames River or the lakefront.

Before the end of 1851, their second year of settlement, William King saw the economic imperatives.

> During the clearing of the land I saw that there was great waste in the burning of valuable timber that could be made a

source of profit to the settlers if they could only get a sawmill to cut it up into lumber . . . The ashes also from the wood burnt in clearing was allowed to go to waste, that if manufactured into pot and pearl ash would be a source of profit to the settlers . . . I saw that it was an absolute necessity to the prosperity of the settlement. We could make no permanent improvements without lumber and without bricks. I called a public meeting. . . .

And in the human resources of the colony itself King found the answers. At that meeting two of the former slaves revealed that they "had wrought at brick making in the U. States," had constructed kilns, and knew how to burn brick. They had seen an abundance of clay on the land, and there was no dearth of wood for the fires.

William dug into his own pocket to start the brickyard. Within a few months his loan was returned to him. In the first year, the Buxton kilns turned out 300,000 brick and there was no other kiln nearer than Chatham to the east and Windsor to the west. Essex County, adjoining Kent on the west, was settling rapidly and there was a market for all the brick that could be produced.

At that same meeting two new settlers spoke up. One was William R. Abbott and the other Henry K. Thomas. Both had come to Buxton because of their children. Abbott had been one of the wealthiest Negroes in Toronto and moved to Buxton so that his children would receive the Christian education possible there. Thomas had managed to sell his business and possessions in Buffalo, New York, but was an escaped slave and feared the slavecatchers after passage of the Fugitive Slave Act. He too chose land in Buxton for his children's education.

The problem was the lack of a sawmill and the capital needed for its expensive equipment. Both Abbott and Thomas volunteered to go to Toronto and Buffalo to approach well-to-do Negro friends and see if the enterprise could not be capitalized by their own people.

But nobody at the meeting had volunteered any knowledge of how to prepare the valuable "black salts," the pot-and-pearl ash much sought after as fertilizer in the eastern worked-out lands. King solved that himself. He went to Delta and there found one F. Gates engaged in the manufacture of pearl ash from the Six Mile Woods. When told of the vast tract of virgin timber at Buxton and the amount of burning going on, Mr. Gates packed up his family and took land near Buxton himself. He not only taught the settlers how to treat wood ash to make potash, he bought their total output and paid cash for it. King relates:

> This gave quite an impulse to clearing, as a settler could now stay at home and work for himself instead of having to go out and work among the farmers to get cash for groceries and clothing. He could now stay at home, clear a piece of his own land, log and burn the timber, convert the ashes into black salts and sell them at home for cash.

The Canada Mill and Mercantile Company, with a capitalization of four thousand dollars, was announced on March 27, 1852, only a few months after the meeting at which Abbott and Thomas volunteered to raise the money. It was such an ambitious cooperative undertaking for Negroes who had been slaves or penniless a few years before that it attracted the attention and admiration of all Canada. The *Toronto Globe* gave it such fervent praise that George Brown must have been sold by his own editorials. He and King were the only white shareholders allowed in the company. Three thousand dollars of the estimated capitalization was taken up immediately among Negroes in Toronto and Buffalo. That represented thirty of the forty shares. The rest of the capitalization was never necessary because the company was an immediate success with William Abbott as its treasurer. The purpose stated in the preamble to its constitution was realized within two years: "We unite ourselves together in order to establish a sawmill, a grist mill and a good country store, believing that this is the only way for us to become independent and respectable in business transactions."

There was one specification in the Constitution that puzzled the public. Article III declared that "the steam saw mill shall be the first object of the company and shall be propelled by an engine of 15 horsepower." That was a lot of horsepower in those days and the machinery could only be found in Detroit. The opinion of experts, voiced in Chatham, was that it was a lot more horsepower than was needed even for high lumber production. But Chatham, where the nearest sawmill was located, would be critical anyway. They would be astounded, however, when the purpose of all the extra power was revealed.

King went shopping, and in Cincinnati he found a portable corn mill which he shipped up the Wabash and Erie Canal, across the Detroit River and to Buxton. There, another belt power-takeoff was attached to the steam sawmill—and Buxton had its gristmill. That was the reason for the extra horsepower.

King organized the industrialization of Buxton and he did it with his usual efficiency. No sooner had Abbott and Thomas returned with the capital than gangs went to work framing the sawmill structure. The brickyard devoted all of its output to construction of the mill's smokestack, a brick engineroom and an extension for the gristmill machinery. King was off to Detroit, Delta, and Cincinnati for the machinery and Mr. Gates. The mill was ready when the machinery arrived and the entire settlement was in frenzied activity.

> There was now a boom in the settlement, getting logs out for the sawmill, clearing land, logging and burning the wood

to get ashes to make black salts for the pearl ash factory . . . The brick yard was also carried on; lumber and brick could now be obtained in the settlement for building purposes, and improvements now began to appear of a more permanent character. The puncheon floors of the early settlers now gave place to fine, planed oak floors and the primitive mud chimneys of the log cabins were replaced with brick, and some of the log cabins themselves gave place to frame buildings, and one settler named West erected a fine, two-story brick temperance hotel, the first brick building erected in the settlement.

The activity was so great and production of logs, lumber, brick, and pearl ash was so high that King was confronted with an old problem, one with which he was familiar. Any productivity is fruitless if nothing gets to market, and water was the most inexpensive highway for freight. And so he called another meeting of the settlers.

The provincial laws, he explained, required not only that each freeholder maintain the road bordering his property but also perform what was called "statute labor" to maintain roads through public tracts. They could perform this service at so many days a year, but their situation was this: parts of the Elgin land bordering the proposed Center Road running north and south were not yet taken up. In order to provide for passage from the 7th Concession clear south to the lakefront beyond the 14th Concession, the forest must be cleared all the way. If they wished to sell their timber, lumber, and bricks, ship their crops and reach the markets as inexpensively as possible, they must cut the Center Road for all of its 9½ miles. It was voted to go to work, as a community.

Once more the teams were organized and, when the Center Road was a wide, straight swath through the forest, with only a single jog needed, the path to Lake Erie and all its ports was open. On the following spring, giant logs and stacks of lumber which had been sledded to the cliff edge were tipped over and splashed into a cove where barges awaited them for shipment to many markets. And when the road had been cut, it was found that the pearl ash from the elms alone was sufficient to pay for the cost of clearing.

King may have been an eminent classical scholar, but that in no way adulterated the canny business logic which he demonstrated again and again. He traveled a great deal, in the United States and in Canada West, and always with one eye out for opportunities. An observation he made in southern Ohio in 1852 led to another meeting at Buxton.

He told the settlers that he had seen hordes of pigs running wild in the corn country, and wondered why. Pork was a staple diet throughout the West and more so in the South. During his years in Louisiana the supply of pork coming down the Mississippi never seemed enough. He asked the farmers in Ohio about it and learned that pork could only be shipped in brine. No flatboat could pen up enough live hogs and carry enough food to survive the long journey down the Ohio and then the Mississippi. But the Ohio woods had been cut over and over. Barrels commanded premium prices and could only be obtained from the Alleghenies. The Ohio farmers would be satisfied with barrel staves alone, because they had enough wood to top and bind the barrels.

Once more he found the human resources among his own people. A fugitive from Georgia had made pitch-pine barrels. By the time the sawmill was ready, so was the barrel stave operation. Here was a money crop more profitable than timber, yet one using the smaller growths which they had been burning. Within a few years, barges at the lakefront were carrying mountainous piles of barrel staves as far south as Cincinnati, and as far east as Buffalo.

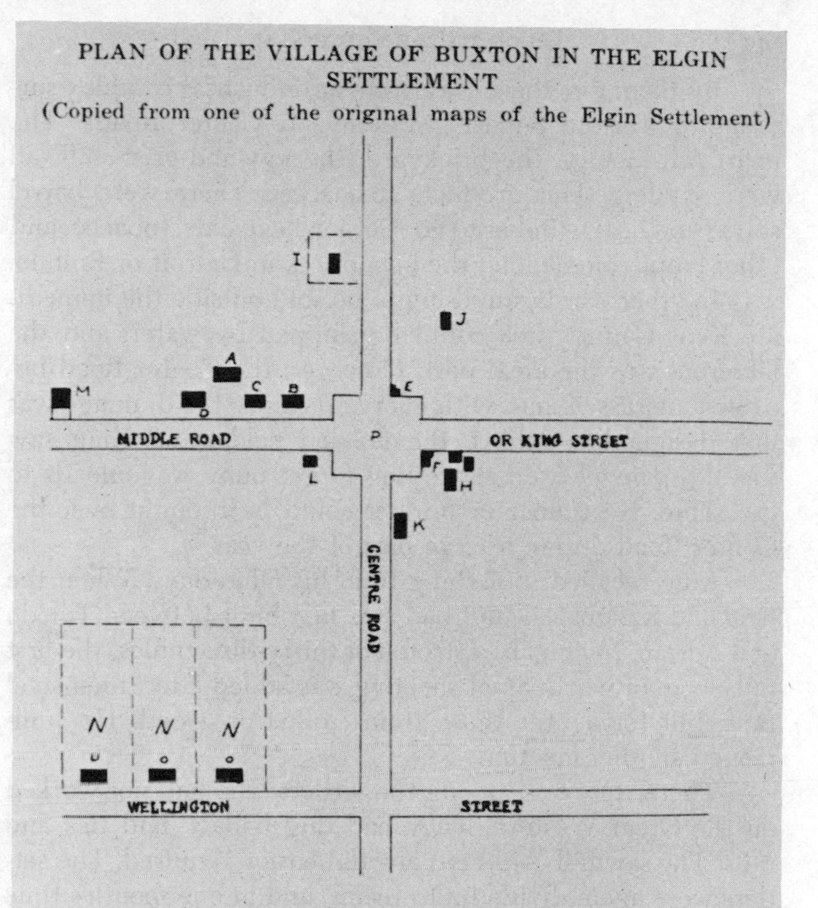

REFERENCES

A	Rev. W. King's House	I	Brick Yard
B	Mission Church	J	Steam Saw and Grist Mill
C	Buxton Post Office	K	Carpenter's Shop
D	Mission School	L	Shoe Shop
E	Store	M	District School
F	A two-storey brick hotel	N	Lots of 50 acres each
G	Blacksmith Shop	O	Houses on Lots
H	Pearlash Factory	P	Buxton Square

EARLY PLAN OF THE VILLAGE OF BUXTON

University of Western Ontario Library

By then, too, there was quite an industrial complex surrounding Buxton Square, Middle and Center Roads. The pearl ash factory, the brickyard, the saw-and-grist mill, all were sending their products to market. There were barrel staves and heavy timber to go. Corn, wheat, oats, tobacco, and other crops commanded the best prices in Detroit or Buffalo.

In other words, anything to be sold outside the immediate Kent County area could be shipped by water, and the lakefront was the ideal port. However, the Center Road became a morass of mud with every rain since the drainage was first designed to relieve the flooded fields, and King saw double spans of oxen struggling to get puny wagonloads to the shore. No timber or lumber could be brought over the Center Road during a large part of the year.

King recalled something from his Ohio days. When the Erie and Kalamazoo Railroad was first built between Toledo and Adrian, Michigan, a stretch of thirty-three miles, the first rails were of wood. Steel sheeting was added later, then steel rails, but for a year those trains rolled on wood. He summoned another meeting.

There were few among the settlers who had not worked on the Great Western. They had dug ballast, laid ties and rails. The sawmill could cut any dimension required. The settlers were again divided into teams, and in one month's time they built a wooden tramway from Buxton Square to the Lake Erie cliff edges. Now a single span of oxen could roll huge cargoes on reinforced wagon beds along the greased wooden rails.

Since the Center Road was a public highway, King needed legal permission to build the tramway; he petitioned the Raleigh Township Council and it was granted unanimously.

> It was moved by Mr. Slade and seconded by Mr. Crow that the petition of the Rev. Mr. King be entertained and

> that the Petitioner be allowed to place a tramway on the west side of the Center Rd. from Buxton Mill to Lake Erie, said railway not to occupy more than eight feet of the present road and to be built at the expence (sic) of the Petitioner. . . .

But the Township Council appeared to distrust Rev. King's aggressive performances. At their very next meeting another motion was carried.

> It was moved by Mr. Crow and seconded by Mr. Dolsen that Mr. Slade be a committee to look after the laying of the Tramway on the Center Rd. and if possible not to allow the main travelled portion of the road to be encumbered or the ditch obstructed.

By its fifth year Buxton was an economic success. By its tenth year Isaac Riley's sons, with five others from Buxton, were attending Knox College in Toronto and their parents had the money to pay for them.

All of William King's predictions came true. All of Larwill's predictions proved false. No spoken testimony to the fact that Buxton had earned the admiration and friendship of its white neighbors could surpass the afternoon of September 14, 1856, when, at two o'clock the Reverend William King asked God's blessing on approximately one thousand guests, mostly the white residents of Chatham.

Their hosts were the nearly one thousand men, women, and children of Buxton, all of them Negro. The guests sat crowded into a pavilion made of lumber from Buxton's own sawmill. It was 120 feet long, covering the entire lawn in front of St. Andrews Church, was 14 feet deep and was shielded from the sun by an arbored ceiling 12 feet high. There were flowers everywhere, from Buxton's gardens, on the long trestle table and on the tables hurriedly set up on the lawn to accommodate the overflow. Flowering climbers grew high on the church walls, following ropes produced in Buxton's own rope-walk.

They dined on venison and wild turkey, both hunted in Buxton's own forests. They also had a choice of beef, mutton, and pork from Buxton's own herds and drank milk from Buxton's two hundred milk cows. They ate bread baked from flour ground in Buxton's own gristmill out of wheat raised on the one thousand acres of land cleared and under cultivation only seven years after the first Negroes arrived. The vegetables came from approximately two hundred front-yard gardens of two hundred homes in Buxton.

After the hearty meal and the lengthy speeches, the guests stretched their legs and inspected Buxton's two schools, all flower-bedecked. Then they visited the three churches, St. Andrews Presbyterian, First Baptist, and British Methodist Episcopal. There were speakers from Toronto, Dr. Willis and Dr. Reid from the Synod, Dr. Irvine of Hamilton. And they had two unexpected guests from London, England, who had seen nothing like this in their tour of the West Indies, where emancipation had been completed ten years before the Buxton Settlement was founded. They were Althorp, the future Earl Spencer, and a member of the British House of Commons named John W. Probyn.

But the speaker who roused them to cheers was their own Archie McKellar who, in the name of all Kent County and Canada West, thanked the Negro hosts for settling among them. In his audience were most of the men of Chatham who had signed the Larwill petitions and their presence was a confession of their error. These Negroes had never been a public burden and obviously never would be, for they had a brickyard, a pearl-ash factory, a blacksmith's shop, a thriving barrel stave business, and an even more prosperous timber business. But, most of all, each of their hosts *owned his own land*.

This Indenture

made the first day of January in the year of our Lord One
Thousand Eight Hundred and Sixtysix in pursuance of the
Act passed in the Thirteenth and Fourteenth years of the
Reign of Her Majesty Queen Victoria Chapter one hundred and
fortyfour entitled "An Act to incorporate the Elgin Association
for the settlement and moral improvement of the coloured
Population of Canada" **Between The Elgin Association**
of the first part and **Levi Anderson** of the Township of
Raleigh in the County of Kent yeoman of the second part
Witnesseth that the said Elgin Association for and in consideration of the sum of **Three Hundred Dollars**
of lawful money of Canada now paid by the said party of the
second part the receipt whereof is hereby acknowledged the
said Elgin Association doth grant unto the said Levi Anderson his heirs and assigns forever **All and singular**
that certain parcel or tract of land and premises situate
lying and being in the Township of Raleigh in the County of
Kent being composed of the northwest half of lot number six
in the thirteenth concession containing one hundred acres
more or less **To have and to hold** unto the said Levi
Anderson his heirs and assigns to and for his and their
sole and only use forever Subject Nevertheless to the reser-
vations limitations provisoes and conditions expressed in
the original grant thereof from the Crown The said Elgin
Association covenants with the said Levi Anderson that
they have the right to convey the said lands to the said
Levi Anderson notwithstanding any Act of the said
The Elgin Association And that the said Levi Anderson
shall have quiet possession of the said lands free from

The land now belongs to Levi Anderson—
first page of a typical document.

North Buxton (Ontario) Museum

The County of Kent was now receiving taxes on approximately four thousand acres of land which had never before contributed to public needs. The lands surrounding Buxton had doubled and trebled in market value due to the crude beginnings of drainage systems. These Negroes would never depreciate property.

Conflict between the races? In all seven years there had been just one incident between a Negro and a white man, and that was settled amicably; it had nothing to do with the difference in color, and the two lived until their deaths as friendly neighbors on adjoining hundred-acre tracts.

And who else, Archie McKellar pointed out, was responsible for the new, fabulously successful money crop in Canada West except the Negroes from Louisiana, Mississippi, the Carolinas, Kentucky, all the South? Who else had knowledge of tobacco cultivation that was making Kent County leaf the most sought after crop in all Canada?

William King should have been a proud man on that beautiful Indian summer day of September 14, 1856. He had not just created his "City of God" for his Negroes. He had spread its influence much further, into the hearts and minds of white men who now realized that they had been filled with the poison of prejudice. He had accomplished something an entire country had failed to do, this Presbyterian preacher. In September, 1856, just a hundred miles south the presidential campaign was reaching its crescendo based on "Bleeding Kansas," and Buchanan was to be elected on the platform of non-interference with expanding slavery. He was to be made President the following year by the Larwills of fourteen slave and five "free" states.

Even while William King was building men and women as well as a settlement, south of the "Line" the Fugitive Slave Act of 1850 was either destroying men, women, and children or sending them to him at Buxton. Even while Buxton's people were marching to the polls at each election, Chief Justice Taney and a majority of the U.S. Supreme Court declared that no Negro can be a citizen of that country. That was the Dred Scott decision. While Rev. William King was receiving multiple honors for his work among escaped slaves, Rev. Theodore Parker was defending himself in Boston against charges of helping slaves escape.

In fact, while all of Canada was struggling toward Confederation, all the United States were whirling toward disunion. There were strange contradictions above and below the "Line."

IX : EMANCIPATION FROM IGNORANCE

BUXTON SETTLEMENT'S MATERIAL success proved only that, given the opportunities, Negroes can achieve economic independence to the same extent as any white group. It disproved the familiar and perpetual charge that Negroes are lazy, irresponsible, and incapable of sustained effort.

But what about the Negroes' incapacity to learn, the mental inferiority which prohibits intellectual achievement? Today, the fallacy of the charge is too well known to repeat, but in William King's day it was an accepted axiom, even among the Abolitionists. He disproved it as will be related later, but also demonstrated something far more important.

Within twelve months of its founding, William King's crude log schoolhouse became the first integrated public school established in North America.

There was more than historical significance in this. The events leading to establishment of the school itself, and the fact that the whites themselves sought the integration, are much more important. Those events began almost immediately, on December 3, 1849, just five days after King and his flock reached Raleigh. It was a Sabbath, and he was invited to preach by the white settlers. They had been served irregularly by circuit riders and, most Sundays, could not make the long, muddy journey to Chatham, which had the nearest church. King joyfully accepted and he set out with Mr. and Mrs. William White, from whom he had bought his own land, with his 21 Negroes, to the District Schoolhouse on the Middle Road which was always used for religious and social events. They found a large group of white families waiting there.

But the common school was locked tightly. It was done

by order of the School District Trustees, even though it had always been used for services whenever a minister appeared.

The old settlers were angry and wanted to break in. King knew that it was Larwill's work and that, as a member of the School District Trustees, he could punish them. The children would be the ones to suffer. He restrained them and announced that he would return to his home and hold services. It would be crowded and uncomfortable, but any who wished to join them could find room.

He did not reckon with a woman. Mrs. White spoke up angrily to tell the neighbors that they had paid for this common school and were entitled to its use. Then she dug into her pocket and waved a key high. She refused to explain how she had obtained it, but she apparently had anticipated trouble.

Mrs. White took command and ushered King and the entire congregation into the schoolhouse over his protests. She must have been a most formidable woman, because the School Trustees left the schoolhouse door unlocked every Sunday thereafter. It may have been due to Mrs. White's anger—or perhaps to the fact that Larwill was planning to be a candidate for the Provincial Parliament the following year.

But King refused to hold services in the schoolhouse again. After his sermon on that first Sabbath he announced that services would be held at his own home and all were welcome. He apologized for the delay in building a church, but so long as they had his home as a place of worship, the building of houses would take first priority.

His house was crowded every Sabbath. And when the first log cabins were up, roofed and snug, all of the Negroes set to building the first church-schoolhouse near where St. Andrews Church stands now. Without a single request made, when the news spread along the Talbot Road that King was building his church, the whites joined the Negroes and they worked side by side as they were to do through all the years.

King built for the future. The log church-schoolhouse was twenty-four by thirty-two feet and sat two hundred at services. Its construction cost him, personally, $400 because he insisted on paying for the labor. The timber was taken from his own land and the lumber for the benches and tables was sawn in Chatham. By then King was out of money and he borrowed back from William White enough to pay for the church-school. This was the first of five mortgages taken out on his land to meet the immediate needs of the settlement. This one was not repaid until 1854.

On the first Sabbath in April 1850, King announced that the school would open the next day for enrollment and all children were welcome. Then he announced that Sabbath School and services would be in the new church-schoolhouse, and that prayer services would begin the following Thursday evening and be held weekly.

From Chatham came warnings that a mob would prevent the opening of the school. There was reason to worry about the rumors: gangs of whites had periodically roamed the woods around the new log cabins and were known to have inspected those that were empty. Their purpose, according to King, was to "so annoy the settlers as to cause them to leave with their families and thus break up the work that had begun."

The first Monday morning in April 1850 was wet and the trees dripped. Again unbeknown to King, the Negroes of Chatham decided to go hunting. They ringed the new school in the forest and watched all paths from Chatham. It is not recorded whether the Vigilantes appeared. But something did happen that was to end the invasions of the settlement.

On that Monday morning, fourteen Negro children old enough for school enrolled and with them were two white children, part of Joshua Shepley's large family. They had left the District Common School.

One reason was young John Rennie, the volunteer teacher King had obtained from Knox College in Toronto. The divinity student was a handsome young man, with both teaching and musical ability. He had led the congregation in singing the day before and had spoken a few words. With his background and ability, the new school was in good hands. On the other hand, the teacher at the District School apparently was typical of Kent County at that time. Teaching appointments there were made on the basis of oral examinations alone, and candidates were examined by the school trustees who could barely sign their own names. The standards were extremely low. There was no high school in the entire county.

Within a few months, more white children came in. Then, as King expanded his educational program to include a night school, white adults appeared. Among the first were Joshua Shepley and his two older daughters. All three of them were in the ridiculous position of having less learning than the youngest children. King himself taught them English, grammar, geography, and arithmetic, and saw all three qualify for teaching licenses.

Meanwhile, a year had passed and there were more white children in King's school than in the District School. The parents of the remainder, led by John Broadbent, came to King and asked permission to enroll their children. Their neighbors who had already sent their children to the Buxton school were delighted with their progress. King was happy to welcome them, more so because retribution was sweet. Larwill now became a School Trustee without a school. The District School was closed down, and the Buxton school became the only common school in the Township. It was an integrated school too, but not in the usual circumstances. There was no Supreme Court decision and the whites sought out the Negro school.

That was all the more remarkable because at that time there were segregated schools in Chatham. A year before, the Provincial Parliament had adopted a Separate School Act for Canada West. The reason stated was that Negro children were being prevented from attending the public schools "by causes arising from the prejudices and ignorance of certain other inhabitants." The children were being barred by the local authorities in much the same way segregated schools are continued in the South today. There are no segregated schools in all Canada today, for the law was tested in the courts sufficiently by 1864 to reach a definition that the right of a separate school is granted any Negro or religious group, as in Roman Catholic parochial schools, but Negroes could not be prevented from attending the public schools.

But this example set by the Buxton School was only one cause of amazement in Canada West. Another was King's own adult education program.

> I also opened a night school for adults and took charge of it myself. It was interesting to see men and women from twenty-five to thirty years of age and some even older who had never tried to learn before, begin with their ABC's and try to learn the names of the letters and put them together in syllables. All the ones who could not read seemed anxious to learn and applied themselves with diligence, although they found it a hard task to master the elements of the English tongue. But, by diligence and perseverance, they soon began to make progress and by the end of six months quite a number of them could read a little, and by the end of the first year many who did not know the letters when they came to me were able to read slowly large print in the Testament. They were quite delighted when they came to the Bible Class

to bring their Bible with them and read the verse with the rest of the class and, what was more pleasing still, many of them when they learned to read learned the way of salvation and became humble followers of Christ.

Within a year King had approximately two hundred men, women, and children in his day school, night school, Sabbath School and Bible classes. There were sixty children in the day school, both white and black.

The enrollment increased explosively due to the influx of fugitives. The refugees from the "free" states were generally able to bring their families away from the menace of the Fugitive Slave Act, but not until they reached Canada were their children to experience a mixed school.

Within five years the day school had 147 children and it was simply too crowded. A second school was built on the Center Road at what is now North Buxton, and its initial class was sixty pupils. It was a log school, twenty-six feet square. Two years later a third school was built. Eventually there were 250 pupils in Buxton's schools, all integrated.

The Buxton schools differed from any others in another respect. With very few exceptions, such as Oberlin and Prudence Crandall's school in Canterbury, Connecticut, which the whites burned down, education of Negroes had the single goal of vocational training. Nowhere else, in Canada, the United States or in England, had the antislavery societies, the interested churches or the Quakers established Negro schools to prepare pupils for the standard classical education. Even Josiah Henson, when Dawn Institute was being discussed, proposed:

> I urge the appropriation of the money to the establishment of a manual labor school, where our children could be taught those elements of knowledge which are usually the occupations of a grammar school; and there the boys could be taught, in addition, the practice of some mechanical art,

and the girls could be instructed in those domestic arts which are the proper occupation and ornament of their sex.

To King this was tacit admission that Negroes were to be forever condemned to work of the hands, that work of the mind and spirit was beyond their potentiality. Therefore, it would follow, God had placed on this earth a people distinctive not only in the color of their skin but had molded them with definite limitations in their capacity to think and to possess faith. This he could not accept.

He had listened to that thesis before. In Edinburgh the Tories had declared that God, in His infinite wisdom, had ordained a lesser manhood to the residents of West Port so that they would assume a modest but rightful place in the social order. It was so ordained, and all who protested the ignorance, degeneration, and poverty of West Port were uttering blasphemy. In Louisiana, during long hours of discussion concerning the divine purpose of slavery, exactly the same arguments were repeated.

Therefore, his own "City of God" was to be a demonstration of the intellectual as well as the economic capacities of the Negroes. With their own land, they were freed from economic bondage. With their own church, they were freed from spiritual poverty. With equal intellectual opportunity, they would be completely free. The formula he propounded was not new in his day and age, but his faith in the capacity of the Negro to take full advantage of it was revolutionary.

While all the arguments concerning the mental capacities of the Negroes were almost a daily debate, and even the Boston Abolitionists expressed their doubts, King simply went ahead and proved his belief.

Within a few years, as observers visited Buxton, King took a sly delight in astonishing them with performances by his star pupils. For the churchmen of all denominations he had ten-year-old Sarah recite the Testament and the Catechism. On January 24, 1850, two months before the school building was opened, he reported that Sarah "has committed all the Shorter Catechism to memory since the first of December."

Sarah would be followed by ten-year-old Jerome Riley, Isaac's oldest boy. He was the prize pupil when academicians visited Buxton. Not one of them failed to report that they had heard this Negro boy recite long passages in almost faultless Latin from Virgil's *Aeneid* and then translate, in a child's vocabulary, the sense of the verses.

The visitors came from Ireland, England, France, and the United States, and their reports of the miracle at Buxton made it possible for King, some years later, to see his appeals for funds with which to build a church and a schoolhouse oversubscribed.

The first Latin class, with six Negro boys in it, began in November 1850, less than nine months after the day school was begun. The first Greek class began a year later. By 1856, King had a class ready for Knox College—all of them just seven years away from slavery, all of them a justification of his belief in the capacity of the Negro, so totally at variance with his times.

It is difficult today to transplant ourselves to the early 1850's while King was prosecuting his plan for Christian education. It is almost impossible to accept the fact that his objectives were so revolutionary. But the press of the time gives some indication of the kind of thinking he was challenging.

Immediately after publication of *Uncle Tom's Cabin* and the stirring of so many consciences regarding slavery, William Lloyd Garrison's *Liberator* was deluged with letters asking "What can we do?" His reply was to point to Buxton, then two years old, as a way to help find homes for fugitive slaves. "This plan has succeeded so well that the friends of the fugitives have every encouragement to extend the experiment."

There were other reasons why attention was given so widely to King's pattern of education. From one of the earliest commentators on Buxton in 1851 to its most recent in 1896, the most cogent observation repeated was that, barring Larwill's agitation, there was a process of integration beginning at the school level, *but not stopping there*.

John Scoble was the first to note this. He was the secretary of the British and Foreign Anti-Slavery Society sent to Dawn Institute in an effort to halt its disintegration. During his investigations he made several trips to Buxton in 1851, and became a devotee of William King's. In his report to the first convention of the Canadian Anti-Slavery Society Scoble noted:

> I am not the advocate for exclusively coloured schools; I believe that one mode of breaking down the prejudice which exists against colour will be educating the children of all complexions together. An important fact came to my attention at Buxton which illustrates this point. At this interesting settlement an excellent school was opened by the Rev. Mr. King, at which superior education was imparted, and the result was that the white school in the neighborhood was given up, and the children transferred to the coloured school where I had the pleasure of seeing them distributed through the various classes, without distinction, and found that they studied harmoniously together.

The superiority of the Buxton school broke down all color antipathy and soon applications for admission came from whites as well as Negroes in all of Canada West and some of the United States, as far south as Alabama. King early recognized the need for a high school and set about obtaining Kent County's first one. He was appointed its trustee in March, 1851 by Lord Elgin, and he was to hold that post for twenty-eight years. With his guidance it became the Chatham Collegiate Institute, the only qualified college preparatory school west of Toronto.

Its founding arose from the needs of Buxton. While all the "higher branches" of a classical and mathematical education were taught, and a "female teacher" had been hired for the little girls who were to receive only a "common education" plus the domestic sciences, there was not room for all who wished to prepare for higher education. The fact that the mission school was preparing classes for college spread throughout the Province. As a result, "some came from a distance, both white and black, to get the benefit of a liberal education."

Some time before, Rev. Egerton Ryerson had been appointed by the Crown to install a common school system in Canada with standards and facilities to match the rapidly growing needs. King had prepared an application for a charter for a high school at Buxton when he learned that Dr. Thomas Cross, the first superintendent of schools in Chatham, was contemplating the same plan. "I considered that one high school was enough for this county then." He joined forces with him and took the petitions himself to Lord Elgin and Dr. Ryerson. The first classes were opened in the old military barracks in Chatham's Tecumseh Park with one teacher.

> I saw it rise from a class of 12 pupils to be the first collegiate institute in the Dominion with a full staff of teachers and 300 pupils on the roll, sending out annually a number of well-qualified school teachers and others who enter the University to qualify for the different learned professions.

He was to become secretary of the Board of Trustees, and when the new log building of Chatham Collegiate Institute was dedicated in 1855, King was the principal speaker.

He also served in similar capacities for the Wilberforce Educational Institute. This was an effort to save the educational features of the Dawn Institute. In 1873, King was instrumental in having the institution moved from Dawn into Chatham and renamed.

While there was self-interest accompanying King's motives (the Chatham Collegiate Institute solved many of Buxton's educational problems), there was none in his equally long service on the Kent County Examining Board for teaching licenses. It was the mixture of preacher and teacher in him, without demarcation between the two. None of his activities strayed far from this combination.

Not all of the Buxton settlers became classical scholars, or scholars at all. They differed in no way from their white schoolmates. However, there was a by-product of the Buxton schools shared by them all. These Negroes who had been slaves a year before joined with their fellow-settlers who had been fortunate in learning to read and write before arriving at Buxton and all became articulate. King was startled early and often by the forces of expression being unleashed by the meetings and by the ability to read.

The first instance of self-expression took place in February 1850, a few months after the settlement was begun, and before Parliament had met and chartered the Elgin Association. Led by Wilson Abbott, the settlers decided to do some lobbying in Parliament themselves to help get the incorporation bill through over Larwill's opposition. They chose a committee of three, Abbott, Adolphus Judah and David Hollin, to compose the following letter to Malcolm Cameron, M.P., at that time leader of the anti-Tory, Reform (Grit) party:

To the Hon. Malcolm Cameron:—

Sir, We the undersigned committee have been appointed

by a number of colored stock holders of the Elgin Association to ask your views on a subject that chiefly concerns our civil rights. Your long residence in the western part of the province, where most of our people are settled, makes you well acquainted with our condition, and the many disadvantages under which we labor, in consequence of an unjust prejudice, which deprives our children, in a great measure, of the use of the common schools, and excludes us from participating in the rights and privileges guaranteed to us by law. This prejudice has lately assumed a hostile form, in an address published at Chatham in August last, the object of which is to prevent us from settling where we please, and if carried into effect, would eventually drive us from the province. As you represent the county where the Elgin Association has purchased land for colored settlers they wish to know if you are in favor of our settling there, or any other place that we may select in the province, and if you will aid us in obtaining all the rights and privileges we are entitled to by law. An answer at your earliest convenience will oblige the committee.

They sent this letter off without King's knowledge and requested a meeting when Cameron's reply was received. There, King was to learn that his people were capable of coming to his assistance already, and that the process of self-emancipation was much faster than he had thought. Besides, Cameron's reply was a most valuable assist in the political uncertainties of the day:

GENTLEMEN:

In reply to your letter of this day I beg leave to say that the evil you complain of, relative to your position in common schools, was fully provided for in the new school bill which I had the honor to conduct through Parliament last session and which comes into operation in January next.

I regretted very much the tone and sentiments of the resolution and address to which you allude as having been passed at Chatham in August last, and I feel quite sure they are not the sentiments of the great mass of the County of Kent. For my own part I have ever advocated the perfect equality of all mankind, and the right of all to every civil and religious privilege without regard to creed or color. And under the constitution we now enjoy all men are really "free and equal" and none can deny to the African anything granted to the Scotchmen and Irishmen or the Saxon; they have the right to purchase where they please, and settle in groups or singly as they like; and wherever they are, they will find me ready to defend and maintain the principles of civil and religious freedom to all, as the principle I hold most dear to myself and most sacred to my country. I have the honor to be your obedient servant,

MALCOLM CAMERON

This letter was a commitment by the Reform Party that, when the question of chartering the Elgin Association came up in Parliament, Larwill and the Tories would have a fight on their hands.

King's next surprise at the initiative among his people came in the summer of 1851, when he called a meeting to offer the second annual report to the stockholders of the Elgin Association.

When he finished reading the report, there were objections from the floor. There had been an omission. King had written nothing to the stockholders countering the false reports being circulated by Larwill and his cohorts through the Chatham, Windsor, and Toronto Tory press. The frequent letters, news reports, and editorials should be answered, the stockholders maintained. They were now a legally constituted body by Act of Parliament, and had every right to speak up. Besides, a copy of the Association's annual report went to Parliament too.

King agreed heartily and promised to append any statement they wished to make to his report and forward it to the members of the Elgin Association. It was the first result of his schooling and inculcation of a pride that was to become a most powerful force. A committee was elected and wrote the following:

> In order to correct certain falsehoods and misrepresentations concerning the coloured settlement at Raleigh, that have been circulated by the enemies of the social improvement of the coloured people in the Province we consider it a duty which we owe both to you and to the public to correct these by a statement of facts.
>
> Twelve months experience have enabled us in some measure to judge of the location, its soil, climate and production. The soil varies from a stiff clay to a sandy loam and on the south side of the block where the land is level, it inclines to a black vegetable mould. It produces wheat, Indian corn, potatoes, oats, tobacco and hemp. It is better adapted to the growth of wheat than any other grain. Although the land is new, and we could get but little cleared for wheat last fall, yet the sample produced is excellent. The grain is full and plump, and weighs 62 pounds to the bushel. The tobacco is said by those who have raised and manufactured the article in the states to be equal to the best leaf raised in Virginia.
>
> The climate is mild and healthy, and is free from those fogs which usually prevail on the lake shore and the river.
>
> Peaches, sweet pickles and every kind of melon grow well in the open air. The snow is seldom more than 6 inches deep and lies but a few weeks at a time.
>
> There is scarcely a day during the winter that a man cannot work at clearing. It often happens during the thaws which are frequent in winter, that we have very mild weather. The Spring commences in April. The summer is warm and we have seldom any white frost until the first of

October and Winter does not set in until the middle of December. We have had but little sickness and the general health has been good.

After one year's trial, we are highly pleased with the location and would not change it for any other in the Province.

We avail ourselves of the present opportunity to express our grateful thanks to the members of the Elgin Association for the interest they have felt in our social and moral improvement and hope for the blessing of God on our industry to show to our enemies that when placed in favorable circumstances we are able and willing to support ourselves.

From that time on, through many attacks against Buxton, Archie McKellar and King, throughout the next thirty years in fact, the people of Buxton became more and more articulate. Their letters, resolutions, and memorials were seldom given space in the Chatham newspapers but *The Voice of the Fugitive*, the *Toronto Globe*, and the Abolitionist press in the United States had them as regular contributors. They were alert to any and all criticism, including the weather in Kent County. On March 29, 1852, a committee was elected to reply to stories of starvation among Negroes in Canada due to the extreme cold.

A register of the weather was kept at Buxton, Canada West, during the month of January. The 19th, 20th and 21st were the coldest days. On the 20th the thermometer stood at 10 degrees below zero. At Chicago on the same day, it is reported to have stood at 20 degrees below zero, and at Cleveland, 19 degrees; at Philadelphia, 7 degrees and at Baltimore, 8 degrees, showing that Canada West was 9 degrees warmer than Cleveland and only 2 degrees colder than Baltimore. There has been a great deal of misrepresentation about the climate of Canada West. It is milder than most states north of the Ohio River and persons from Louisiana enjoy the best of health in it. Indeed, the southern planter loves to breathe

the air of our lakes and recruit his shattered constitution by a summer ramble in our healthful and picturesque country.

Messages "back home" to the northern free states were frequent. Ezekiel Cooper, a fugitive from Northampton, Massachusetts, in 1852 wrote to the *Liberator:*

> I consider that Canada is the place where we have our rights. We might stay in the United States and preach for rights and liberty until our heads are laid beneath the soil, and the result will be that our children will still be under the yoke. But let them come into this Province and all join in one united place and we can work wonders for our redemption. We have purchased fifty acres and are now at work on it. We have got a flourishing school here and the teachers appear to take a lively interest in teaching the coloured people. There are some noble coloured scholars here who may do much hereafter to elevate the race.

There are many such communications but one is a classic of satire. It is signed by Edward R. Grants, Samuel Wickham and Robert Harris as "a committee from Buxton" and answers the wave of Southern inspired diatribes set off by publication of *Uncle Tom's Cabin,* all accusing Canadian Negroes of being lazy beggars. It concludes thus:

> We wish the people in the United States to know that there is one portion of Canada West where the coloured people are self-supporting and they wish them to send neither petticoats nor pantaloons to the County of Kent. Those who are too lazy to support themselves and live on the bounty of others must be a disgrace themselves. We hope in a short time to clothe ourselves in the wool grown on our own sheep, raised on our own farms. We trust the day is not far distant when it will be considered a disgrace for a woman to let her husband appear in public without a suit of homespun on his back, made and woven by herself. The few cases of real want which arise from sickness or old age can with a trifling effort

be relieved here without making it a pretext for a system of wholesale begging in the U.S.

There is little question as to the temper of this statement. It declares unmistakably "No Help Wanted," and asserts the fierce independence that King knew was in his people. It was not the fact of their independence that surprised, it was the speed with which it developed from the opposite pole of slavery.

Once more it must be pointed out that the slaveowners were entirely justified in fearing education of their slaves. But even more to be feared by the slaveholders was William King's accent on "Christian education." His ultimate purpose in education was to train a nucleus of Negroes—a core group like his cabin raising crews—to Christianize and elevate their own people, not just in Canada but in the United States and Africa as well. He believed that a "City of God" was possible anywhere.

☆

X : COUNTING SOULS

IT IS DIFFICULT to separate the preacher from the teacher in King's actions. Just as his concepts of economic and intellectual self-emancipation differed so from all others of his times, so did his emphasis on the "Christian" in education. Within a year of settlement the day school, to him, was a fact accomplished. The Synod was sending him the teachers, he himself was teaching the adults and the advanced students. This course was clear.

Not so clear was the development of his church, the Sabbath Schools, and the Thursday night Bible classes. There was no money, for one thing, and the first St. Andrews Church was overcrowded by whites and Negroes alike. There were few books in his religious library, actually only those books he had brought back from Edinburgh and a supply of catechisms from the Synod.

But the concrete problems of the settlement's religious life were minor in the light of his purpose. His "City of God" was never to remain isolated from the world and exist only as a monument to the accomplishments of a comparative handful among the millions of Negroes still in slavery. Buxton Settlement was to be a fountainhead of Christianity and, from his very first message to the Toronto Synod in 1848 until his last recorded expression on his "City of God" in 1892, William King was an indomitable advocate of Christian education for his people, not for themselves alone, but for all their race. Only the outbreak of the Civil War prevented the sailing, from New York, of his first group of Negro Buxton missionaries to Africa in the Fall of 1861.

For this purpose William King subordinated his pride

and went begging in Canada, the United States, and the British Isles. For it, he himself went heavily into debt. For the first five years, until his own people again asserted their independence and demanded a share in building their religious community, he carried the burden alone. It would have been easy to merely count noses in his church and say that these are Christians. It was what the ecclesiastical apologists of the South were doing. Prof. David Christy, in *Pulpit Politics* cited King and the Buxton Settlement as the only example among free Negroes anywhere in the world where "proper moral control" is exercised and therefore "any real progress can be made by the blacks." His statistics were totally unreliable but Christy's argument had force in church councils of all denominations, both North and South. The standard argument he had used in *Cotton Is King,* to the effect that slavery made Christians and freedom made heathens, was repeated in the later book. Christy's misinformation concerning Buxton has colored the thinking of the few historians discussing King's work. He writes:

> In Canada, the mission of the Rev. Mr. King, in 1859, had a membership of seventy, and an attendance of two hundred to three hundred. We have no other statistics from Canada, as to the colored churches, but have seen a newspaper statement that the membership is about three hundred.

In 1859 there were at least that many Negro fugitives entering Canada every week. The Negro population there has been variously estimated at between thirty-five thousand and fifty thousand and these fugitives fled into their churches immediately after crossing the "Line." Those from the plantations had never had their own churches, and in the cities of the North, only the most populous could afford established congregations.

By that time King had 112 in the Sunday School at St.

Andrews alone. He had over two hundred communicants in the church and over one hundred in the adult Bible classes. The Baptist and British Methodist Episcopal congregations by 1860 had their own Sunday Schools. By that time each Sabbath saw over eight hundred Buxton people in the three churches. Well over a thousand Negroes in Kent County, in addition, attended their own churches. If Christy had wished to study the *Liberator* he would have learned that, in proportion to their population, more Negroes in Canada supported their churches than the whites.

William King's kind of religious instruction, however, demanded Scriptural knowledge. He refused to count bodies as souls fully and freely able to partake of the Lord's Supper. Among his many sermons pleading for the making of Christians, perhaps his purpose is best expressed in a letter to the children of the Sabbath School at Knox Church in Toronto. Early in 1853, they had written to notify him that they had adopted the Buxton Mission as their responsibility. King wrote to them:

> Most of the people among whom I labour at Buxton were formerly slaves in the United States where they were compelled to work for others without receiving any wages, and, what is worse, without being taught to read the Bible. The children, like the parents, were left to grow up in ignorance and vice—no person to take them to the Sabbath School—no kind teacher to tell them about Christ, and the way of salvation. A number of these people have fled the bondage and are now living among us, in that ignorant state in which slavery left them. . . . Some of them have made considerable progress in scriptural knowledge, and we fondly hope that some of them have found Christ to be a precious Saviour. All are anxious to learn the word of God. Parents and children are often in the same class, endeavoring to improve the privilege, which has heretofore been denied them, of reading the Bible.

It is pleasing to see some of the old people, whose eyes are dim, put on their spectacles to spell their way through a lesson in the New Testament with their children. Some of the children at the day school have begun to learn Latin, and we hope that a number of them will enter College—give themselves to Christ, and go to their father-land and tell their ignorant countrymen of that Saviour whom they have found themselves. . . . My dear children, it is a sad and solemn thought that one hundred million of our fellow creatures are now living in Africa without hearing of Christ and dying without knowing anything of salvation. We are endeavoring at the Buxton Mission to prepare the preachers to go to proclaim it. . . .

On the other hand, the children attending King's own Sabbath School understood his purpose full well. His pride in them was obvious in an early report to the Presbyterian Synod announcing that the contribution box of the Juvenile Missionary Society of St. Andrews Church was opened on its first anniversary. The box contained eighteen dollars which the children voted in behalf of the mission at Calabar on the African coast. King was so delighted that he asked the *Presbyterian Ecclesiastical and Missionary Record* to make special note of that fact, and that was done.

William King's kind of religion was based on the Gospel and he was bound by no narrow sectarianism, just so long as his people heard the Word and read it for themselves. He himself organized the first raising bee for the First Baptist Church in 1853 and gave them his blessing. They had been holding their services in various homes until then and the charter members of the congregation were only nine. Among them were natural leaders in the community, George Hatter, Alfred West, William H. Jackson, and Isaac Washington. They worshiped as they chose and attended the Presbyterian

Mission School quite without theological conflict. Before the post-Civil War exodus, the Baptist congregation numbered one hundred and had built itself a new church. In 1855, when a group who had been raised in the influence of the Anglican Church planned their own congregation on the Center Road, again there was a raising bee, with Baptists and Presbyterians now, helping to build the first British Methodist Episcopal Church.

William King did not have to assume the Buxton Mission as a personal obligation, but he did. To each of the fugitive slaves reaching his haven he explained that all that was expected of them was economic self-sufficiency. His Church, the Presbyterian Church of Canada, had assumed all responsibility for St. Andrews and the schools through establishment of the Buxton Home Mission. Until their land was paid for, he told them, they had no financial obligation toward upkeep of the church and schools.

The collections for the Buxton Home Mission were never sufficient to meet the outlay for the purposes of Christian education. The influx from the United States resulting from the Fugitive Slave Act of 1850 had never been anticipated by anyone connected with the founding of the Elgin Association, nor by King himself. Such rapid growth found both the Church and King himself totally unprepared financially. Collections from the various Presbyterian congregations for the Buxton Mission averaged approximately $400 annually during the first five years. There was never enough money to pay the subsistence scale needed by the volunteer teachers, so King boarded them out of his own pocket. Nor was there money for enough books, Bibles, blackboards, or pencils; King bought them himself.

During the very first year, the summer of 1850, King

entered a financial crisis, and within two years he was heavily in debt. All of his Louisiana savings had gone toward divinity school. All of his Louisiana inheritance had been spent in bringing his people to the North Star. During the more than three years between his appointment as a missionary to Canada in 1846 and September 11, 1849, when the Colonial Committee approved his new mission, he had received fifty pounds in salary. On the latter date the Synod authorized him to draw one hundred pounds against the Colonial Committee and this was applied at once to purchase of his own land.

Being in debt did not seem to bother King. What was a burden on his conscience was his failure to provide for the church and school as he had promised his people. They had not failed the Mission, he had.

The worst happened on August 12, 1850. The month before, the Synod Committee had authorized another draft for one hundred pounds on the Free Church, and King promptly spent it in payment of debts. Then the draft "bounced" for non-payment in Edinburgh and King was served with a demand payment notice for that amount plus interest and costs amounting to £14 *7s. 3d.* It seems that King had been dropped from the Colonial Committee payroll in June 1848, when he received his appointment from the Canadian Synod. Neither the Synod nor King had been notified.

By then King and the Buxton Mission were widely known in three countries, and such a catastrophe was a menace to the future of them both. King negotiated another mortgage on his land through the London Building Society to meet this crisis.

King did not care about being paid. All that he had or could borrow would be applied to the religious needs of his people. They were thirsty for the Gospel and he had pledged that one security of faith to them. It was that problem and not the multiple cares of settling his people in the wilderness that gave him the most anguish during the first year.

Strangely, it was due to Larwill that William King found a pattern for the future in meeting the religious needs of the settlement. If Larwill had shown more restraint in his campaign against King and the Elgin Association, perhaps the Presbyterian Congregations in Pittsburgh, Pennsylvania, might never have heard about the Buxton Settlement. They did read about it in Frederick Douglass' newspaper, *North Star,* because a remarkable young Negro, Dr. Martin R. Delany, had practiced medicine in Pittsburgh and won the hearts of its stricken inhabitants for his services during the cholera epidemic of 1854.

Dr. Delany, who had many talents, left his practice to help Douglass edit the *North Star* in Rochester, N.Y. He was to devote the rest of his life to the cause of the Negro, as slave, soldier, and freedman. The columns of the *North Star* carried the story of Buxton back to Pittsburgh and several of the Presbyterian congregations, both white and black, wrote to the Canadian church for more information about the settlement. These letters reached Dr. Robert Burns, then Moderator of the Presbyterian Assembly and he proposed to King that they seek help for the Buxton Mission church and schools there. Pittsburgh was a center of Presbyterianism, the result of the first Scots-Irish settlers who raised their first church there in 1787 on Sixth St. while the city was but a wilderness fort. The Western Theological Seminary was founded in 1825 across the Allegheny River in Allegheny City. As a result of the stand taken on slavery by all but one of the Presbyterian congregations in Pittsburgh, a large proportion of its approximately two thousand Negro freedmen were of that church.

After a trying journey, King and Dr. Burns arrived in Pittsburgh early in November 1850. In a report on the mission, King makes quite clear the separation in his "code of secular independence for his settlers and their spiritual dependence."

> We regularly draw the line of distinction between the interests of the (Elgin) Association in the purchase and settlement of the land, and the arrangements made for the spiritual benefit of the settlers upon it. This last was the single object of our visit to the States. . . . To assist in defraying the expenses thereby incurred, and to provide for the keeping up of the religious establishment thus effected, was the single object of the appeal. . . . In the second place, while we made no secret of our views, both on slavery in general and on the refugee law in particular, we did not assume the attitude of anti-slavery or abolition pleaders. We sought to lay before all whom we addressed, a specific case of benevolence.

King took pains to make the point clear for a very good reason. At the time of their mission, Pittsburgh was in the same throes as both the New England and New York merchants, the first fearful for loss of the supply of cotton, and the second the loss of the South's shipping. Pittsburgh, already a burgeoning blast furnace, was at the head of the major supply line to the South, the Ohio and Mississippi rivers. The South was its natural market for the iron forgings and finished goods of the growing manufacturing city. King describes very well the attitudes he and Dr. Burns found:

> It cannot be denied that we did not find that ardent interest we expected in behalf of the coloured man. A strong sentiment of freedom, and even of anti-slavery, exists in those parts, as generally in the Northern States, but there are many powerful counteractives. The prejudice against colour is strong. The pecuniary interest of the North, in the

> good-will of the South, is deep. The species of loyalty which bows to all law, as such, irrespective of the character of the law (Fugitive Slave Act) is rampant. Something like a censure on the institutions of the Union is supposed to be conveyed by the very proposal to help those whom one of these institutions has driven from their homes.

He has nothing but praise for the "free blacks" of the city and for the "Scots and Irish Presbyterians" whose churches had taken a firm stand for antislavery and against slaveholding. All of these congregations welcomed the two Canadians.

A busy three weeks were spent and each of them lectured as much as six times in a single day. In actual dollars, the results were small, approximately four hundred dollars in all, but the aftermath of the mission was startling. There was an invitation from Philadelphia, William Lloyd Garrison's *Liberator* in Boston spread the news and the early fame of William King and his mission spread among the Abolitionists. Later they were to call on him as a skilled "conductor" on the Underground Railroad. And the word about William King reached Brunswick, Maine, where Harriet Beecher Stowe was working on *Uncle Tom's Cabin* which was to appear six months later. The invitation to visit her resulted from the Pittsburgh news.

The most significant result of the Pittsburgh mission was that it decided the future course of King's actions to fulfill his promise to his people. For the next ten years he was to go "begging" in three countries and he only stopped because his goal was achieved. By 1860 there was more than enough money.

Meanwhile there were two more gifts from Pittsburgh and both had more value for the Buxton Settlement than money. Shortly after his return he received the following letter from the white "Ladies of Allegheny City" accompanied by several heavy boxes:

ALLEGHENY CITY, 25 NOV. 1850

To the Rev. Wm. King

DEAR SIR:—

We have long felt a deep interest in the spiritual improvement of the Colored population. It gives us great pleasure to hear of the effort now being made by the Presbyterian Church of Canada to improve their moral condition. We rejoice that they have found with you what our own law denies them here—a home and an asylum.

We feel it a duty to aid you in giving the gospel to those persons whom our law has driven from us. As a token of the interest we feel in your School and Mission, I have been requested by the ladies of Allegheny City to present you with the "Presbyterian Library," and five Missionary maps for the Sabbath School, hoping that these may be the means, in the hands of God, of leading some young men of piety to devote themselves to the cause of Christ in a foreign land; and the prayer of the Committee is, that God may bless your efforts in training up a native ministry to preach the gospel to their own people both here and in Africa.

HARRIETT C. MARSHALL
ELIZA DEAN
And others, on behalf of the Committee.

This gift was very close to William King's heart, but there was more to come from Pittsburgh and it arrived shortly after the Presbyterian Library. It was the Liberty Bell.

A hundred years later that Bell was still pealing out its message to the dark-skinned families of North Buxton. For a hundred years, unto the fourth generation, it has sent across the flat fields of Raleigh Plains the call to the spirit that sustained the men, women and children of the settlement. It rang at six in the morning and nine at night day in and day out and it tolled the passing years with a message that is eternal. It still hangs in St. Andrews Church and the inscription is still on it: "Presented to the Rev. Wm. King, by the Coloured Inhabitants of Pittsburgh, for Academy at Raleigh, C.W." To the people of Buxton, it was a gift second only to the Emancipation Proclamation. The letter accompanying the bell expresses a wistful envy applicable today, as well as the deep reverence of the Pittsburgh Negroes.

PITTSBURGH, 23rd Nov., 1850

To the Coloured Settlers at Raleigh, C.West

DEAR BRETHREN,—

We have heard with great pleasure from Dr. Burns and the Rev. Wm. King of your settlement at Raleigh. We rejoice that you have met with Christian friends who cheer and encourage you in your efforts to improve your social condition.

You are now in a *land of liberty*, where the rights and privileges of freemen are secured to you by law. Your future position in society will depend very much on your own exertions. We sincerely hope that by your industry and good conduct you will put to silence those who speak evil of you, and show yourselves worthy of the respect and confidence of the members of the "Elgin Association", who have nobly advocated your cause.

We feel a deep interest both in your temporal and spiritual welfare. As a lasting memorial of our kindness, we send to the Rev. Wm. King, a Bell for the Academy, that when we shall be mouldering in our coffins, will call your children to the house of instruction. While your children are brought up under the blessings of a Christian education, we trust that in the land of your adoption you will not forget the God of your fathers. Love and serve him; remember the Sabbath day to keep it holy; and when the bell, with its solemn tones, calls you to the house of God, remember your brethren who are in bonds; and let your prayer ascend to

God, that He may, in His own good time, break every yoke and let the oppressed go free; that he may turn both the hearts of the Masters and Servants from the bondage of Satan to the service of the one living and true God.

J. C. Peck
J. B. Vashon
On Behalf of the Committee.

All of the Buxton settlers turned out on the very next Sunday when their Liberty Bell rang out for the first time, and after services they held a meeting. Isaac Riley was elected chairman of a committee to thank "the Coloured Inhabitants of Pittsburgh" and to do so "On Behalf of the Coloured Inhabitants of Raleigh." Isaac and William Jackson wrote and signed the letter, men who had been slaves two years before:

Raleigh, C.W., 17th Dec., 1850

To the Coloured Inhabitants of Pittsburgh
Dear Brethren:—

We have received your letter dated the 23rd Nov., and the bell presented to the Rev. W. King for the Academy at Raleigh. We are delighted at all times to hear from the friends that we have left in a land of pretended freedom, and although separated in body, we are present with you in spirit; and we fondly hope that our prayers often meet before the throne of God for mutual blessings. We will endeavor to observe and practice the advice which you have kindly given us, by loving and serving God and obeying the laws of our Sovereign. We will not cease to implore the Divine Blessing on that Government which has given us liberty not only in name but in reality. The bell has been raised to the place erected for it, and for the first time the silence of our forest was broken on last Sabbath morn, by its joyful peals inviting us to the house of God. We would return to you our sincere thanks for this memorial of your kindness, and we trust that while its cheerful peal invites us to the house of prayer, we will then remember our brethren who are in less favorable circumstances; and our constant prayer will be that the Bible, the gift of God to man, may no longer be withheld from you by the unrighteous acts of professed Christian legislators; that the power of the oppressor may be broken, and that those who have long been held in bondage may be set free.

Through all the years of his travels in behalf of the Buxton Mission church and school, William King was never to forget the mission to Pittsburgh. He was to recall it all the years later in sermon after sermon, in his writings and speeches. Twice he was to welcome to Buxton families who had contributed to the cost of the Liberty Bell, after anti-Negro riots in Pittsburgh were to drive them to the North Star. The Liberty Bell was rung especially for them and for each fugitive family to reach Buxton during the decade of the Fugitive Slave Act. He insisted on it, for the Liberty Bell "proclaimed liberty to the captive."

Thereafter, King set out on his journeys without his hat in hand, knowing only that if his God could provide a gift so precious, He would continue to provide.

At his own request, King was authorized officially by the Synod, in October 1851:

> . . . to visit such localities in the Province and in the adjoining United States from time to time as he may think proper —with the view of explaining the object and management of the Mission, and of urging its claims on the prayers and beneficence of Christianity generally, carefully reporting the contributions he may receive for this object and also his proceedings in behalf of it to the Committee from time to time.

He was to leave for Ohio the following spring, when the ice was out, and annually until 1855 after the crops were in and the teachers assigned from Knox College had met with his approval. He weathered the five years by these "begging" trips in behalf of Christian education.

In February 1855, the settlers of Buxton revolted against King's assumption of full responsibility for financing the church and the schools. He could not keep from them the fact of his own poverty or his sorrow when unable to meet a vital need of the Mission. They themselves called the meeting and took the vote that forced King to accept their help. At the end of the year he was able to report with jubilant pride that not only had the settlers decided to bear the burden of their own congregation, but they also accepted all the responsibilities of being a church affiliated with others. He reported to the Synod:

> It was resolved that the Church should contribute to all the schemes of the Synod, besides taking up a collection every Sabbath; also that the scholars attending the missionary schools should pay a small sum toward the support of the teachers. . . .

It was also mentioned that those who could not pay would be taught free so that all the children might have the benefit of a good school ". . . but we wished to give an oportunity to such as were able and willing to pay for the education of their children to do so."

> The result has been most gratifying, notwithstanding the pressure felt by the settlers during the past year. Of those families who have sent to both schools, more than one-half of them have paid something, one-fifth have paid the whole rate bill charged, and only twenty-two have paid nothing. The Synodical and Sabbath-day collections have been regularly taken up in the Church. The whole amount raised, from both Church and schools, is about seventy pounds.

Thereafter, King was never to struggle alone. Just as he had underestimated his people's potential in earning and learning, he had never anticipated the immediate dynamics of his pattern of Christian education and the human potential it had unleashed. Buxton had many visitors through all the years and many sang the praises of his accomplishments. He prized most of all the tribute given to his people by Rev. Samuel Ringgold Ward of Syracuse after his visit in 1852. Known as the "Black Daniel Webster" due to his oratorical abilities, the Underground Railroad "conductor" at Syracuse, N.Y., who had saved Jerry Happy in that city, among many others, was himself a fugitive from the Fugitive Slave Law. In 1855 in London, England, he wrote:

> But I know of no community (I have travelled all over the United Kingdom) where stricter, better attention is paid to religion than in Buxton. The whole population attend church. Their attention—their deep, serious interest—their intelligent love of the gospel—their decent, dignified demeanor—their freedom from gaudiness in dress, their neatness of person and, best of all, the lives they exhibit in daily transactions—render them a most agreeable congregation, either to worship with or to address. . . .

☆

XI : PROUD CITIZENS

THE MIRACLE AT BUXTON—achievement of economic independence, freedom from ignorance, and realization of Christianity as a faith, not a label—these would have no real meaning without the dynamics of citizenship that they generated. What kind of social beings emerged from slavery after reaching Buxton?

The record is a revelation worthy of study by the United States today. King nurtured and demanded of his people a brand of citizenship that set a pattern and was copied by the surrounding whites. He began early in 1850 when he called one of the numerous "town meetings" for the express purpose of establishing the structure of self-government.

In Upper Canada, he explained, the Negro had every right accorded to white citizens. They had all the protection of the laws of the Province. They could hire lawyers and go to court with the assurance of equal judicial treatment. They had the right of petition to all branches of government for redress of injustices. The laws of the Province, and more important, the enforcement of those laws, was color blind.

But, he continued, disagreements in all families and communities are inevitable. They are disruptive and leave enmities behind, even when settled. Would it not be wiser for the settlers to resolve those disputes themselves in view of the hostile world in which they lived? In fact, wouldn't it be wiser for them to so govern themselves in all secular matters that such internal disputes are minimized?

He proposed that the settlers elect a Court of Arbitration before which disagreements could be brought by all who had previously agreed to abide by the decision rendered. The election was held immediately and a five-member Court of Arbitration, to which King declared himself ineligible, was constituted. During the next two years there were just five cases heard and they were settled without difficulty. In the succeeding years, there were fewer and fewer cases in dispute, but an increasing number of community matters were considered by the Court of Arbitration. It became the governing body of the Settlement. While it was King's responsibility to accept or reject new fugitives, as director of the Elgin Association, it became the Court's obligation to house and feed the fugitives until they could move into their own log cabins.

The Court of Arbitration gradually took over the management of Buxton's industrialization, its emergencies and celebrations, the general welfare of each individual in the community. It was to the Court of Arbitration that the settlers brought their complaints, recommendations, and crises. It became an advisory body to King and, at the same time, the executive branch of government in Buxton in all secular matters.

There is no question that King dominated the successive Courts during the first years. But, as he traveled more in behalf of the schools and church, as he took on more duties as a missionary and as Buxton's representative before the whites, authority gravitated from him to the settlers themselves.

As an example, there never was a policeman or a constable assigned to Buxton, not to this day. Even at the height of its population there was need for police authority only once, and that incident in 1854 is somewhat humorous.

It happened while the Great Western Railroad was being built through the Elgin tract. In one of the road gangs there was an Irishman whose language was foul and he persisted in using profanity before the women and children.

King was in Toronto on Elgin Association business, and so the Court of Arbitration met to consider the problem. Was profanity a crime? None of them knew. The railroad worker could be shut up, of course, by turning him over to some of the young men, but there had never been violence in Buxton. The Court decided to delegate two of its members to journey to Chatham and consult with the Sheriff of Kent County. If profanity was a crime, they would prefer a complaint and return with a constable to arrest the man. This was done; but when they returned with the constable, they found a jurisdictional question. The road gang had moved on to another township and the crime was moot.

In that same year of the founding of the Court of Arbitration, 1850, another problem presented itself—liquor. Drinking was as much a national institution in Canada as elsewhere, despite the emerging temperance societies. Aside from home stills, the village of Chatham alone had three distilleries in 1850 and two breweries. Whisky, corn liquor, peach brandy, beer, and ale could be had cheaply, in "cash or barter" in any of twenty-one taverns. Scattered through Raleigh Township were thirteen taverns. There was no wedding, funeral, raising bee, birth, camp meeting, militia muster, horse race, any social occasion at all—plus some quite un-social—without hearty and unrestrained drinking. At a Temperance Society meeting in Chatham once, the complaint was made that the preacher at one hilarious wedding had to be propped up while somebody else read the service.

But elections, which lasted from three days to a full span between Sabbaths, were perhaps the greatest brawl of all. Whisky was free at any of the tavern headquarters of any of the candidates, and some voters were carried to the polls to make their marks properly.

None of this affected Buxton until an Englishman named Woods bought one of the old settler's farms on the Middle

Road just beyond the Elgin boundaries. He opened a grocery store and with it obtained a whisky license.

Nothing in all the years, not Larwill or mobs or his political battles frightened King more than this threat. "If this traffic was to continue in the settlement, I knew it would do more to demoralize the settlers than I could do by the gospel and education to elevate them." He had seen what liquor could do, in West Port and in East Feliciana, to rich and poor, to master and slave. He had no legal authority to stop the sale of the whisky. No sale could be made on Elgin lands, but Woods was outside them.

He called another meeting and pleaded with the settlers to solve this problem themselves. He asked them to recall their slave days, when a kindly master or overseer became another man, less than a man, when in liquor. He did not preach temperance. He begged for abstinence and urged that "their only safety was not to go where it (whisky) was sold." In other words, he advocated a boycott of Woods' store.

> The settlers were temperate; drunkenness was not their besetting sin. Woods, when he sold out the first cargo of whisky which he brought in, bought no more. The coloured people did not patronize his store, but when he quit selling spirits he got their custom.

No other merchant ever attempted to sell liquors in the vicinity of Buxton, nor is liquor sold there to this day. Yet there has never been a temperance society in Buxton. Instead, a conviction was freely accepted. Though he was to preach hundreds of temperance sermons, King never delivered one in Buxton. It was not necessary.

Another problem became evident early in 1851. The possession of cash was a totally new experience for most of the settlers. Only those who had lived in the northern states or had purchased their own freedom were accustomed to handling cash. King feared the habits he had seen at West Port Mission when a laborer received his day's pay and immediately spent it without thought of the future. His people could not default their land payments or they would again be adrift. They should not buy clothing but rather weave their own. The "store-bought" luxuries should await their total independence. This problem at West Port had been on its way to solution before William had left Edinburgh in 1846. Dr. Chalmers had founded a savings bank limited to members of the congregation only.

And so a passbook to the Buxton Savings Bank became a badge of honor in the settlement. Every Tuesday and Friday evening between six and seven o'clock the bank was open in the church-schoolhouse for deposits or withdrawals. Deposits as small as ten cents were accepted and entered in a Cash Ledger as well as the Pass Book, "such entries to be made in both words and figures." The whole or any part of the depositor's funds could be withdrawn with a week's notice to the Treasurer. There would be a semi-annual audit and report to the depositors. Only those settled on Elgin Association lands were eligible to be depositors or officers in the bank.

Having experienced the vagaries of Louisiana banking, King demanded that the depositors be protected by the Elgin Association and the accounts were guaranteed by that group. A committee of three shareholders in the Elgin Association and three depositors were to oversee the affairs of the Buxton Savings Bank as Trustees. All funds were to be deposited in the Bank of Upper Canada, and at no time was cash on hand to exceed twenty-five dollars.

Unfortunately, the records of the Buxton Savings Bank have not been found. It is certain though that the bank was an important factor in the unusually rapid payment for the Elgin Association lands. By the second crop season, the settlers were selling, for cash, all the grains and vegetables they

THE

Buxton Savings Bank,

IN CONNECTION WITH

THE ELGIN SETTLEMENTS.

OPEN every TUESDAY and FRIDAY Evening
From Six to Seven o'Clock.

Sums of 10 Cents and upwards received.

TITLE PAGE OF A PASSBOOK

By permission of Mr. and Mrs. Charles H. Carnahan, Merlin, Ontario could spare from their own needs. By the second winter, they were receiving cash in payment for their timber sledded to the lakefront. By the third season they were selling their live hogs in Chatham. By the time the railroad bonanza came to Kent County, they had acquired the habit of saving in their own bank accounts against future needs.

It should be emphasized that each of these measures proposed by King called only for *voluntary* participation. That was the essential difference between Buxton and other Negro colonies in Canada. At Buxton, each measure was adopted by the settlers themselves and each settler was individually responsible for adhering to them. There was no compulsion to utilize the Buxton Savings Bank, nothing but disapproval of their fellow settlers preventing them from getting drunk. (While the churches and schools of Chatham were separated for black and white, the tavern keepers never drew the color line at cash.) Nor was attendance at church or school demanded. Existence of the Court of Arbitration did not deny any man the right to go to the civil courts of Kent County, though none did.

A most idealistic kind of morality developed in Buxton as a result of the total development of the individual and the community. The minds and hearts of these former slaves were never completely apart from slavery. Most of them had relatives still in slavery, some of them husbands, wives, and children. They could never forget their own slavery. As a result, when they realized fully the implications of freedom, they were fiercely independent. They had a burning wish to own all of themselves, without obligation to anyone for their freedom. A curious example was the settling of a J. Levy in Buxton during the summer of 1852. He had come to Buxton for land and a permanent home only after he had resolved the moral problem illustrated by the following letter to his former master:

SANDWICH, Jan. 12, 1852

J. A. LEVY, ESQ.

RESPECTED SIR:—

When you purchased me, you promised that whenever I paid you the sum of $380, I should then be manumited and set free. I should have staid with you, and paid the balance due you which is $50; I was truly unwilling to leave you until you were paid in full; but, respected sir, liberty is ever watchful, and I got an impression that you were about to sell me. This induced me to leave you, unwillingly I confess, but security to myself demanded the sacrifice. I am now free and in a free country. Still I wish to pay you the fifty dollars due, and if you will place my freedom papers, properly executed, into the hands of anyone in the city of New York, I will send a person with the balance due you to them, the same to be paid on delivery of the proper papers.

You will please to address me, per mail, Post Office, Sandwich, Canada West.

With respectful regard, believe me, Sir, to be your sincere well-wisher.

J. LEVY

Levy's action could be interpreted as an ultra-fine sense of honesty, but King named it a desire to be a whole man, one who was free through his own effort. In 1851 he lost a most valuable addition to the settlement, a skilled blacksmith, due to this same desire.

Tom Gordon was only twenty-two when he reached Buxton but had been owned by a Governor of Kentucky and was trained as a blacksmith. In 1847 he escaped to Ripley, Ohio. There his skills were sought. He was safe in that famous center of the Underground Railroad because Rev. John Rankin, a Presbyterian minister who could not compromise with Virginia slavery, had a highly organized protection system for the escaped slaves.

But passage of the Fugitive Slave Act made Ripley a target for the slavehunters who reaped large bounties for returning fugitives. Tom Gordon was a valuable slave and his master, armed with the law, sent the slavecatcher after him. A Kentucky deputy sheriff came to the stable where Tom was blacksmith and told him there was something wrong with his horse's hoof. While examining the horse, Tom also examined the man and thought he recognized him. That was enough for him. Everybody knew that the slavecatchers were around. The warning system set up by Rev. Rankin was in full operation. After a narrow escape, Tom was hidden by the Underground Railroad and sent on to Buxton.

He was a valuable addition to the settlement and immediately entered school. About six weeks later King received a letter from Kentucky inquiring if Tom was with him. Three months later a letter came from Rev. Rankin in Ripley reporting that the owner of the horse used by Tom in his escape had been fined one thousand dollars. Under the Fugitive Slave Act such a fine was levied on anyone aiding a fugitive slave, even to the extent of food. By paying the fine, the Underground Railroad conductor was given Tom's manumission papers. According to King, there was no choice for Tom when he saw the letter. "Tom said he would go back and work to pay the fine, which he hoped to do in a few years now that he was free."

In 1852 when in Ripley on one of his "begging" tours, King visited with Tom and reported: "He informed me that he was working at his trade and going to school at night and he hoped to have the whole fine paid in another year."

There was another reason, aside from the high morality of the people of Buxton, that made them emancipated citizens. They were informed citizens. King had seen to that in 1852 when he brought post offices, not only to Buxton but to three other villages nearby—East and West Tilbury and

Maidstone. He organized a petition campaign through all of the four townships. The nearest post office had been Chatham, until he acted in 1852, and he reports: "I found a great drawback to the intellectual improvement of the whole country west of Chatham." Sometimes, the state of the roads prevented travel to Chatham for long periods and there just was no contact with the outside world. King himself carried the petitions to the Postmaster General, had himself named postmaster at Buxton and also named the other three. "As soon as the new offices were established the people began to write letters and to get newspapers, to reach and know something of what was going on in the world around them."

As a result of the newspapers, the settlers of Buxton not only received an "education in citizenship," as King put it, they also received assurances that the laws of Canada applied equally to them and to the whites. They were given such assurances with almost every newspaper they read, for few of them failed to report on the question closest to all of them after the passage of the Fugitive Slave Act. Would Canada extradite them to the United States if the slavecatchers came across the border after them?

In all Canada's history only one slave was returned over the border with a semblance of legality. But even that was reassuring to the fugitives. They could agree with Rev. Samuel R. Ward, then secretary of the new Canadian Anti-Slavery Society who said: "Such is the even handed justice and impartiality of the British Courts. Thank God for this. There is a resort to which we may go when robbed and insulted." They could agree and wonder about the one slave who was returned to slavery, because as much justice as was possible was rendered.

This was the Archy Lanton case. He was arrested on the charge of horse-stealing in the States (his master's horse), held in jail in Windsor until the slavehunters arrived and, without a hearing, was surrendered to them by two magistrates named Wilkinson and Woodbridge. These magistrates were immediately discharged.

When the Sheriff of Montreal, in January 1855, was approached by a sheriff's deputy from Fredericksburg, Maryland, to help return fugitives who "were without the pale of the Fugitive Slave Law and can only be restored by cunning together with skill," the indignant Canadian officer immediately made the offer public. The Maryland man had suggested that the large bounty rewards be split fifty–fifty with "a good assistant in your City who would induce the Negroes to the frontier." The bounty hunters did not dare go "too far into Canada, for fear of being arrested." The Sheriff not only made the offer public in all the Canadian newspapers but assured the slavehunters that their fears of arrest were entirely justified.

The settlers in Buxton read of these and other cases and they were proud in the summer of 1851 when their own Elgin Association treasurer, John T. Fisher of Toronto, answered one of Larwill's "Black Code" proposals in the *Toronto Patriot*. Larwill had cited a Grand Jury in Toronto which included one Negro. He declared that the whites refused to serve with him. Fisher's reply contributed greatly to Larwill's defeat in the elections that fall. Not only was the Negro juror accepted, but "I will only add that I am happy to say to the gentleman [Larwill] that the coloured man in question has been appointed foreman of the jury 3 times in one day—that is, on three different cases."

Very early in the life of the settlement, while King's copies of the *Toronto Globe* were being circulated among the families to be read aloud for those who still could not read, the Negroes of Buxton received an assurance that, no matter what Larwill did, they were safe. The event related to the meeting in Colchester, in October 1849, when the whites adopted Larwill's motion to deny suffrage to the Negro residents of their village.

During the following spring, while Larwill was most active in attempting to prevent incorporation of the Elgin Association, the first proof of equal justice was given Buxton by the Canadian courts. Larwill escaped punishment because he was not a legal officer of the village of Colchester; he merely wrote the resolution. But the chairman of the meeting was charged with sponsoring violation of the suffrage laws, was convicted and fined.

Almost daily, through the Negro newspaper *Voice of the Fugitive* which was published in Sandwich by Henry Bibb, and through George Brown's *Toronto Globe,* the people of Buxton were able to contrast their legal lot with that of their relatives in the United States. In Canada, theirs was not a freedom written in indelible ink and invisible in their daily lives. The Canadian law, faulty as all man-made law must be, was equal both in its blessings and its inequities. Of this they were assured.

In 1863, Samuel Gridley Howe reported to Congress after interviewing nearly one hundred Canadian Negroes that their standard reply to his question why they had not remained in the "free states" was: "The law's the difference."

As a result of the *feeling* as well as the fact of full citizenship, in 1856 the settlers of Buxton demonstrated the first assertion of political "black power" on this continent. There was nothing cataclysmic or menacing about it. They voted, and that is all. Their assertion of democratic suffrage differed in no way from today's elections in the United States when the "Irish vote" in South Boston, the "Italian vote" in Cicero, the "Creole vote" in New Orleans, and the "German vote" in Cincinnati, are the accepted and everyday assertions of "ethnic power" courted by practicing and practical politicians.

The genesis of "black power" in what is now western Ontario in the 1850's is essentially the story of two men—Edwin Larwill and Archibald McKellar. It is a political adventure.

Politics in Canada has always been a brawling expression of growing pains and, in the 1850's, Kent County was the lustiest infant of them all. From election to election only the party labels were identifiable. The political bedfellows were totally unpredictable.

For instance, that inexhaustible source of Kent County lore, Victor Lauriston, repeats a story so delightful it should not be questioned. It was of the time in 1842 when an agricultural society was being formed in Chatham and the meetings took place in Jamie Taylor's new Commercial Hotel. Among other persons present at the extended meetings in the tavern common room was twenty-six-year old Archie McKellar, already a prominent farmer in Raleigh Township, and John Dolsen, who was to be Archie's partner in the lumber business. They engaged in a drinking bout with rollicking Ed Larwill and he outlasted both the partners. That was the first time Larwill beat McKellar. He helped put him to bed.

But the Tory tinsmith already had his eye on politics and supported popular young McKellar for the presidency of the Kent Agricultural Society. Spurred on by Larwill, young Archie put himself in the public eye by sponsoring horse races—from tavern to tavern—agricultural fairs, and plowing matches. He made his first public speech, coached by Larwill, as a result of winning second prize in a plowing match in 1844. McKellar figured prominently in the pages of the *Chatham Journal* during the brief period in 1843–1844 that Edwin Larwill was its emergency editor.

In 1848, Larwill persuaded McKellar to join him under the Tory label in the election of the Kent County Provisional

Council and both were elected. It is likely that McKellar's disillusionment with his political pal took place during that term. One of the duties of the Provisional Council was to build "a court house to accommodate the lawyers and a jail to accommodate the other rascals" as Victor Lauriston quotes it. Larwill was appointed chairman of the building committee, and when the courthouse was completed in 1849, it received the nickname "Old Tin Top." The roof was made of tin and Larwill was the only tinsmith in town. When it had rusted through, it was replaced with more durable slate.

But even more disillusioning was Larwill's seizure on Negro settlement as a political cause and his unprincipled attacks both on William King and on the Negroes in general. McKellar was a man of principle and he came from the same Scots-Irish background as King's. He knew Larwill's political purpose, to run for Parliament in 1851.

Instead of a carefully nurtured Tory ally, Larwill found McKellar a political viper. He not only spoke out against Larwill's attacks on the Elgin Association but utilized all the training in electioneering he had received from the demagogue. Archie McKellar adopted the Reform Party label, for the rest of his life, and called the Kent County convention in Dresden to choose a candidate. As its chairman, he swung the invitation to George Brown of the *Globe* who had purchased land in Bothwell, Kent County, and therefore was eligible to run for Parliament from there.

In spite of one of the perennial splits in the Reform Party, in which three other Liberals were entered in opposition to Brown while Larwill stood alone as the Conservative candidate, the count was Brown—836; Larwill—739. McKellar had beaten him.

This vote, late in 1851, was King's first essay into Canadian politics. One reason, of course, was his personal and profound attachment to McKellar, which was to last all of their lives and through many a battle. Besides, George Brown personally and through the already powerful *Toronto Globe* was giving the new Canadian Anti-Slavery Society tremendous support.

But there was little he could do in this election.

> When I came into the township, very few of the coloured people had votes; the greater part of them were without the property necessary to qualify them for voting, and some who had property were not naturalized so their voice was not heard in the politics of the country. Three years residence in the township was necessary to qualify them for naturalization.

The Buxton voters were able to help a little more in the next Parliamentary elections in 1854. "In the third year of the settlement, I collected all the settlers of twenty-one years of age who had been three years in the Province and had them naturalized."

But Larwill was victorious in this one. At the last minute, Kent County was split as an election district and Lambton County was formed, taking George Brown to that constituency where he won easily. There was no other candidate in Kent County until McKellar himself stepped in to fill the breach. It was too late.

The next election was in 1856 and this time Larwill and McKellar were face to face. This time too, the Negroes of all Kent County had responded to King's naturalization call. "I found in our own settlement some three hundred over twenty-one who had the proper qualifications to vote when naturalized."

All Kent County knew what had happened in that election. King had seen to that. If, to be victorious in Canadian politics, a degree of theatricality was necessary, King went at it like a stage manager. A short time before, he had had the one thousand residents of Chatham as guests, with Archie

McKellar, his candidate, as the principal spokesman for the Reform Party's staunch support of Negro rights. At the election itself, the entire province was made aware of a new political force emerging in Kent County.

That morning, three hundred Negroes gathered in front of St. Andrews and they took the short-cut to Chatham through Duck Pond Swamp. They marched down King Street as a tight and proud unit, no doubt joking about the name of the street and King's prominence in having a street named for him, a standard joke among them.

They entered the Court House as a unit, and in the voting none of them had to make his mark. Each man signed his name on the register. That was not true of approximately fifty percent of the whites who voted. Among the Negro settlers too was represented a larger number of rate (tax) payers than any similar white group in all Kent County. Nor was a single one of them drunk, while all through Chatham there was free whisky and the usual election party. They voted as a unit too, for McKellar beat Larwill by 778 votes, the largest majority for any candidate for public office in Kent County until the turn of the century. Their 300 votes and the other Negro votes gathered up by King through intensive electioneering reversed the result of the 1854 election in which McKellar was defeated by Larwill for the Provincial Parliament.

The election of 1856 was highly significant in Canada West, and not merely for its political result. Many of those who voted were little more than three years away from slavery. They had reached the ultimate in democratic expression only a few years from the lowest human state known to any civilization. A few of them had voted in the 1854 elections but for most of the three hundred, this was their first experience in political equality.

King had come to realize that the ownership of the land his people had bought and the intellectual abilities he was helping to develop would be as permanent as the degree of political participation they would assert. The ballot was the enforcement clause of their democracy. Without it, even the laws of Canada could be changed to those proposed by Larwill. And he knew that the political language of the people was exactly the flamboyant manner in which his men had marched to the voting.

The politicians in Chatham took heed of King's dramatic assertion of political power and began to revise some of their calculations. Larwill himself was politically extinct from that day on. Except for an occasional outburst, his fangs had been drawn and organized prejudice ceased to be a political factor.

King noted: "From that time forward all opposition both to me and the coloured people ceased. They were now clothed with political power and rising fast both in a social and moral point of view."

He meant that the community as a whole was "rising fast" politically, socially and morally. This was literally true. Buxton, by 1856, was the "Negro capital" of Kent County, yet at the same time, a most integrated member of all its communities.

In Raleigh Township itself there were township councilmen, pathmasters, and other officers from Buxton elected as early as 1854. It was supplying teachers, both black and white, to all the common schools of the County by 1857. It was contributing, by then, to the financial structure of the Presbyterian Church of Canada. The tax revenues derived by the County were contributed by more rate payers from Buxton, in proportion to population, than any other community in Kent.

In fact, King and Buxton were responsible for the creation and continuation of agricultural prosperity of the county to the present day. In 1852 George Brown, M.P., on urging by King, attempted to obtain a Parliamentary appropriation

Archibald McKellar

for drainage of the Raleigh Plains but his Reform Party was a minority. In 1854 Larwill was elected and, of course, would not even introduce any such measure. But Archie McKellar, in 1857, was able to justify an appropriation of $400,000 by the Provincial Parliament to carry through the drainage plans resulting from surveys made by the Elgin Association.

These surveys had begun in 1851 because King knew the uses of water. He sought and obtained permission from the Elgin Association's Board of Trustees to drain, not just the Elgin tract, but the entire watershed. The final report to Parliament of Elgin Association finances shows that $4,102.12 was expended for preliminary surveys and drainage before the Government adopted the plan.

Approximately ten thousand useless acres were reclaimed and the flood of farmers into Kent County during the 1860's and 1870's was a direct result of Buxton's existence. Economically, Negroes made excellent neighbors in Kent County for land values increased as each acre was drained, cleared and planted; as the roads were cut through and King's tramway offered Raleigh's own "port" at the lakefront for all the markets of the Great Lakes; as the three Buxton schools and the three churches welcomed students and supplicants; as each new generation of Negroes and whites grew up together.

Raleigh Plains became the most fruitful agricultural section in Canada West. All land increased phenomenally in value, and there was a land boom and speculation, with all its attendant evils. However, all who held onto their land until 1880, when King retired from active management of the settlement, profited much more from increased valuation than those who surrendered to the speculators. In that year, after the land frenzy had subsided, there was a new tax appraisal throughout Kent County. A random sampling of the settlers of Buxton who had paid $2.50 per acre for their land reveals the following official values placed by the tax assessors in 1880:

Green Due, 8th Concession, settled 1851; 150 acres—$10,000.

Daniel Duckett; 10th Concession, 1855; 50 acres—$5,000.

Charles Henderson, 10th Concession, 1852; 100 acres—$7,000.

Ezekiel Cooper, 8th Concession, 1852; 50 acres—$2,000.

William Carter, 11th Concession, 1854; 100 acres—$8,000.

George Hatter, 11th Concession, 1850; 250 acres—$20,000.

All Buxton settlers who remained on their land experienced similar increases in valuations, in accord with the extent of improvements and fertility. The same increase was experienced in all the surrounding townships. Rev. Josiah Henson, for instance, the "Uncle Tom" of Mrs. Stowe's novel, had paid $4 per acre for his land in 1843. It was in Camden Township near Dresden and, in 1880, was valued at $20,000 on 200 acres. The neighboring whites in Raleigh Township also shared in the increase. Daniel White, on the 11th Concession near Charing Cross, paid Crown Land prices averaging $3 an acre for 175 acres. In 1880, it was valued at $10,000.

As the realization grew among Buxton's white neighbors that this group of Negroes in no way resembled the descriptions of all colored people imported from the United States, the color prejudice began to disappear. As the early years passed and the blacks and white shared the same schools, the same churches, the same prosperity, and the same degree of democracy, the very consciousness of "black" and "white" differentiation also began to disappear.

In all the history of Buxton settlement there was just one incident of collision between black and white neighbors, and that had nothing to do with color. In fact, the great-grandson of the white man involved, is still living on the hundred acres settled by John Roe in 1847, and is still surrounded by black and white neighbors. Roe was one of the early settlers who bought the "front hundreds" on the old Talbot Road which later became the Middle Road. This was the southwest half of Lot 11 in Concession 11. A location ticket was given to a fugitive named Robert Harris for the abutting fifty acres of the northwest half of Lot 11, part of the Elgin tract.

Harris, with the help of other settlers, began to clear the land when Roe ordered him off, claiming that he had bought the "back hundred." King reports that he threatened "he would drive him off by force." Harris left without further incident, to await King's return from Toronto.

> I called Mr. Harris and Mr. Roe before me and heard their story. Mr. Roe said that he was informed by a certain person in Chatham that I had not bought the land, and that anyone of the white settlers on the Middle Road who owned the front hundred, might send down to the land office and purchase the back hundred, that he would get the land for him if he would give him the money. He gave the man the money. I asked Roe if he had got the deed; he replied that he had not got it. I then showed him my title to the land and to all the back hundreds on the Middle Road, and I have been informed, I said, that you have been cutting some valuable timber on the back hundred and that some of it is still lying on the lot, cut. Now I do not wish to put you to any trouble for what you have done by driving a man off a lot that was his and not yours. I will give you permission to take the timber off the lot that you have cut there, but I warn you to cut no more, nor to give any trouble to Mr. Harris who has settled on the lot, and to Harris I said to go and settle on the lot and if anyone gives you annoyance, let me know and I will see that you get justice. . . .

The incident was fully reported by King because it resolved a potentially disastrous situation between the Negroes and the whites. Among the dozens of annoyances prompted by Larwill was the rumor that all of the back hundreds along the Middle Road belonged to the early white settlers. When Roe attempted to collect his money from the unidentified man in Chatham, he had to threaten suit in order to get it. The story spread along the Middle Road and removed a possible cause of friction over land titles.

There were no other incidents. Within a few years the whites too came to the Court of Arbitration to resolve any questions, not only between themselves and the Negro settlers, but also with other whites.

Any community acquires definite institutional characteristics, and Buxton was no exception. Outwardly, it resembled all of the other white agricultural communities of Canada West. They were all carved out of the forests under the same conditions. The difference between Buxton and the rest was not only in the color of the inhabitants.

These ex-slaves had, for the first time, an opportunity to obtain what all the Scots and Irish and United Empire Loyalists from the States had had throughout their generations—a family. Today, a family is accepted as a social truism although poverty destroys as many Negro families now as slavery did a century ago. In slavery though, there was not even a hope of creating a family. There were kind masters and they died and the heirs had no regard for slave families. They commanded a higher price individually. There were cruel masters and, if a father or a mother resented a daughter being taken to a master's bed, they were sold and the daughter retained. Children were apprenticed away with a view to their future economic worth. A boy with muscles and the slightest indication of rebellion was sold away because "Can't let a peach get ripe." The preachers in all the churches prayed for families—"For Whites Only."

For the first time in their lives and in their parents' lives, the settlers in Buxton knew that they might see their grandchildren some day, and that miraculous change in their status was the dominating compulsion in each of the cabins.

Why did the Isaac Rileys follow the North Star? Both of them explained that their masters in Perry County, Missouri, were exceptionally kind. Isaac's even taught him to read and "spell," but not to write. Neither of them ever saw a whipping, let alone having had one. And yet, Isaac said in 1854: "After I had a son, it grieved me to see some small boys in the neighborhood, who were hired out to work twenty miles from home. I looked at my boy, and thought if he remained, he would have to leave us in the same way, and grow up in ignorance. It appeared to me cruel to keep him ignorant." And Mrs. Riley added: "We are well contented. If I do not live to see it, perhaps my children will, that this will one day be a great place."

Harry Thomas was thirty-two when he reached Buxton, after his eighth break for the North Star was successful. He had been sold and re-sold, lashed, imprisoned, starved, and all but killed by more than a dozen masters in nearly that many states—a familiar pattern for a rebel. When finally he escaped from Henderson, Kentucky, and reached Buxton, two miracles happened. Thomas found that he was a most useful person to the settlement, which had no doctor. He "practiced as a physician, from the knowledge I had obtained from a colored man in Mississippi, who knew roots and herbs. . . ." Far more important though was his discovery in Buxton that he, a vagabond slave, could be a husband, a father and keep a family.

Even the "free" fugitives from the northern states experienced the same full realization that this was their first opportunity for family security. Henry Johnson had eight children. "I lived twenty-three years in Massillon, Ohio, and was doing well at draying and carting—wanted for nothing—had money when I wanted it, and provisions plenty." Then why leave?

"But my children were thrust out of the schools, as were all the colored children—one *must* know how I felt about it. . . . I left the States for rights, freedom, liberty. I came to Buxton to educate my children. . . . I have bought, paid for, and have a deed of one hundred acres of land."

The family was an overwhelming compulsion directing the settlers of Buxton because it had not been possible at all in slavery, and was restricted in the North. King recognized that and fostered it, though it placed the church second in their motivation. He had seen, in the Felicianas, what the alternatives had been. That is why he was so happy when he married Anna Maria Weems and Alfred Hooper, and then baptized their children.

Anna Maria Weems must have been a remarkable young lady. She was just 12 years old in 1853 when she sat on a rail fence alongside the road bordering her master's Virginia plantation, some thirty miles from Washington. Her mother had been sold to South Carolina rice and her father to Alabama cotton. Anna was not sold because she was well-developed, strong and healthy. She could breed crop after crop of valuable babies in the quarters. If the male slaves did not service her, the master and his sons would.

That Sunday an elderly slave from a neighboring plantation chanced by, bearing the glad news that his brother had been heard from. He was safe in Canada. He had followed the North Star through an Underground stationmaster in Washington. The jubilant man told Anna the name of the stationmaster, a prominent lawyer in the capital.

Three nights later Anna, dressed as a boy, slipped away

from the slave quarters, and in two nights walked to Washington. She hid in the woods days. She put the stationmaster into a panic. His own spies had informed him that the slave-catchers were looking for a twelve-year-old girl, a most valuable breeder. The rewards were high, even before the newspapers in Washington advertised them. He hid her in his attic.

Anna was hunted up and down the East Coast and that made her a challenge to the Underground. They could not send her north in a group heading for the well-organized Philadelphia station because she represented added danger to all others. She was handled individually through Wilmington, Delaware. She reached Philadelphia as the "son" of a free Negro who had the necessary papers. There she was offered a home and adoption in a free Negro family, but stubbornly refused. She had heard about Canada where she would not have to hide from the slavehunters.

By avoiding the usual routes, she reached the Buffalo, New York, Underground station and that is where King met her, having been notified of this special problem. While the whites of the Underground created a diversion at the bridge, King and Anna walked across into Canada.

Anna was adopted by the Joseph Laisons on the 10th Concession and she met the Hooper boy, from the 8th Concession, in the school. She was not watched for the time when she was ripe for breeding, and then bedded. Young Hooper courted her, like any swain would, and they did not "jump over the Massa's broomstick" but were married with all the pomp adopted by the families who venerated the ceremony because they had been deprived of it. They took up land in Dresden and their descendants are all over Canada.

The family was a consuming passion for the Negroes of Buxton, and to them it was the outstanding fruit of freedom.

A huge part of Raleigh Plains became integrated in all

respects—in education and religion, economically, socially, and politically. Inevitably, they intermarried and the world did not end.

Canada has no laws against intermarriage. In the United States, thirty states have such laws to prevent the "Africanization," the "mongrelization," the "adulteration" of the white race. Conditions such as at North Buxton cannot be duplicated in the United States because of one word—*miscegenation.*

The meaning given miscegenation is one of the weapons of white supremacists and their most effective one. Perhaps the best description of its consequences is given by the learned anthropologist Dr. Brewton Berry:

> Nature, it would seem, is quite indifferent to the whole problem of miscegenation. She neither punishes such unions with monstrous and inferior offspring nor blesses them with supermen. Man, however, has shown much more concern in the matter, and he has produced laws and mores for coping with it. Nature replies to the question of miscegenation with a shrug of the shoulders; man speaks out, but he falters and contradicts himself and talks from both sides of his mouth.

King responded to intermarriage, not with a shrug of the shoulders—since he knew full well the hostile attitudes—but still quite naturally. It was at least marriage, and not the riotous fornication in Natchez "Under-the-Hill" or the furtive slave-quarter raids by his students, or the concubinage of New Orleans. He married them and watched their families grow. He did regret the birth of mulattoes, sharing the genetic fancies of his day:

> I think the mulattoes are not so long-lived as the whites or the blacks. And even in New Orleans, Dr. Stone—very good authority there—stated to me that he was of opinion that the mixed race would die out in four generations. I

> have watched the matter since, and it seems to me that, as a class they have not the same stamina as pure blacks or pure whites.

By 1863 King noted that the children in the schools, aside from the whites, were "about half blacks and half mulattoes." In other words, within approximately 14 years of the first settlement the mixing of the races was considerable. But King merely comments on this as a fact. He expresses no opinion. He has a very definite opinion, however, regarding the high plane of sexual morality in the settlement. Also in 1863, he reported:

> Only four illegitimate children have been born in this settlement; and that is a better state of things than you will find in Europe. In England, Scotland, or Ireland, the proportion of bastards is much greater. The people here consider it a disgrace. I observe that they pay a very great respect to chastity and the marriage relation. They all want to be proclaimed in church three times. There will be cases of infidelity among them, but the guilty parties are not respected. The most blame falls on the woman. Very few cases of adultery have come under my observation. I strongly suspect three or four women, from their conduct among men; but I have no proof of their criminality.

Actually, in Raleigh Township there was no problem as a result of intermarriage, both because of the interdependence of the blacks and whites and the high morality practiced by the community. Not even Larwill's continued fulminations on the horrors of "amalgamation" could disrupt the closer unions of the people of both colors because all of his warnings were refuted in their daily lives. The Negroes saw that the laws of Canada protected them from Larwill and the whites themselves saw each of his dire forebodings refuted.

The Negroes of Buxton did not depreciate land. They increased its value. They were not idle or slothful, but rather the reverse, setting a pace of industry hard to equal. They were not dependent on their neighbors or the community, but instead aided their neighbors and contributed equally in taxation. They were not ignorant and debased, unfit for white social intercourse, but actually set patterns of social behavior unknown even in Chatham. In short, the Larwill arguments, exactly those of white supremacists today, were one by one denied by daily experience.

This was true of intermarriage as well. Such marriages were infrequent due to differing backgrounds and nationalities, just as marriages between the Irish immigrants and English immigrants were infrequent due to differing religions and antecedents. The intermarriage assumed its proper proportions, not the genetic horror of the racists. The people of Canada West knew how mulattoes were conceived, just as well as the whites of the Black Belt knew, but they preferred use of the marriage bed rather than the master's bed. The people of Canada West, as has been said, possessed antipathy toward color, but also a respect for reality. They themselves were only a generation away from pioneering when women were in short supply but Indians were still in the area. They had no such term as "squaw man."

Nor was the word "miscegenation" projected into the horror of the white supremacists. As an example, in the Provincial Parliament in 1856, Larwill attempted to attack the Negroes as prone to criminality. He offered a resolution requesting a report from the government on "all negro or colored, male or female, mulatto, samboes, half-breeds or mules, mongrels or conglomerates" being held in public institutions.

Not even the most conservative Tory could stomach that and Larwill was faced with a unanimous resolution demanding retraction of his motion. He retracted.

Like all of the other problems encountered by the Negroes in their relations with the whites, in Kent County intermarriage became a matter of curiosity, of individual choice and universal gossip, differing in no way from other intermarriages, between English and Irish, Italian and Scandinavian, and the like. Possibly the geneticists, sociologists, and anthropologists of the nineteenth century were not widely read in the county.

☆

PART FOUR: ADVENTURES IN ANTI-SLAVERY

XII : THE NORTH STAR

IT REQUIRES a special brand of provocation to change a man of William King's rigid integrity into a lawbreaker, a deceiver, a conspirator. His conscience was quite clear when he was drawn, so inevitably, into the work of the Underground Railroad.

In this, King was as much a part of the attitude of the 1850's as many another preacher, teacher, farmer, Quaker, poet, merchant, dockworker, or housewife. When the Fugitive Slave Act was adopted as a part of the compromise of 1850, the teeth of the children of the (Missouri) Compromise of 1820 were set on edge.

King's reaction to the Fugitive Slave Act differed in no way from that of another man of the same name, Rev. Martin Luther King Jr., who also practiced civil disobedience in response to a "higher law." Between William's Chatham and Martin Luther's Selma was a span of 113 years but the two ministers, one white and one Negro, shared the same spiritual motivation. To William King the "higher law" was: "Thou shalt not deliver unto his master the servant which is escaped from his master unto thee. . . ." (Deuteronomy 23: 15).

Martin Luther King's compulsion was his faith in the American dream and a naive belief in the seeming fairy tales told by the founding fathers while they ate the cherries from the tree George Washington never cut down. In William's day it was civil disobedience to protest an unjust law of the land; in Martin Luther King's it was civil disobedience to protest the *official* civil disobedience practiced in all states in defiance of the laws of the land.

The pawns of both eras, the 1850's and the 1960's, suffered the very same despair. The Negroes of both periods in United States history had doors closed in their faces, by laws in the earlier instance, and by disregard of laws in the second. The dubious freedom of the half-million Negroes of the North in the 1850's became a daily dread, and any hope whatsoever of change in the path of their return to outright slavery was shattered by the Dred Scott decision of 1857. When hope is stolen from an individual, so are restraints. One of the first Negro militants, Dr. Martin R. Delany, declared:

> All the ideas I have of liberty and independence I obtained from reading the history of the Revolutionary Fathers. From them I learned that a man has the right to defend his castle, even to the taking of life. My cottage is my castle; my wife and children are its inmates. If any man enters that castle to look for a fugitive slave—I care not if it be he who signed his name to that ignominous (sic) law; if he comes with the Declaration of Independence flying in the air as a banner, and the Constitution of the United States upon his bosom as a breastplate—if he enters my house to search for a fugitive slave, and I do not strike him down dead, may the grave refuse my body a resting place, and righteous heaven deny my spirit admission.

The mildest among the free Negroes in the abolition movement became formidable pleaders for direct action. One of the most reasonable, Charles Lenox Remond, Secretary of the Massachusetts Anti-Slavery Society, declared: "I am irritable, excitable, quarrelsome—and my prayer to God is, that I may never cease to be irritable, that I may never cease to be quarrelsome, until the last slaves shall be made free in our country, and the colored man's manhood acknowledged."

Among the white abolitionists it was a time for heroes, and in his quiet way, King was one of them. He had a detailed knowledge of the Underground Railroad even before his own first involvement in the spring of 1852. The Buxton Settlement received many of the most famous fugitives, and from each of them King received their stories of escape. It was the temper of the times and his own natural inclinations that involved him with the Underground Railroad. It was no accident that he became an emergency "conductor." He was ready and willing.

Like his initial "begging" trip to Pittsburgh in 1850, the financial results from southern Ohio were meager in 1852, but the repercussions from the trip were enormous. After preaching at the Ripley, Ohio, Underground Railroad headquarters run by fire-eating Rev. John Rankin, King went east along the Ohio River into what was known in the Underground as "Stewart" country. The name was due to the activities of another Presbyterian minister, Rev. William Stewart, his five sons, and a Negro couple in nearby Poke Patch. Their name was Stewart, too.

King rode circuit with Dr. Stewart, speaking to all congregations about the Buxton church and schools, as well as to local antislavery meetings. When they returned, Dr. Stewart organized a big meeting, notifying the Stewart clan to gather and bring their neighbors. It must have been a curious meeting.

In the audience were most of the area's Board of Directors for the Underground Railroad, each with a southern price on his head. There was also a party of Kentucky planters in the audience. They were on a slavehunting mission, flushed with the initial success of the Fugitive Slave Act, then in operation little more than a year. Despite the Stewart boys guarding the church, and their number appears to be legion, the planters knew they were safe in the church. They shared a curious morality. Mayhem was perfectly legitimate on the road and in Underground depots, but only native white Ohioans could use violence in breaking up an antislavery meeting.

When King finished his speech and Dr. Stewart pleaded for contributions, the question period began. One of the planters asked about the effect of the Fugitive Slave Act on Canadian Negroes and it unleashed an answer from the audience. King records: "The meeting expressed forcefully their hatred of the law and their determination to resist its enforcement in every possible way."

His own answer was given eagerly. As a result of the Fugitive Slave Act, the refugees were pouring into Canada. He cited facts and figures, though no names, and did give the names of Kentucky counties from which many of his settlers came. The audience enjoyed the biting satire. By the time he was finished, King made it appear that the South had bestowed a blessing on its slaves by forcing the Fugitive Slave Act through Congress. He was very popular at the antislavery meeting.

When it was over, one of the planters named Edward Thompson questioned King closely regarding the Buxton Settlement and the conditions there. Dr. Stewart took him aside to warn him that the Kentucky gentleman was in search of an escaped woman and her child owned by him. The Underground was fully informed about it. The woman was about to be sold South and separated from her child. She was twenty-six years old and valuable as a breeder.

But King could honestly tell Mr. Thompson that he knew nothing of the fugitive slave. He and Dr. Stewart returned home quite late, and there he met the very woman the planter was after. Her name was Eliza, and her story was repeated many times over along the Ohio River as well as in *Uncle Tom's Cabin*. Her child, a daughter, was five years old. "They were both good looking and would no doubt have brought a good price in a southern slave mart for house servants."

The next day it was proposed that King, who was heading due north for home from the port of Sandusky, Ohio, should conduct Eliza and her child. King readily agreed but Dr. Stewart, whose word was final, negated the plan. He proposed that one of the most reliable of the conductors, young Jacob Stewart, organize the "traffic" for Eliza and her child, and asked King to act as a decoy. He was a marked man, Dr. Stewart pointed out, and the professional slave-hunters now assigned to Eliza would be certain to follow him. With explicit instructions, King started north and "acted suspicious." He made certain that he contacted, openly and loudly, the notorious Underground conductors in each settlement. He stopped at crossroads, as though awaiting companions.

He must have been very convincingly guilty. When he reached Sandusky and made his last contact, freeing him to book passage on a steamer for Amherstburg, "two slave hunters came on board to see if I had any coloured person with me. . . ."

Their visit was more than useless. At the Sandusky depot, King had received a message from Dr. Stewart. Jacob had scored again! While King was making his slow, diversionary way north, Eliza and her child had been speedily transported by another route and were safe in Canada.

The Ohio exploit was to have many repercussions as King's name became known in Philadelphia and Boston in a new light. He was not only the founder and guardian of the new Buxton Settlement to which the Abolitionists sent the fugitives, but a willing Underground worker. That is why, in the fall of 1852, they honored his strange request to reverse the wheels of the Underground Railroad.

The first and perhaps the most famous case in Abolition history after passage of the Fugitive Slave Act was the rescue of Shadrach from the Court House in Boston—an audacious defiance of the law, described by the zealous Theodore Parker as "the most noble deed done in Boston since the destruction of the tea in 1773. I thank God for it."

The Shadrach rescue roused the entire South. The Yankees were openly violating the law of the land. If nothing was done about it, then the uneasy Compromise of 1850 which temporarily patched the Union together would prove worthless. Once more there were mutterings of secession, and the pressure in Washington caused President Fillmore to issue the statement written by his Secretary of State, Daniel Webster, on February 18, 1851. It amounted to orders to all citizens "who shall be found within the vicinity of this outrage" to turn informer and help recapture Shadrach, or else be prosecuted for violation of the Fugitive Slave Act. The North was aroused.

Two weeks later, Shadrach, whose real name was Frederick Wilkins, was safe in Buxton, forwarded there through Rev. Samuel J. Ward's Underground station in Buffalo. Once in Buxton, Shadrach took up land in the 11th Concession, fifty acres of Lot No. 6, for which he had paid £31 5*s.* in full by September 3, 1857.

When he had cleared his land and had a comfortable cabin, Shadrach asked Rev. King's help in locating his wife and child. When he had escaped from Boston, his owner had sold them South. The family was found after a year through William Still's omnipotent Underground information center in Philadelphia. The woman and the child were still together and on a plantation in Douglas County, near Atlanta, Georgia.

The Underground Railroad took Shadrach a thousand miles south to the Georgia plantation, where he stole his family, and then the thousand miles back with them. The journey took a little over two months. All that is known about the route is that King sent Shadrach to the Stewart boys in southern Ohio, and that they escorted the family back to Lake Erie. Meanwhile, in Boston, the trials of suspects in the Shadrach rescue were going on with Wendell Phillips and Richard Henry Dana challenging the constitutionality of the Fugitive Slave Act while defending the violators.

King was on another fund-raising trip early in 1853 when he assumed his role as a "conductor" on the Underground Railroad. It was entirely unexpected. He was in Boston and journeyed to nearby Andover, Mass., to visit with Harriet Beecher Stowe, by then internationally famous as a result of *Uncle Tom's Cabin.* King told Mrs. Stowe of his life, about Mary and the Buxton Settlement, and she later wrote *Dred, a Tale of the Dismal Swamp,* published in 1856. Her Nina Gordon was patterned after Mary Phares and the lofty-minded Edward Clayton was William King, in appearance, thoughts, and ideals. Mrs. Stowe had a footnote in the first edition of *Dred:* "These statements are all true of the Elgin Settlement, founded by Mr. King, a gentleman who removed and settled his slaves in the south of Canada." And King named his home in Buxton "Clayton House."

He returned to Boston after a "pleasant" stay with Mrs. Stowe and found the Abolitionist capital in another uproar over a fugitive slave case. It was the Dick Sims case.

Dick Sims has been confused with the Thomas Sims case in 1851 when the Boston Abolitionists failed to rescue him and he was sent back to slavery. Perhaps the confusion resulted from similar circumstances as well as names. Both slaves escaped from Savannah to Boston aboard lumber ships. However, Dick stowed away while Tom bribed a sailor to hide him in the hold, and was betrayed. Dick was found and the skipper of the ship telegraphed his owner, hoping for the reward.

The Abolitionist Vigilance Committee, headed by Dr. Samuel Gridley Howe at that time, heard about the wire from a sympathetic telegraph operator. The substance of it was requesting extradition papers so that Dick could be turned over to the U.S. Commissioners.

Wendell Phillips and William Lloyd Garrison both applied for a writ of habeas corpus and then boarded the ship to see that it was served. They took Dick off with them and he was seen next in court. King wrote:

> I was in the court and heard the [habeas corpus] trial. When Dick was set free, Wendell Phillips who acted as his lawyer came to me and asked me when I was going to Canada. I told him in two days. He said he intended to send Dick with me as he expected the extradition papers every day and he would have to defend the case in court, but he wished Dick to be in a place of safety before the trial began.

The extradition papers arrived the next day and the Sheriff started searching for Dick. However, the Vigilance Committee was skilled by then and Dick was safely out of the city. King's instructions were simply to pursue the course he had planned and he had no further contact with Phillips, just in case he would be watched. The young lawyer was always followed when there was a fugitive sought.

On the following morning, King boarded his train bound for Syracuse, Rochester, and the bridge crossing the Welland Canal to St. Catharines in Canada. Ten miles out of Boston, the train made an unscheduled stop and a strange white man, followed by young Dick, came aboard. They came through the cars and stopped at King's seat. The white man said nothing except to present Dick and a ticket for his passage, then he disappeared. Later King was to learn that in the courtroom, Phillips had pointed him out to this "conductor."

Dick was quick to learn his role. King told him he was to take charge of his "portmanteau" and be a body servant. If anyone on the train were to ask, Dick had been his servant for years.

Everything went smoothly during the long journey across New York State but King was uneasy. He knew that he was playing another man's game, that the Sheriff was more skilled in hunting fugitives than he was in evading officers.

It was his eternal caution that prompted King to switch trains somewhere beyond Rochester. His own train stopped at a siding with an overheated funnel. While waiting there for it to cool, so that the train could crawl on toward the bridge, another train pulled up alongside. The conductor informed King the train was from Batavia, New York, and was heading for Buffalo.

"I changed my mind and concluded to go to Buffalo."

Actually, King had reasoned it out. There were few possible escape routes for Dick, since Canada was his only refuge. The Boston waterfront would be covered by the Sheriff and that left only the few trains headed west out of Boston. He figured that the Boston train would be searched.

But in Buffalo, they would not search a train from Batavia and they did leave it undisturbed. He was right so far. What about the Buffalo bridge to Fort Erie? That would be guarded.

He and Dick went to a hotel, the young servant carrying the "portmanteau" and waiting while his master had tea. Over the tea King pondered and then enquired. There was a train leaving Buffalo for Niagara Falls at 9:00 P.M., and they were on it.

> On arriving at the Falls, Dick took my portmanteau and we both walked over the suspension bridge. When half-way across, I showed him the line to the Canada side. I told him he was now free and all the power in the United States could not take him back over that line which separated between freedom and slavery. The poor fellow was frantic with joy to think that he was now free from his master.

King's fears had been entirely justified. His first train had been searched and so had the other Boston trains arriving at Buffalo. At both bridges, crossing to Fort Erie and to St. Catharines, slavecatchers armed with the necessary seizure documents had been waiting. The Sheriff had used the telegraph. The suspension bridge at Niagara Falls had not been guarded at all.

There are many fantastic legends about William King's battles of wits with slaveowners, but the best-documented and perhaps the cleverest was the Raglan plot. It became known and laughed about throughout Canada, because the government and the courts were involved. It was a plot worthy of a professional "con" man.

The Buxton School attracted students from all over Canada and the United States and one of the Negro pupils later became a U.S. Congressman from Alabama and fierce spokesman for the first Civil Rights Bill of 1875. He was James T. Rapier, son of a wealthy mulatto free Negro whose large plantation was only a few miles from Florence, Alabama, where King had once been offered a school. The elder James Rapier recognized the early brilliance of his boy and was determined that he would receive an education and live in a free land. In such cases, light-colored sons were usually sent to Europe by either their white or mulatto fathers. But

Rapier knew Canada, having made investments in Toronto as a safeguard against further tightening of the Alabama Black Laws. It was entirely possible that some day he would have to take his family and all his own slaves there. He sent the boy to Toronto and then to Buxton.

Rapier visited his son and during one visit King told him that the Canadian authorities were advertising for the heirs of one Sam Raglan who had escaped from Alabama some twelve years before, had worked in Toronto as a skilled carpenter and accumulated four acres of valuable downtown land, a home, and some cash. He had never married and there was no will. The estate was valued at about five thousand dollars.

Rapier had a neighbor near Florence by that name, a white man with lots of slaves. He promised to investigate when he returned south. Soon Rapier wrote that it was his neighbor Raglan from whom Sam had escaped, and that Raglan believed he had the right of inheritance since he had owned Sam. But he also owned a younger brother named Milton, the only surviving relative. King visited a lawyer in Toronto and determined that Milton, not Raglan, was the heir since there was no slavery condition recognized in Canada. And so the plot was made.

With Raglan and Milton, Rapier came north. He was a good neighbor and would see to it that Raglan had his rights. Raglan remained in Buffalo while Rapier took Milton to Toronto, satisfied the government as to Milton's identity and relationship to Sam. That had been made easy by Raglan, who provided all the documents necessary. The estate was promptly transferred to Milton's name. Now the classic touch was added.

Rapier returned to Buffalo *with Milton.* His good offices were no longer needed and he wished to return home. He had deposited Milton back on U.S. soil, with title to all that property, and into the hands of his master. His work was done. All that remained was for Milton to transfer the property to Raglan. Rapier departed.

The transfer of title could only be made in Toronto and Raglan innocently set out with Milton. Why not? Milton had returned, hadn't he? At the lawyer's office they were welcomed by King; Milton said a polite goodbye to his former master, and made ready for the journey to Buxton with King, who refused to allow him to sign any transfer papers.

"The master now saw the trap into which he had fallen. He returned to Alabama a wiser man, and Milton came to Buxton and purchased one hundred acres, married and lived comfortably on it until he died."

Why didn't Milton just go free during his first visit to Toronto with Rapier? Because Rapier then could be charged with slavestealing and, being a Negro in Alabama, no doubt would lose his own freedom and property. However, Raglan could never bring the matter to court. Hadn't Rapier left Milton with him in Buffalo, New York, on U.S. soil? Hadn't Raglan himself, out of his own cupidity, taken his slave across the line to freedom?

Meanwhile, Milton Raglan's rapid rise from slavery to wealth was perhaps the fastest in slave history.

One of King's most able adult students in the night school was also the cause of the greatest agitation in the South until Harper's Ferry. He was William Parker, to the North a hero, but to the South the villain of the Christiana, Pennsylvania, riot of September 10, 1851.

A Maryland planter, Edward Gorsuch, was killed and his son Dickinson was seriously wounded in an all-night siege of William Parker's home near Christiana. With a U.S. marshal notorious for his slavecatching abilities, Henry H. Kline, and fifty whites pressed into duty under authority given him by the Fugitive Slave Act, the Gorsuch party had sought the capture of four escaped slaves in the Parker home.

But the Negroes in the countryside had been warned in advance of the raid by the Philadelphia Underground, and some thirty of them holed up with Parker. He was their acknowledged leader in a defense organization created as a result of the numerous slavecatching raids in southern Pennsylvania. Some of them were free, and some were fugitives like Parker, who had escaped from Anne Arundel County, Maryland, three years before.

After the battle, when Gorsuch lay dead and only two of Parker's men were slightly wounded, the Negroes went to the attack and scattered the whites. The four fugitives were hurried off, and the Negroes scattered to their homes when word came that Kline had sent out a call for mobilization of all the whites in the area. Parker left his family with his mother-in-law, and with the ringleaders of the resistance started north for Rochester, New York, and Frederick Douglass' home.

It was the only fugitive case in which the charge of treason was made, against two innocent white Quakers, Chester Hanway and Elijah Lewis, because their beliefs forced them to refuse to aid the U.S. Marshal in performance of his duties. They, with thirty-three Negroes from the Christiana area, were rounded up by a special detail of forty-five Marines from the Philadelphia Navy Yard on President Fillmore's personal orders. None were ever convicted but all spent months in prison.

The Parker fugitives were welcomed by Douglass. In his autobiography he declares: "Had they been pursued then and there, my home would have been stained with blood. . . . I could not look upon them as murderers. To me, they were heroic defenders of the just rights of man against manstealers and murderers."

However, they reached Rev. Hiram Wilson, the Underground Railroad agent in St. Catharines, and were safe. He gathered up a quick collection and gave them ten dollars to send them further from the border. The news had come that Governor Johnston of Pennsylvania had made a demand on the Governor-General of Canada for their extradition under the terms of the Webster-Ashburton treaty. Instead of disappearing, Parker and Abraham Johnson, his neighbor in Christiana and soon to be his neighbor in Buxton, went directly to Toronto. They arrived in the evening of September 23, and William Parker took exactly the right action in dealing with the Governor-General, Lord Elgin. He went to his offices in the Government House and asked for him. The Governor-General saw him at once, shook his hand and asked him to sit down. "His genial, sympathetic manner it was that convinced me he meant well." Lord Elgin confirmed the demand from Governor Johnston and questioned Parker as to whether he was a fugitive from slavery or from justice. Then he asked the Negro to return at three o'clock that afternoon. When he did, Parker found a message from Lord Elgin: "You are as free a man as I am."

With Abraham Johnson, he worked in Kingston, awaiting his family. The Underground Railroad had promised to deliver them. In March 1852, Parker heard about Buxton Settlement and determined to go there. With his family, Abraham Johnson, and a letter of introduction to Henry Bibb in Sandwich, they took the ship to Windsor and arrived in Buxton in April. Henry Bibb released all his florid prose in a lengthy welcome to William Parker in *The Voice of the Fugitive.*

> This man in our estimation deserves the admiration of a Hannibal, a Touissaint L'Ouverture or a George Washington. A nobler defense was never made in behalf of human liberty upon the plains of Lexington, Concord or Bunker Hill than

was put forth by William Parker at Christiana. . . . We bid him with his family and all others from that hypocritical republic welcome to this our glorious land of adoption where no slave hunter dare to step his feet in search of a slave.

Far from being the ravening beast of the Southern press, William Parker was a most solid citizen. He was soon elected to the Court of Arbitration, and then to the honor of representing Buxton on the Raleigh Township Council.

But the story about the Christiana riot probably would have been lost if not for William King's adult classes in which Parker enrolled. He was thirty years old when he reached Buxton and could neither read nor write.

Within a few years, Frederick Douglass' Kent County correspondent for the *North Star* was William Parker, and he was writing many of the communications for the Court of Arbitration. Before the Civil War he wrote an account of his adventures as a slave, the Christiana battle and the escape, and this was published by *The Atlantic Monthly* of Boston in two parts in 1866.

The editor who procured the manuscript was James R. Gilmore, President Lincoln's unofficial emissary in July 1864 to Jefferson Davis in Richmond, Virginia, in a vain search for a basis for peace. Gilmore, writing as Edmund Kirke, provided a preface to "The Freedman's Story," which was a tribute to Parker and his teachers:

> The manuscript of the following pages has been handed to me with the request that I would revise it for publication, or weave into its facts a story which should show the fitness of the Southern black for the exercise of the right of suffrage. . . . It is written in a fair, legible hand; its words are correctly spelled; its facts are clearly stated, and—in most instances—its sentences are properly constructed. Therefore, it needs no revision. On reading it over carefully, I also discover that it is in itself a stronger argument for the manhood

of the negro that any which could be adduced by one not himself a freedman; for it is the argument of facts, and facts are the most powerful logic. Therefore, if I were to imbed these facts in the mud of fiction, I would simply oblige the reader to dredge for the oyster, which in this narrative he has without the trouble of dredging, fresh and juicy as it came from the hand of nature,—or rather, from the hand of one of Nature's noblemen,—and who, until he was thirty years of age, had never put two letters together. . . . This man is a doer, not a writer; though he gives us—particularly in the second part—touches of Nature and little bits of description, which are perfectly inimitable. . . .

King was justifiably proud of his pupil and historians may be grateful for William Parker's account of the events. The trial records give nothing of the spirit of the times, shared by many Negroes like William Parker. The choice of freedom or death was made by many of them, including those fugitives conducted along the Underground Railroad by King. But, without knowing it, William Parker reveals in a single paragraph of the article a total lack of awareness of his own contribution:

When I first settled in Buxton, the white settlers in the vicinity were opposed to colored people. Their prejudices were very strong; but the spread of intelligence and religion in the community has wrought a great change in them. Prejudice is fast being uprooted; indeed, they do not appear like the same people that they were. In a short time I hope that the foul spirit will depart entirely.

It did, and settlers like William Parker were responsible for the change. He was one of the most respected members of the Raleigh Township Council and was re-elected year after year by both white and black voters.

The Buxton Settlement was most definitely right in time

and place. It served not only the escaped slave but the free Negro of the North whose freedom became more and more questionable as the slavehunters more and more disregarded manumission papers and local authorities. There was one free Negro from Lorain, Ohio, who did not arrive until 1855 after all of his illusions had been blasted. This was William Howard Day, a delegate to the Ohio Negro Convention in Cleveland in 1851, who declared at that meeting:

> Coming up as I do, in the midst of three millions of men in chains, and five hundred thousand only half free, I consider every instrument precious which guarantees to me liberty. I consider the Constitution the foundation of American liberties, and wrapping myself in the flag of the nation, I would plant myself upon that Constitution, and using the weapons they have given me, I would appeal to the American people for the rights thus guaranteed.

William Day's appeal was not heard and he escaped to Buxton. His experiences were to prove invaluable to the settlement when he went abroad with King to tell Irish, Scots, and English audiences that no Negro could ever be free so long as one slave lived in the United States.

☆

XIII : YEAR OF THE PILGRIMAGE

THE YEAR 1856 was a crucial one for William King. By all external evidence, he should have been the happiest of men, filled with pride in himself and the settlers, basking in the high praise from all quarters. Nowhere in the public prints, in his letters, speeches, or sermons, however, is there a hint of the loneliness and sense of failure that he confessed in the privacy of his study.

By then the settlement was such a success that it was the example adopted by the very first convention of the Canadian Anti-Slavery Society. Henry Bibb, in founding the Refugee's Home Society, copied almost exactly the pattern set in Buxton for his Essex County Colony. The only differences were that the lots were sold to the fugitives in twenty-five-acre pieces instead of fifty acres and the terms of settlement before the land could be transferred was fifteen years rather than ten, as under the Elgin Association agreements.

By then Buxton had 147 students in the day schools and his hopes for the grand design of attack on the African slave trade at its source were high. He wrote:

> The school connected with the mission is progressing, and we trust the voice of its pupils will one day be heard to advantage from one end of the Province to the other. Nay, the time we hope may not be too far distant when they will vie with each other, and more highly favored lands, in carrying the lamp of eternal truth and planting the cross on the remotest shores of Africa.

In that same year, 1856, he received the highest honor yet from his own church. The Synod ordered that his annual report be printed in the Church's permanent record and "that the Synod expresses its gratitude to God for the success which has crowned the Buxton Mission."

That high praise had been given him by the Synod consistently since his very first report on his search for a settlement site in 1849. The Synod approved the report at that time and adopted a resolution: "The Synod agreed to tender their thanks to Mr. King for his diligence and zeal in prosecuting his mission to the coloured population of the province."

By 1856 too, the names William King and Buxton Settlement were known throughout the United States and the British Isles, particularly in Edinburgh. Frederick Douglass had seen to that. When he learned about the Buxton Settlement, Douglass came to Buxton and in St. Andrews Church before King's own people made a public apology for the indictment he had made in 1845. He printed the public apology in his newspaper, *North Star,* and sent copies to Scotland. This not only exonerated King but also was in keeping with Douglass' stature.

In 1856, Horace Greeley sent one of his *Tribune* correspondents to Buxton from New York, and the lengthy report in praise of the settlers and their accomplishments ended with, "We left Buxton with the belief that we had seen one of those rare men who, by a single-minded devotion to one worthy object, not only accomplished great ends but ennoble our common humanity."

By then there was scarcely a holiday in Chatham without King as one of the speakers. There was not one Presbyterian Church in all Canada West from Windsor to London in which King had not preached during any given year. There were no elections, provincial, county, or township, without Reform Party candidates seeking King's endorsement. The Conservatives did not approach him because they knew his loyalties were only with the political party or officeholder showing no taint of anti-Negro prejudice.

All of the contemporary descriptions of William King during those crowded years of the 1850's agree. He was a calm man, given to fire only in the pulpit or in debate. He was a patient man, with time to explore the least of his people's problems. He was absolutely implacable in the constant application of his energies and capacities toward the one goal. He possessed warmth, for the children of the settlement loved him and their parents confided in him. He commanded respect wherever he went, among the lowly and the mighty.

But this outwardly serene man revealed his inner turmoil in fragments of diaries. At the very time he was working on the annual report to the Synod which was placed in the permanent record of the Church, King also wrote: "Began to make preparations for the Sabbath. Found myself unable to compose. Mind distracted with care, none to sympathize or support. Oh, God, be there any dwelling place to which I may ever resort?" Time after time, in his study, he noted his loneliness in the fragmentary diaries, but it was hidden from all others.

William King was surrounded by love during that year 1856. True, he had only one confidant, but Robin Phares was more of a beloved dependent than a companion. Robin was King's outstanding "failure" among his own slaves. He had allowed his "Moses in the Wilderness" (Robin's own name for King) to teach him to write just a little but to read all of the Bible. He then refused to pay for more than twenty-five acres, and was adamant in grubbing out only enough to feed himself. He would not raise a money crop. As a result, King was forced to meet his payments on the land, and Robin did not work off the indebtedness until October 1, 1870, a full twenty years after raising his cabin.

Robin was not lazy. He was the first to volunteer for community work projects or cabin raisings. He was not shiftless, because his cabin and patch of garden were meticulously in order at all times. He was always merry, and was the only man in the settlement who dared laugh at King's sternest lectures on the virtues of economic independence. He never cared for money but was supremely happy with his garden, his pipe, his fireplace, and his Bible. There was nothing King could do with him.

Yet he visited Robin's cabin nearby on the 10th Concession frequently, whenever he could sit for a few minutes and listen to the man tell about his childhood with Mary Phares. Robin was two years older than Mary and had played with her and Eliza at the East Feliciana plantation. He and Eliza were of an age, and for a time it was hoped that Robin would marry her and "make something of himself" but she married a fugitive from Kentucky.

King sat with Robin only to listen to his tales of the Phares plantation and then retreat to his study. After one such visit, he scrawled in his April 1855 entries: "Found some comfort drawing near to God, but oh, the distracted thought and wandering imagination. I can hardly derive any comfort from spiritual exercises but Oh, God, I put my trust in Thee. Strengthen and support me by Thy Grace. Make me such as Thou wouldst have me be." Again and again he prayed on paper, begging some relief from the suffering of loneliness.

But in 1856 William King was not alone. He had been married for three years to Jemima Nicolina Baxter, the volunteer with whom he had worked in the West Port Mission during 1845 and 1846. Yet he had "none to sympathize or support."

The tragedy of William King's second marriage was never revealed by anything he ever said or wrote. Indeed, his scribbled autobiography contains only one mention of "My wife . . ." in connection with an incident in 1866. Not even her death is noted. Her name may be found in only two other places, in a brief history of the King family written by William for a reunion in 1893, and on her gravestone beside his:

Hic Jacet
Jemima Nicolina
the beloved wife of
Rev$^{d.}$ William King
daughter of the late
Rev$^{d.}$ David Baxter
Presbyterian minister of Lillies-Leaf,
Roxborough Shire, Scotland
Died November 6th 1887
Aged 74 years

The hour is now coming, in the which
All that are in their graves shall
Hear His voice and shall come forth.
Jn V: 28

Actually, more is known of her father than of Jemima after her arrival in Canada. Rev. David Baxter had been one of the original Disruption ministers in 1843 and the congregation he held in Lillies-Leaf was formed by him. Jemima spent some time in Liverpool before Canada and that is all that is known of her.

There was a deliberate attempt by King to suppress mention or memory of his second wife, and the reason can be found in the legends of the settlement. Within a few years of the marriage, Jemima showed sufficient evidence of mental derangement that all of King's thirty years of domestic life must have been filled with frustration. It would have been still more bitter if one of the stories about Jemima is true, that she began to be "queer" after the stillbirth of a baby some time in 1855. That would have been sufficient to cause a man who had already lost two children and a wife to cry out to his God. But in sifting the tales told by three elderly Buxton residents of the second generation and those generally accepted in the settlement, the cause of the second Mrs. King's mental illness is not confirmed. Its evidences, however, are clear.

For three months Harriet Rhue Hatchett received piano lessons from Jemima King in the King house which was named the "Clayton House" in memory of the Harriet Beecher Stowe character based on William King. But her lessons terminated suddenly when Mrs. King had one of her "spells." These were a total withdrawal from the world and her immediate surroundings. Mollie and her children, who took care of the Clayton House, brought her food and William moved a bed into his study shortly after their marriage. The piano was placed in the bedroom and, for hours on end, Jemima would play. Apparently, during her schizophrenic "spells," she only embroidered and played the piano. Finally, she ceased doing either and merely sat at the window of the bedroom throughout the day. That was where she was found whenever her food was brought to her.

During the first few years, her only contact with the settlers was in playing the piano at services in St. Andrews Church next door. But even that stopped after her strange actions were repeated. When she ventured outdoors, Jemima took to wearing a black shawl and hid her head in it when passing others. Many times, she dressed up two of Mollie's children, a girl and a boy, as attendants, and wearing a bridal veil, paraded with them down the Middle Road.

Only once in all the years was Jemima King to perform any duties customary to the wife of a minister and that was during an emergency. In 1866, one of the young men who had returned from the Union army after the Civil War brought with him a case of smallpox and King, who had never had the disease, fought its spread through the settlement with the assistance of only one woman, the only one among the settlers who had recovered from it and was therefore immune. For ten days he took care of the children while the woman cared for the young soldier, Harry Thomas, and a six-month-old baby. The entire family contracted the disease and a fourteen-year-old boy died. In the midst of this, the word came that Dick Sims was down with what appeared to be smallpox.

King hurried to the home of the young man he had brought from Boston more than fifteen years before, now owner of his own land and father of three children. There he found not only that Dick was down with smallpox, but that Mrs. Sims had given birth to a fourth child, alone. The mother and the baby needed care, but there was smallpox in the house. William isolated them. "No one could be found to attend her. My wife went and attended her for a few days until she got better."

There is no question that Jemima, daughter and wife of a minister, would have been by his side during that crisis had she been responsible.

> There were eighteen cases in all, and I only lost one patient, the boy of the Thomas'. I was thankful that God in His Providence stopped the disease; it spread no further and no white person had it. The house was cleaned and fumigated and all the settlement were vaccinated and the disease disappeared entirely.

By 1873, Jemima had retreated to her bedroom and seldom emerged until her death fourteen years later. In the prior years, King had taken her to England, to visit in Liverpool with her remaining relatives, in hopes of some recovery. There was none.

Whatever the causes or extent of Jemima's illness, it was a burden King was to bear for over three decades without a word of complaint except in his diaries. The full realization that his second marriage, too, was to be a tragic one struck him at the end of 1855. Immediately after Christmas he left Buxton—alone—on a journey that expressed his emotional crisis. He went to Louisiana, to the Felicianas, to New Orleans. He stopped at Natchez. In other words, William King re-lived his earlier years.

Ostensibly, the reason for the trip was that finally his father-in-law's home plantation was to be sold and the estate liquidated. The will had declared that Frances Emmaline and the daughter Clara were to have possession for ten years, and those had passed. But there was no need for King to be there. He had waived all claim to the residue of the estate in order to get his slaves in 1848.

William lingered on in East Feliciana. He reached Bayou Sara on January 7, and the sale was held on the 10th.

Of the sale itself King says with restraint, that he "was affected by seeing Negroes for sale, and seeing the furniture which formerly belonged to myself being sold." It was the furniture he and Mary had used.

Most of the three weeks he was in East Feliciana were spent with his brother James and with old John McKaeven, father of his original students on Colonel Brian's plantation. At Dr. Phares' he saw Frances Emmaline and her daughter, but he was safely married now.

He wandered around Jackson, too, trying to find some of his old friends and students, but he "found few of them living; the yellow fever and cholera had done their work." And on Sunday, January 13, he was touched by an invitation to preach at the Presbyterian Church in Jackson, Dr. Buller's church, which he had attended. "It was a new house, a new preacher, and a new congregation."

He preached in Plains too and found that death had struck down his old friends there. Throughout the three weeks King was in search of other friends, and perhaps other days. He found Henrietta in Bayou Sara and reminisced about the old days when she was his servant at the College. "She was pleased with meeting me." And he journeyed to Dr.

Phares' plantation twice, not to see the family as much as to spend the time with his father-in-law's former slaves, now owned by Dr. Phares. He was able to report to them the life their friends and relatives among his slaves were living in Canada, and particularly to Solomon's father what his son was like in school.

All this visiting was done in miserable weather, with sleet and raw rain almost constant. The roads were difficult, and yet he used them constantly in search of friends. He also spent four days in New Orleans before boarding the steamer *Crystal Palace* for the long voyage north. There he saw George Race, one of his free students at Mathews Academy. He found him living "in a princely mansion" on St. Charles Street, and "married to a lovely and amiable wife, with all that this world can give."

Held up by the weather and the vagaries of the Illinois Central Railroad of that day, King was ten days in returning home; in fact he made it just in time to hold Thursday night prayer services.

That Sunday, he chose as his text Hebrews 12: 1 and 3, and closed the door on Mary and the Louisiana years. He was never to return.

> 1 Wherefore, seeing we also are compassed about with too great a cloud of witnesses, let us lay aside every weight, and the sin which doth so easily beset us, and let us run with patience the race that is set before us. . . .
>
> 3 For consider him that endureth such contradiction of sinners against himself, least ye be wearied and faint in your minds.

The journey south in 1856 was an emotional turning point in William King's life. It was then that he buried Mary.

As though ashamed of his emotional lapse, King returned to his mission to "run with patience the race" before him. Into the next turbulent five years he crowded even more accomplishments than during the first five years of the settlement. During the balance of 1856 his diaries show only one complaint. He found little time for his own spiritual life and often prayed: "Oh, God, deliver me from the secularities of this station." With the schools, the mission work, the Elgin Association business, meeting and preaching all over Canada West, his own church, and continued involvement in the industrial life of the settlement, it is a wonder he found any moments at all for himself.

His study was no refuge. Only late at night could he work without interruption, for his days were filled, during the infrequent intervals at home, by a stream of visitors or obligations of his missionary work. No matter what the crisis, King continued his visits to the families, both for the purpose of prayer and to see if the families were progressing as he wished.

In March, 1856, for instance, he visited in the 7th, 8th, and 9th concessions and found "two very bad with consumption, and one of them ignorant of Christ." A few days later, he had "some pleasant intercourse with the Shadds of the 7th Concession and learned that they had been refused seats in a church some distance away. King knew the minister and notes scornfully ". . . and yet he professes to preach the Gospel to every creature making preparation for the Sabbath."

Over on the 8th Concession three days later—"Composed a difference between two settlers and prevented a law suit. . . . Found Thomas Brown very sick; little hope of his recovery." And on the 9th Concession the following week: "Conversed with fourteen families and prayed with them." Continuing still to visit the 9th Concession, ". . . had some religious conversation and found them very willing to converse with me on religious subjects. Visited one family where death had made a breach in the family circle. . . ."

During this same month King had preached four sermons at regular services in Buxton, two in East Tilbury, held four Bible Classes, a meeting of the Sessions, dispensed the Lord's Supper, and examined a number of "candidates for admission to the Sacrament."

Meanwhile, he also attended the affairs of the school, which included conferences with John Rennie and packing him off to London to care for some business relating to the school.

There was infinite detail in the transactions of the Elgin Association and the economic affairs of the settlement. For instance, he went into Chatham twice. On March 4, it was to obtain insurance on the sawmill to the extent of five thousand dollars. On March 20, it was to take care of another mortgage, and to forward some papers to the treasurer of the Elgin Association.

During the month, in one of the infrequent periods he was at home, he caught up with his correspondence, which was international in character and related to the settlement and all its transactions with the business world, the Elgin Association, the Hamilton Presbytery, the Synod, and the Buxton Mission and his continuing efforts to raise money for the church and school.

The month did begin happily. On March 1, he noted: "Making preparation for the Sabbath, found it delightful to retire from the world and commune with Christ." He had some more time before the Thursday night prayer service on the 13th, for he "remained at home writing and making some arrangements about my own private affairs." But he had only one other day to himself. That was on March 21. "Remained at home reading and making preparations for the Sabbath. Found it agreeable to have some time to read and study."

But that was an exceptional month and was not to be repeated for at least the rest of that year. There was a personal note for machinery he had signed for at the Detroit Locomotive Works to the amount of $165, and he had no money. But he managed to obtain a sixty-day loan for two hundred dollars from the Corn Bank in Chatham which postponed that crisis. He preached several times—in Chatham, Detroit, Mersea, Port Sarnia, and Ridgetown—attended a meeting of the Presbytery in Hamilton, went to a meeting of the Synod in London—all within the next two months.

During that period too, aside from the regular stream of visitors, he was host to the Rev. William Ferrie of New Brunswick; John Scoble of Dawn Institute, who insisted that King officiate at the marriage of his daughter; Rev. Angus McColl, his friend from St. Andrews in Chatham; William Clarke from London, Ontario; and others whose identities are not specified.

It was after the Louisiana turning point that William King began also to discover a new personal satisfaction. His first crop of students was ready for the harvest of Knox College. The first one was Jerome Riley, and even the antagonistic *Chatham Planet* grudgingly reported: "we are informed that young Riley intends to enter the University next Winter; the youth has fair talents, and if properly cultivated may yet become a blessing to his people."

"Fair talents"! That made King fume. Jerome was one of the most promising classical scholars he had ever taught, and his brother John, two years younger, was not far behind him. The only trouble with Jerome, as far as King was concerned, was his tendency toward medicine, rather than the ministry.

There was Wilson Abbott's boy Anderson, almost ready for college too, and James Rapier, the Alabaman. King had no worry about the ability of these boys, either scholastically or financially, to support a full college course.

But there were four more boys in his first college-bound class whose parents were far from wealthy. They lived comfortably, as did most of the settlers after the first year, but cash was always a problem. King assumed that problem as his own, as part of his promise to provide all possible educational opportunities. From 1856 on, he waged a distinct campaign for funds with which to send all deserving Buxton boys to college. This was an additional begging chore for he still needed almost all the capital available for building the church and new school.

The Buxton boys were King's intellectual children. He concentrated all his teaching skills on them, and often postponed his duties for the Elgin Association to spend hours with them. In his expressions of pride, worry, and disappointment concerning their individual performances, he reacted exactly as any parent would. He gave them as much of himself as he would have given Theophilus had the boy lived. His Buxton boys *must* be sent to college.

In November 1856, in his report to the Synod, he stressed the situation in which he found himself:

> There is a class now learning Latin and Greek, some of them will enter College as soon as they are prepared. Two were ready to enter last November but their parents being unable to support them at College they were under the necessity of returning home. The same difficulty will be felt by the class now preparing. One of the boys farthest advanced, who is reading the second book of Virgil, the parents are in humble circumstances and will not be able to support him in college. A Bursary fund, capable of supporting two or three students, during their first and second years at College, would be a great boon. Unless some assistance be rendered to those, who with much difficulty have prepared themselves for College, very few will have the means to enter. . . .

One could well imagine the Synod's reception of his proposal for a Bursary fund applied to his own particular mission. All over Canada there were deserving students unable to attend college for lack of money. But they were white students, not black, and they would not serve King's larger purpose which he went on to repeat, as he did in every report to the Synod:

> Unless this can be remedied one great object of the mission will be frustrated, namely, the training of young men of piety and talents for further usefulness in the Church. Never was there more need for such young men as at present. Already "the fields are white to harvest"—the light is breaking in on the dark continent of Africa, from almost every direction . . . The Slave Trade is still carried on along the coast, notwithstanding the vigilance of the British Navy. Nothing but the preaching of the everlasting Gospel will put an end to that inhuman traffic. . . .

There was a calculated audacity in King's program to find funds for college. He seized upon the results of the Synod meeting in London, Ontario, on June 16, 1855, when that body highly approved his annual report, and notes: "The Synod further strongly recommended this object to the liberal support of the congregations of the Church."

King thereupon went directly to the "congregations of the church" and asked each member for a contribution of eighteen cents annually to the Buxton Mission. He made it a public appeal in the *Ecclesiastical and Missionary Record*, and was somewhat chiding in his comments. Some congregations, he said ". . . have felt no interest whatsoever in the Mission and have contributed nothing." One congregation expressed its interest in the Mission by two cents per capita and another by three cents, King calculated.

This may have been a bit blunt, but the alarming drop in the Buxton Mission fund was halted, and within two years was back above a thousand dollars.

Another result of King's campaign for his college-bound boys was actually the start of a Bursary Fund as a result of a legacy. One James Thompson of Beverly, Canada West, left one thousand dollars to be devoted to missions, and King put in his bid for all of it. He had the motion offered and seconded at a Synod meeting in Kingston, but an amendment was made and carried to divide it somewhat among the other missions of the Church. King's portion was four hundred dollars.

Then he began to receive small donations, one of twenty dollars "to be applied in assisting coloured youths who are now prosecuting their studies for the ministry." There was £22 2*s*. from the Ladies Society of Edinburgh for Emancipation. There was to be help for the college fund within Buxton too, for William Field's will left his land and property to his wife Hardinia for "the rest of her natural life." Should his daughter Mary escape from slavery she was to inherit from Hardinia, otherwise all of his property was to be used "for the purpose of educating poor colored students for the Presbyterian Church of Canada."

It was not an easy task he had set for himself, raising money for college for his boys. There were compensations, though. Here and there pennies were gathered by groups and sent to Buxton for his Bursary fund with apologies for their small amounts. But King knew the sources and knew the sacrifices entailed in raising just pennies. There was one contribution that gladdened his heart and gave him the courage to fight on from day to day. He was so proud of it that he requested the *Presbyterian Ecclesiastical and Missionary Record* to print an announcement about it.

"The Rev. Wm. King, minister to the coloured population at Buxton, thankfully acknowledges the receipt of a draft for £1 10*s*. sterling from the children of the Sabbath School of the West Port Church in Edinburgh. . . ." This was from

Rev. William Tasker's church, directly from the "City of God," from the heart of Dr. Chalmers' concept.

If this was possible within so few years of the founding of the West Port Mission, under difficulties so much greater than he had found in Buxton, how could King lose faith in his own mission, no matter how slowly it was realized? Dr. Chalmers had never hesitated, had never questioned the inevitability of a "City of God." And so William King kept on. He found money for his first class ready for college in 1856, for two students he mentioned in his appeal to the Synod in November. One of them, Alfred Lafferty, went to Trinity College in Toronto with Anderson Abbott. Another, Richard Johnson, went to Edinburgh to study medicine.

In none of his boys was his faith misplaced. Within a few years they had each made their marks, and in 1862 King was able to boast about them to the famous Dr. Samuel Gridley Howe when the latter visited Buxton in behalf of the Freedman's Enquiry Commission. The following is Dr. Howe's report of an interview with Dr. McCaul, president of Trinity College:

> We had a mulatto here this last examination (1861) who took the "double first" in both classics and mathematics. He has very great ability. There are very few whites who can do what he did. It would be considered a rare thing to have a "double-first" got once in five years, and that amongst the highest "honor-men." The "honor-men" as we call them, are in a ratio of one to thirty. He expected to come out first of all in mathematics, but he failed in that; but he came out in the first class of honors, in both classics and mathematics, as no one else in that year did; and I do not think there have been more than three instances in which it has been done since the University was opened twenty years ago. Lafferty is the young man's name. His father was of very humble capacity, and I think, a full black. There was another man

who was a student here who did very well in medicine—Dr. Augusta. There was another medical student here—Mr. Abbott—who got along very well. I do not hesitate to say, in regard to Mr. Lafferty, that he is fully equal to any white man, and as I mentioned to you, far superior to the average of them. It was a great subject of astonishment to some of our Kentucky friends, who came over here last year in October, when they saw this mulatto get the first prize for Greek verse, which he had to recite; and he was the crack man of the day, with all the others listening to him with great pleasure.

It may be assumed that King boasted mightily to Dr. Howe about his boys in that first class of 1856, for over at Knox College both Jerome Riley and James Rapier had graduated with honors. Then there was Richard Johnson in Edinburgh. He had had no money either. His father, Henry Johnson, told Benjamin Drew in 1854: "I left the States for Canada, for rights, freedom, liberty. I came to Buxton to educate my children."

Richard Johnson proved to be one of the most helpful of the students. He not only turned out to be an ambassador of good will for the Buxton Mission, but pointed the direction toward solving all King's financial problems.

King received a letter dated February 15, 1859, from Mrs. William B. Borwich of Dundee, Scotland, enclosing an order for ten pounds "to assist a Scholarship for any promising pupil of yours that may wish to prosecute his studies at college with a view to the ministry."

The gift was from the Dundee Ladies Anti-Slavery Society, of which Mrs. Borwich was treasurer. It was prompted by the following incident:

> We had your friend Mr. Johnson with us at Dundee during his Christmas holidays and in public he acquitted himself very creditably. Every person was pleased also with him in

private—at his unassuming manner, at his considerable intelligence and his earnest and apparent sincere piety. A number like him would roll back the tide of obloquy from the race. The students at Dundee speak highly of his standing in his classes, especially in the department of Anatomy.

This was followed by an inquiry from Glasgow as to the amount necessary to send a Buxton boy through college. There were other letters, from Ireland, and from England. One was from Henry Christie, the founder of the famous hat firm in London, England.

During that same year there was a deputation from the Presbyterian Church in Ireland, Rev. William McClure from Londonderry and a Professor Gibson from Belfast College. These two spent an entire day examining King's students, and they too were enthusiastic in their reports.

As a result of their visit, the Irish Church issued a formal invitation through the Synod asking King to appear before their Assembly and describe his work.

But the final push that was to send King, William H. Day, and his traveling companion of the Pittsburgh pilgrimage, Dr. Robert Burns, overseas for a momentous journey was a visit from an old friend.

Dr. Frederick Monod, the eminent French divine William King had been awed to meet in Dr. Chalmers' home, arrived to investigate Buxton with his son Theodore. Dr. Monod preached to the settlers at special services, marveled at the settlement—though somewhat disillusioned by the sight of a party of Indians encamped in the Elgin woods on a hunting trip—and left King with something to think about.

Dr. Monod had been in the United States and was in Canada raising money to build himself a church in Paris. He had been highly successful. A Protestant church in Paris was a most worthy objective in New England, and the wealthy businessmen who also financed anti-Negro riots in Boston took to this project. He was successful in Canada West, too, although of course, not in Catholic Quebec Province.

Dr. Monod had scarcely disappeared aboard the train for Toronto when King, his usual deliberate thinking in the discard, was preparing his petition. If Dr. Monod could plow such fertile ground on this side of the Atlantic to build himself a church, why shouldn't he seek funds for his own Buxton church in the British Isles where anti-slavery attitudes were pioneered?

He went to Toronto for the 1859 Synod meeting and came home with their approval of

> Rev. King's visit to the mother country; authorize that gentleman to proceed forthwith to Great Britain and Ireland, with the view of diffusing information in regard to an experiment in behalf of the coloured population of Canada, the success of which has been so gratifying, and empower him to receive subscriptions for re-building the Church and School House, and for the general objects of the mission. . . .

☆

PART FIVE: DREAMS OF CONQUEST

XIV : WILLIAM KING AND JOHN BROWN

BEFORE GOING OVERSEAS, William King was to have a most potent influence on the course taken by John Brown on his road to martyrdom at Harper's Ferry. The many historians who have kept the man's soul marching on in the study of American history appear to have overlooked King's influence on the events in Chatham, Kent County, during 1858 and 1859, which led to the climax of the Dark Decade.

It was Dr. Martin R. Delany, a Negro, who made the famous Constitutional Convention in Chatham possible on May 8–10, 1858.

It was Rev. William King, a white man, who made an invasion of Virginia by Canadian ex-slaves impossible in October 1859.

These two men, both committed to an ending of slavery in the United States, were poles apart in 1858 as to the methods to be used. Both were to be abroad at the time of Harper's Ferry and both were to join hands in London, England, in June 1860, as the most important cogs in King's old dream of ending slavery at its source, in Africa. In Chatham they were practically neighbors and both were engaged in activities in behalf of the Negro, but their totally different approaches made them distant acquaintances rather than the close friends and co-workers they were to become in England.

They had worked together before, in behalf of electing Archie McKellar to the Provincial Parliament in the previous years. Dr. Delany was McKellar's organizer among the Negroes in Chatham itself where he was practicing medicine. King did the electioneering through Kent County, among the Negro settlements and rural concentrations of Negroes. They had shared the same platforms, but not the same beliefs, in the antislavery action.

All three men—William King, Martin Delany, and John Brown—personified the three differing viewpoints resulting from the hopelessness of the 1850's. Out of his own experience King knew that slavery would never end voluntarily, only by ending the slave trade. Out of his own antislavery years of frustration, Dr. Delany had given up the fight and believed only that emigration to Africa was the slave's solution. John Brown too had given up, but only on the forms of persuasion advocated by his Abolitionist patrons, the "Secret Six." By then he was Jehovah's avenging hand.

With passage of the Fugitive Slave Act, John Brown returned to the Old Testament, and the texts which made Harper's Ferry inevitable. Very soon after passage of the Act, on January 15, 1851, in Springfield, Massachusetts, he had organized his League of Gileadites to fight the Midianite slavecatchers, eye for eye and tooth for tooth. These Negroes pledged to "Stand by one another, and by your friends, while a drop of blood remains; and be hanged, if you must, but tell no tales out of school. Make no confession. . . ." As the Lord instructed Gideon, "Whosoever is fearful or afraid let him return and depart early from Mount Gilead," so John Brown instructed his followers and supporters. He arrived in Chatham on April 30, 1858, after the battle of Ottawotomie, an event which was termed justifiable homicide in the North and massacre in the South. Violent destruction was his course as the only method of ending slavery.

In Chatham, John Brown sought out Dr. Delany, and with good reason. Martin Robison Delany was one of the most amazingly versatile men of any color in American history. Born of free Negro parents in Charles Town, now West Virginia, Delany won his medical education largely with the help of a Pittsburgh physician.

As a doctor he had won the hearts of whites, as well as fellow Negroes, by his work in the Pittsburgh cholera epidemic in 1854. Before helping Frederick Douglass start the *North Star,* he had published the antislavery Pittsburgh periodical *Mystery,* and had almost been mobbed in Ohio as an Abolitionist speaker. He was an inventor, novelist and writer, explorer and soldier. It was Major Delany, the first Negro combat Major in the U.S. Army, who in Charleston, South Carolina, commanded the 104th United States Colored Troops in April 1865, when news of Lincoln's assassination reached that city. It was the same Delany who was a candidate for lieutenant-governor of South Carolina in 1874, when the unsuccessful Independent Republic Party was formed there.

Dr. Delany had been practicing medicine in Chatham for two years when John Brown reached there. He had given up the antislavery fight temporarily, and turned to emigration to Africa as the only solution for his people. In 1854, while practicing medicine in Pittsburgh, he issued the call for the first National Emigration Convention, and for the second in 1856. He then moved to Chatham for Canadian freedom. He was, temporarily, a beaten man.

Between Dr. Delany and Rev. King there was honest disagreement regarding emigration of the slaves to Africa. It was not only the impracticality of transporting four million

RESIDENCE OF ISRAEL D. SHADD IN CHATHAM
The publisher of the *Provincial Freeman,* Shadd was an important member of the Negro community; John Brown stayed here when he was in Chatham. The house is now destroyed.

F. H. Brown Historical Collection

people there that influenced King. It was more his belief that only the end of the slave trade would end slavery in the United States. By 1858 that trade had trebled since the founding of Liberia in 1821, some of it from Liberian ports. Only about nine thousand slaves had been manumitted for Liberia in all that time, while hundreds of thousands of slaves had made the Middle Passage for America. But first and foremost in King's opposition to emigration was its lack of realism in regard to the ending of slavery. He had lived with slave-owners, and knew that so long as slavery was profitable, it would never be relinquished.

On the other hand, Delany was a victim of despair. The Negro would never be free in the United States, he believed, until there was a country somewhere, with its own independence, military force, and power among nations to demand such freedom. In this, Dr. Delany pre-dated Dr. Theodor Herzl and Zionism for the Jews of Europe. His beliefs were well-documented in his book published in Philadelphia in 1852, *The Condition, Elevation, Emigration and Destiny of the Colored People of the United States Politically Considered.*

In advocating settlement of East Africa Dr. Delany declared:

> The land is ours—there it lies with inexhaustible resources; let us go and possess it. In Eastern Africa must rise up a nation, to whom all the world must pay commercial tribute . . . We must make an issue, create an event, and establish a position for ourselves and never may we expect to be respected as men and women until we have undertaken some fearless, bold and adventurous deeds of daring contending against every odd—regardless of every consequence.

With such sentiments, it is small wonder that John Brown turned to Dr. Delany when he reached Chatham. They had never met, though both were close friends to

Frederick Douglass until Dr. Delany left the *North Star* in 1849. John Brown sought him out for aid in organizing the Constitutional Convention. He explained his purpose, and at no time did King speak out against that purpose. Three months after the Constitutional Convention King was to speak out publicly against the "Kansas aggressions," in total agreement with John Brown.

Brown proposed no Harper's Ferry in Chatham. Nor did he propose the overthrow of the United States government, as Governor Wise of Virginia charged when he declared: "With God's help we will drive all the disunionists together back into Canada. Let the compact of fanatics and intolerance be confined to British soil." At Harper's Ferry there was only one Canadian, Osborn Perry Anderson, a freeborn Negro fugitive from Pennsylvania.

What John Brown did propose to Dr. Delany in May 1858, and which was agreed to by King, has been reported with all the inaccuracies of Southern historiography. Dr. Delany's own account, apparently neglected, is as follows:

> The convention, when assembled, consisted of Captain John Brown, his son Owen, eleven or twelve of his Kansas followers, all young white men, enthusiastic and able, and probably sixty or seventy colored men, whom I brought together.

Among them were several Buxton men: Abraham Shadd, Ezekiel Cooper, William Howard Day, Thomas W. Stringer, and others. King, being white, was not invited to the meetings held in Buxton homes but he was fully informed throughout the period of the convention. How could he oppose John Brown's plan when the domain of slavery was being extended northward into Kansas, and the Missouri Compromise of 1820 limiting its boundaries was discarded? This is what John Brown proposed, according to Dr. Delany:

His scheme was nothing more than this: To make Kansas instead of Canada, the terminus of the Underground Railroad; instead of passing off the slave to Canada, to send him to Kansas, and there test, on the soil of the United States territory, whether or not the right to freedom would be maintained where no municipal power had authorized.

This plan included settlement behind fortifications so that the slaves would not be dispersed, as the anti-slavery whites had been in Kansas. This route was to be called the "Subterranean Pass Way," with the initials S.P.W. to distinguish it from the Underground Railroad—which meant Canada to all antislavery forces. In effect, John Brown, fresh from fighting the proslavery armies from Missouri, proposed building a free state out of the thousands of fugitives pouring into Canada. What would be more sensible than to divert the fugitives to Kansas and establish pockets of resistance? John Brown's plan was in keeping with his times.

There is the further question: why the trappings of a constitution, elections, and a provisional government? Dr. Delany also provides that answer, from his report on the Chatham Convention:

The whole matter had been well considered, and at first, a state government had been proposed, and in accordance a constitution prepared. This was presented to the convention; and here a difficulty presented itself to the minds of some present, that according to American jurisprudence, Negroes, having no rights respected by white men, consequently could have no right to petition, and none to sovereignty . . . Therefore it would be a mere mockery to set up a claim as a fundamental right, which in itself was null and void . . . To obviate this, and avoid the charge against them as lawless and unorganized, existing without government, it was proposed that an independent community be established within and under the government of the United States, but without the state sovereignty of the compact, similar to the Cherokee nation of the Indians, or the Mormons. To these last named, references were made, as parallel cases at the time. The necessary changes and modifications were made in the constitution, and with such it was printed.

The precedent was there. Before Utah was accepted even as a territory, it was the independent State of Deseret, headed by Brigham Young. Its transition into statehood took so long only because of opposition to polygamy.

The preamble to this constitution, a printed copy of which was produced for John Brown's trial, makes unmistakably clear that the Negro strongholds in Kansas resulting from the S.P.W. operations were to have a political character only to establish a legality for eventual absorption into a free United States. Following the "Whereas" declaring that slavery in the country was no more than "unprovoked and unjustifiable war of one portion of its citizens upon another portion,"

> Therefore we Citizens of the United States, and the Oppressed People, who, by a Recent Decision of the Supreme Court are Declared to have no Rights which the White Man is bound to Respect; Together with all Other People Degraded by the Laws thereof, Do, *for the Time Being,* Ordain and Establish for Ourselves the following Provisional Constitution and Ordinances, the Better to Protect our Persons, Property, and Lives and Liberties; and to Govern our Actions.

Among Negroes in Kent County, there was to be only one secret kept from King—when they guarded him from Larwill's gang in the beginnings of Buxton, and when they watched over his safety as an old man. John Brown's activities and plans were known to him from the day of the man's arrival with his sons and the other white veterans of the Kansas Wars. The story spread around Chatham, that these strangers were in the town to found a new Masonic Lodge, thereby explaining the secrecy, was believed by no one but the Constitutional Convention. The fact that Brown lived in the house of Israel Shadd on King St., where the Negro newspaper *Provincial Freeman* was published, was a giveaway. There were no mixed Masonic Lodges.

King knew when the meetings were held in Buxton, at the home of Abraham Shadd, Israel's brother, and at Ezekiel Cooper's. While he deplored John Brown's past history of violence, how could he dispute the necessity of it? The initial violence was in the Kansas-Nebraska Act and the proslavery guerilla armies terrorizing the settlers in Kansas. But he was uneasy, worried about the part the Canadian Negroes should play in this crisis.

On August 2, 1858, King was the principal speaker at Kent County's annual observance of the 1833 West Indian Emancipation. This was a holiday for the Negroes of Canada, and they marched in uniform as part of the Kent County Militia, picnicked in Tecumseh Park, and at night danced in the barracks. But each of the thousands of Negroes who gathered in the Park on that day in 1858 knew why he declared:

> A spirit of uneasiness is manifesting itself. The fugitive slave bill, the Dred Scott decision and the Kansas aggressions are the symptoms of an incurable disease . . . Hate and a festering sense of undeserved injury, prompting to revenge, together with a despair of attaining to its end by lawful means, will goad on to some lawless, desperate act of widespread rebellion, in which the planter and his property will perish together.

Further than sounding that warning, King only urged caution on the Negroes who came to him for advice. Perhaps the factor that worried him most was that neither he nor Archie McKellar, both of them proven friends of the Negroes, were ever approached by any member of the Brown party. Nor was any other white man in Kent County. The recruiting was being done exclusively among the Negroes.

King's watchful waiting ended in the spring of 1859, when John Brown returned to Chatham from the dramatic and highly publicized raid in Missouri in which the slave-owner David Cruse was killed. It was then that John Brown told Dr. Delany: "It is men I want, not money; money I can get plentiful enough but no men. Money can come without being seen, but men are afraid of identification with me, though they favor my measures. They are cowards, Sir, cowards!"

King was apprehensive about the future because of the Missouri raid. The rescue of the twelve slaves and their triumphant escort by Brown and his small band all the twenty-five-hundred-mile route to Windsor was as dramatic as Harper's Ferry, but without the climax of a trial. All along the route there was little secrecy in the flight. There was even a letter by John Brown himself, giving a detailed account of the raid, published in the *New York Tribune* in January 1859, though the party did not reach Canada until March 12. By then Brown had a price of three thousand dollars on his head.

To King, the Missouri raid spelled an irresponsible defiance of the enemy. While the rescue of twelve slaves was entirely praiseworthy, and the death of Cruse was to be deplored, the open challenge could only be condemned if the Kansas scheme was still in Brown's plans. That did not seem likely because he had burned his bridges behind him. The S.P.W. and concentrations of fugitive slaves would be impossible because the militant proslavery whites had been forewarned. Brown himself had warned them by the arrogant progress of the rescue.

Therefore, when John Brown Jr. returned to Buxton for more meetings and the recruiting drive for an unknown future action was launched, King sent out his warnings. He may not have known what John Brown planned. It is questionable to this day whether anyone knew.

That is why only Osborn Perry Anderson, Israel Shadd's printer's devil, was the only Canadian Negro at Harper's Ferry, when by all logic there should have been a whole army of invasion raised in Kent County alone. Every Negro family had ties with the slaves. Had they volunteered, their own families would have been safe in Canada. Many of them had gone south on rescues, some of them with King's help. King's fear of "some lawless, desperate act," in which the slaveowners and their "property," meaning their slaves, would perish together prevented the recruiting which John Brown had every right to expect. The authoritative Canadian historian, Dr. Fred Landon, points out:

> Chatham was chosen as the place of meeting with specific reference to the effect it might have on the large Negro population resident within the immediate vicinity. There were more Negroes within fifty miles of Chatham than in any other section of Canadian territory, and among them were men of intelligence, education and daring. Some of them were experienced in slave-raiding. Brown was justified in expecting help from them.

In April 1859, while John Brown and his men were vainly trying to recruit their army of insurrection in Canada West, both King and Dr. Delany were busily preparing to go abroad on the assignments that led to London.

Dr. Delany left first, in early May, sailing from New York aboard the bark *Mendi* as head of the Niger Valley Exploring Party which was the first all-Negro scientific expedition sent to Africa. It was the product of Dr. Delany's fertile brain, and was financed entirely by the Negro fugitives from the United States settled in Kent County.

Shortly after his arrival in Chatham, Dr. Delany had

found among the settlers, including some from Buxton, a kinship concerning his thesis of a powerful African state. The men who agreed with him were mostly the more articulate, formerly free Negroes of the northern states, driven to Canada by the Black Codes. There was William Howard Day, elected president of the organization formed in 1858 and named the African Commission. He too was dispirited by the events of the Dark Decade, yet could appreciate the reality of King's criticism of emigration schemes. He was an Elder in St. Andrews and was very close to William King.

All three Shadd brothers, Israel, Isaac, and Abraham, were part of the African Commission. The latter two lived in Buxton, and to this day their descendants are lawyers, teachers, and doctors in Canada and the United States. The unusual family had romantic beginnings, going back to a Hessian soldier, Hans Schad, who was wounded during Braddock's retreat in 1775. He was taken in by a free Negro widow at Chad's Ford, Pennsylvania, and a year later married her daughter.

The Niger Valley Exploring Party was purely a scientific expedition, being explicit in its relationship to possible future exploration. Its purpose was to

> make a topographical, geological and geographical examination of the Valley of the River Niger, in Africa, and an inquiry into the state and condition of the people of that valley, and other parts of Africa, together with such other scientific inquiries as may by them be deemed expedient, for the purpose of science, and for general information; without any reference to, and with the board being entirely opposed to, any emigration there as such. Provided, however, that nothing in this instrument be so construed as to interfere with the rights of the commissioners to negotiate, in their own behalf, or that of any other parties or organizations, for territory.

With Dr. Delany on the expedition were Robert Douglass, the Negro artist from Philadelphia whose work was not shown there but was considered sufficiently meritorious for election to the Royal Academy of Arts in London the following year; Professor Robert Campbell, the naturalist and director of the Philadelphia Institute for Colored Youth, sponsored by the free Negroes of that city; Amos Aray, surgeon; and James W. Prinnel, secretary, both of Kent County.

William Howard Day chose to accompany King to the British Isles and help raise funds for the Buxton Mission. From his own embattled "free" years in Ohio since 1849, when he graduated from Oberlin College, he knew that any future for the Negro at all would require the kind of leadership among them being produced in Buxton.

The three men—Day, Delany, and King—all set sail for the same purpose, to find some hope for the Negroes to replace the despair of the 1850's. All three had rejected John Brown's mysterious plans, knowing only that they spelled fruitless violence. King believed that slavery would be ended by ending the African slave trade. Day believed slavery might be ended by the imponderable force of Negro leadership. Delany believed that slavery might be ended by creation of a Negro Israel in Africa.

The African Aid Society, which they helped initiate in London the following June, embraced all three approaches. They left John Brown behind them in order to pursue his purpose, an end to compromise with slavery.

☆

XV : THE AFRICAN DREAM

AT NO TIME in his life was William King happier than during those months in the British Isles. From Dublin on, he and William Day were on a triumphal tour, welcomed extravagantly in every city and invited to more meetings than they could hope to attend. All through Ireland, Scotland, and England, the two were accorded enthusiastic receptions.

They arrived in Dublin on July 3, and within a few weeks King knew that raising the funds for a new Buxton church and school would be the least of his problems. By the end of August he was able to send the Toronto Synod the first draft toward the Buxton Fund. It was for $1,726.50. Eventually, he was to forward over six thousand dollars, which was ample for the needs. The success was due not only to the immediate and generous approval of the Buxton Settlement he found in every audience, but perhaps also to the substance of his message as well. Another factor, of course, was King's habitual preparation and planning. He had sent ahead printed leaflets describing Buxton and its goals. He had with him letters of introduction to the most influential sponsorship in all cities.

While Dr. Burns went on to the Continent as the official representative of the Canadian Presbyterian Church to the Tercentenary celebrations of the Reformation, Rev. King and Elder Day began with their first appearances before the Irish General Assembly on the day they arrived in Dublin. They were given two full hours.

King confined himself to the report from the Canadian Church as its official delegate, and left to Day the story of Buxton. Again, this was good stage management. William Day's oratory had the power of obvious sincerity, of a simple piety, and straightforward presentation of his own life as a "Free" Negro, in contrast with his life in Buxton. The *Ulster County Banner* was absolutely ecstatic about Elder Day. Then the two men were scheduled to speak before the public at a meeting in the Metropolitan Hall.

The public meeting was on July 12, and the Lord Mayor of Dublin presided. The hall seated five thousand but people were standing, in the back and in the two galleries. William Day spoke first, with his usual effectiveness, but this time it was King who won the ovation.

Granted the existing animus toward slavery's last stronghold, the United States, it must be admitted that King's speech was calculated to turn the audience's pockets inside out.

> In the United States they are erecting a monument to Washington to commemorate his noble deeds. Everyone is requested to give something toward the erection of the monument, and every state is requested to send a stone with the name of the state engraved on it, to be set in the monument as a memorial to the love which the state has for freedom. The names of all the donors are enrolled and laid up in the monument to be kept as a memorial of their love of freedom.
>
> I wish to erect a monument to freedom that will be more durable than granite. When the sculptured marble of Washington's shall have crumbled into stone, the one I propose to erect shall, with God's blessing, lift its head to Heaven and its influence shall be felt not only in time, but throughout eternity. . . .

He then asserted his own right to ask for funds.

> I have contributed to this monument, what is considered property [his slaves] in the United States, to the amount of $15,000. I have devoted nine years of my life in superintending this work and gave $5,000 of my own private means

> to carry on the work . . . I now want $7,000 to complete and I have come over here with my friend to help us in this work. That sum I expect to raise in the three Kingdoms before I return, and it is not till I have asked it, and you have refused to give, that I will believe that the money cannot be raised here to complete the object. I think there are seven thousand persons in the British Isles who would be willing to complete the work already begun, and who would show the hatred which they bear to slavery by their love and liberality to those who have escaped from its cruel bondage.

He told them about Buxton and his pride in its people, and concluded with the story of the visit to Pittsburgh and the gift of the Liberty Bell by the Negro freedmen of that city.

The result of that speech was not only money but a flood of invitations to visit all of north Ireland. It was three weeks before they could leave to keep their engagements in Scotland.

The very day after the public meeting, King was invited to an audience with Lord Morpeth, Viceroy of Ireland, who had served in Canada and for whom the Lake Erie village of Morpeth was named. Having preached often in Morpeth, about 15 miles from Buxton, King was able to tell his Lordship all the details of his village. When King rose to leave, Lord Morpeth gave him a folded sheet of paper containing congratulations on his work for the fugitives. It also contained a check for fifty dollars.

After Glasgow, Dundee, and other cities, King and Day reached Edinburgh. It was a time of memories for William King. He saw the house at No. 1 Lord Russell Place again. Once more he saw the familiar faces of Dr. Cunningham and Dr. Candlish, a good many of his former professors at the New College, and he was able to see the wonders that had been wrought at West Port. Dr. Chalmers was gone but his work was still there.

The first public meeting took place in the very same Queen Street Hall where Frederick Douglass had denounced him, and for the first time in thirteen years William King spoke up in public in his own behalf. He told the audience the circumstances that led to his condemnation. "I was now for the first time before an Edinburgh audience to vindicate myself from the foul slander that had been made by the deputation against me." The Lord Provost of Edinburgh, presiding at the meeting, interrupted to ask the audience for a vote of gratitude to King for the course he had taken.

Day followed King on the rostrum—and then there was a surprise. Archie McKellar had come to Scotland of his own volition to help out, and he took the stand to confirm and adorn all that King and Day had said. And then the Buxton boy, Richard Johnson, the medical missionary, also spoke.

The meeting ended with a standing ovation, and the staid *Edinburgh Witness* reported:

> He (King) . . . gathered round him a little nation of 1,200 souls, slaves once, now free men. He has turned the tide of pro-slavery feeling so far, that no candidate for office has the least chance of election who does not avow it as his creed that the coloured man ought to share equally with the white in all the rights and privileges accorded by the British Constitution. The humanity, energy, and wisdom that could accomplish all this needs no praise of us, or of any man.

The meeting revealed every facet of King's efforts. He told his own story as a slaveowner. William Day had been a slave, and Richard Johnson was the son of a slave. Archie McKellar, M.P., was British Law triumphant.

The public demanded another chance. Queen Street Hall had been unable to accommodate all who wanted to hear these men. A second meeting was held there a week later, and again it was packed. The chairman this time was a General Anderson who had served many years with the British Army in Canada. Once more there was a standing vote in endorsement of all the objectives of the Buxton Mission.

King seized this opportunity to flagellate the "Christian church of America" for its proslavery sympathies. The exceptions he noted were "honorable," some 1,000 ministers in the Reformed Presbyterian, the Associate Reformers, the Free Presbyterians and the New School Presbyterian churches. This brought cheers from the audience. But there was silence when he pointed out that there were between four and five thousand other men of the cloth who accepted slavery.

William Day brought both cheers and tears from the audience. Again without the least display of bitterness, he read them a letter from a white friend in Newport, Rhode Island, who was the host of a Negro girl well known in Edinburgh. She had been educated both there and in England and had returned to the United States to work for her people. The girl was taken to church on a Sunday and sat in the same pew with her hostess. The lady received a note from the church committee telling her that her colored guest should be seated in the gallery and not in her pew. The lady defied the committee, and on the following Sabbath took her guest directly to the pew. She was notified that, with or without Negro guests, her pew was taken from her.

Had William Day told the Edinburgh audience of the floggings he had seen, had he told them of the cruelties practiced, and the families torn apart by slavery, he could not have shocked these Scotsmen more. They were stunned and angry at the same time. This was the antithesis of all for which the Free Church was founded, and was a total violation of what Dr. Chalmers had preached.

In Scotland, as in Ireland, the people gave generously

because King asked only for his church and schools. The leaflet he had distributed at the meeting made this clear.

> The buildings are all of a temporary kind, and will require to be replaced by others of a more substantial and permanent nature. The schools will require the support of friends for some time to come. It is on the spiritual and educational part of the enterprise that we now appeal to you; we ask nothing for their temporal support. We ask you only to aid in the erection of good and substantial buildings, to place the schools on a permanent and efficient basis, and to create a few bursaries for the purpose of preparing young men of piety and talents for future usefulness, either in Canada, the United States or Africa.

By the end of November, King knew that there would be enough money for all his purposes in Buxton. "In December, I proceeded to London to mature a plan which I, with some of my antislavery friends in London had in view, namely, to plant Christian colonies on the west coast of Africa as a barrier against the slave trade . . ."

There has been some confusion concerning the African Aid Society. Its lifetime was so brief that its purposes have been identified with other organizations sponsoring Negro emigration to Africa. It was not an emigration scheme. It was a forerunner of Crossroads Africa, the Peace Corps, and dozens of international efforts to assist Africans. When he returned home, King was authorized to train, in the Buxton Settlement, "pioneers of the Christian colonies to be formed."

The "Christian colonies" were to be composed of natives and the "emigrants," a corps of specially trained young men and women. "I was to furnish the men from the Elgin Settlement who were to act as the pioneers of the Christian colonies to be formed, and the London Society was to furnish the means and protection to the colonists." The teams of "pioneers" were to be Buxton boys who had graduated from colleges in their respective fields, such as John Riley, now a minister; Richard M. Johnson, the medical missionary; and James T. Rapier, who had dual abilities in administration and the cultivation of cotton and sugar. With teachers added to these specialties, the natives of Africa would themselves achieve self-emancipation, and their chiefs would find greater profits in their new cotton and sugar economy than in the sale of their people to the slave smugglers.

King made his proposal for the African Aid Society before the same distinguished gathering that heard Dr. Delany's report on the exploration of the Niger Valley, and his announcement that he had successfully negotiated a treaty with several chiefs of Abbeokuta for the first experiment in aiding that underdeveloped country. The Society received the approval of the Prince Consort, Albert, and Lord Alfred Churchill was named to head it. Governmental and private support was given it after Lord Chancellor Brougham endorsed the plan.

It is impossible to know how much the high and mighty of England were influenced in favor of the African Aid Society by the international incident that took place during the very first session of the International Statistical Congress, on July 16, 1860. It had King cheering for Dr. Delany, with the rest of the audience, and was the substance of numerous columns in the *London Times* and *London Chronicle* for several weeks afterward. The affair certainly influenced British public opinion against the United States.

What happened was that the entire American delegation to the International Congress walked out following a remark by Lord Brougham. Nor did they return. There are two versions of the incident, one given by Dr. Delany, and the other by the head of the American delegation, the distinguished Judge Augustus B. Longstreet of Georgia, who strangely

FUGITIVE SLAVES IN CANADA.

ELGIN SETTLEMENT.

THERE are upwards of 30,000 coloured persons in Canada, mostly fugitives from the United States. Their numbers are increasing rapidly by the operation of the Fugitive Slave Law, which gives them no resting place till they reach Canada, where they generally arrive in a destitute condition, stripped of everything but life. The occasion of the Elgin Settlement, being formed for their social and moral improvement, was this: The Rev. WILLIAM KING having become heir to a number of slaves in Louisiana, set them free as soon as they came into his possession, paid their passage, and accompanied them to Canada, a distance of 1500 miles. On his arrival he found the fugitives in that degraded condition in which slavery had left them, most of them without a home and without a friend, and for whose soul no man cared.

An appeal was made to the Christian community on their behalf, which was responded to by the friends of the slave there. An Association was formed, under the patronage of LORD ELGIN, then Governor-General, which was incorporated by Act of Parliament in 1850, under the title of the Elgin Association. Mr. King was chosen unanimously to superintend the Settlement. Eighteen thousand dollars were subscribed, and nine thousand acres of land secured from Government in the Township of Raleigh, and County of Kent. Those lands were divided into farms of fifty acres each, and given to coloured settlers at a nominal price.

One of the objects contemplated by this effort was to show by practical experiment that the coloured man, when placed in favourable circumstances, could support himself by his own industry, and to refute the charge brought against him by the pro-slavery party in the United States, that he would not support himself when set free. On these lands upwards of two hundred families are now settled, supporting themselves by their own industry.

Lord Althorp, now Earl SPENCER, of England, who visited the Settlement in 1857, and Professor Gibson of Belfast, and the Rev. William M'Lure of Londonderry, who spent two days, in 1858, in visiting the Settlement, speak favourably of their improvement. The Rev. Dr. Burns and Dr. Willis of Toronto are Vice-Presidents of the Elgin Association, and frequently visit the Settlement. They also testify to the success of the experiment, and the industry of the settlers.

On these lands a church has been erected, to supply the adult population with the means of grace; and schools have been established, to give the children a good education. These schools are now attended by upwards of one hundred pupils. The number would be greatly increased by enlarging the accommodation, and erecting permanent buildings.

[OVER.

Front page of the leaflet King wrote and distributed during his tour of England, Scotland, and Ireland.

National Archives, Ottawa, Canada

enough had been President of Centenary College in Jackson, Louisiana, in 1849, after King's departure and the sale of Louisiana College to the Methodists.

The learned Judge Longstreet was an ardent secessionist, had published a newspaper called *States Rights Sentinel* in Augusta, Georgia, and had written several books in behalf of slavery. During those tense months of 1860 he must have been particularly sensitive.

After Prince Albert had welcomed the learned body, Lord Brougham, who was chairman of the opening session, rose to present the guests and delegates. Beside Prince Albert sat George M. Dallas, Minister to the Court of St. James from the United States, and former vice president in the Polk administration, who had presided over the Senate when the Wilmot Proviso, barring extension of slavery into lands conquered from Mexico, went down to defeat.

Lord Brougham turned to him and said (Judge Longstreet version): "I call the attention of Mr. Dallas to the fact that there is a negro present (or among the delegates) and I hope he will have no scruples on that account." Judge Longstreet adds that the delegates responded with "general and enthusiastic applause."

Judge Longstreet's report to his government continues: "Silence being restored, the negro, who goes by the name of Delany, rose and said 'I thank your royal highness and Lord Brougham and have only to say *that I am a man.*' " (Emphasis Longstreet's.)

"This too was applauded warmly by the delegates. I regarded this an ill-timed assault upon our country, a wanton indignity offered to our minister, and a pointed insult offered to me. I immediately withdrew from the body. The propriety of my course is respectfully submitted to my government."

Dr. Delany declares that he said: "I rise, your Royal Highness, to thank his lordship, the unflinching friend of the negro, for the remarks he has made in reference to myself, and to assure your Royal Highness that I am a man."

But on the following day, the first business session of the Congress, a state member of the American delegation, a Dr. Jarvis from Boston, brought Judge Longstreet's paper to be read. Lord Brougham seized the occasion to add oil to the fire already raging in the London press.

> This reminds me of a statement made in the papers this morning, that I had designedly wounded the feelings of the American minister at this court . . . Now, what is this "offense" complained of? Why, on the opening of this august assemblage, possibly the largest in number, and the most learned, that the world ever saw together from different nations, to be among whom any man might feel proud, as an evidence of his advance, civilization and attainments, what is the fact: Why, here we see, even in this unequaled council, a son of Africa, one of that race whom we have been taught to look upon as inferior. I only alluded to this as one of the most gratifying as well as extraordinary facts of the age.

This really set Judge Longstreet off, and he wrote one of the lengthiest epistles ever printed in the *London Chronicle*. It was a discussion of what was said and what was meant, an assertion that England does not understand the slaveowners' burden, and an offer: "if you cannot condescend to our company, we will not complain at giving a place to Dr. Delany, and we can beatify you with four millions precisely such." The diatribe ends with ". . . farewell to Europe forever and forever."

The whole furor amounted to giving the International Congress and England a firsthand demonstration of the emotions that would prevent any expectation of ending the slave trade carried aboard Yankee ships. The need for the African Aid Society became even more obvious.

King himself reports the final act in this drama: "Dr.

Delany, before reading his report, gave a scathing speech denouncing the United States for their hypocrisy, stating that England was the only country where true freedom was enjoyed."

Before returning home, the African Aid Society had commissioned King to prepare the first team of missionaries at Buxton, with funds for two-thirds of their cost for a full year in Africa to be borne by the organization. Dr. Delany was commissioned to head this first group to Abbeokuta. The target date for the first expedition was a year from then, in June 1861.

All through the rest of 1860, King personally took over instruction of his young men and was in constant contact with Delany, in correspondence with Lord Alfred Churchill, the British consul at Lagos, the secretary of the African Aid Society, and all who were engaged in the project. His "team" was ready by the Fall but there were delays. In Africa the chiefs who had signed the agreement attempted to repudiate it. They were fearful of the experience in Liberia where the settlers had driven the natives off their lands and alienated all the interior. However, an agreement that the new emigrants were to live within the walled town and only use uncultivated land for their experiments in raising sugar and cotton was finally reached.

In March 1861, Lord Churchill was highly complimentary in one of his replies to King, answering several of his detailed questions.

> The success which has attended your measures and which is confirmed in a letter we have since received from Dr. Delany who promises to send within a few days, lists of a goodly number of eligible emigrants, is very gratifying. It is only such men as you write of "experienced, intelligent, practical Christian men" who we would consent to send to

> lay the foundation of work in Africa . . . The Secretary will keep you constantly advised of everything that may be interesting or important, and the Committee will be glad to hear from you as frequently as possible relative to the progress of the movement among your people . . . Relying on your indispensible [sic] cooperation, for which I beg you to accept my acknowledgment . . .

While Lord Churchill and others were consistently encouraging, during that same month King received a reply to his enquiry sent to the explorer David Livingstone seventeen months before. It was written by Livingstone aboard the fabled *Pioneer* after his return from the discovery and exploration of Lake Nyasa. Livingstone was not encouraging. Conflict with the natives and susceptibility to the "African fever" were his major reasons. "I entertain, therefore, serious doubts as to the propriety of recommending those who have escaped from slavery trying to emigrate to Africa, though if they could cultivate cotton and sugar they would no doubt in the course of time benefit both Africa and themselves."

But the reply in no way disheartened King. Dr. Delany's report had already answered his questions concerning sugar and cotton. He continued his correspondence with England and Africa and then, in December 1860, the Anderson case aroused all Canada. King was called upon to lead the fight to save the fugitive from extradition to the United States and death.

William Anderson was a fugitive from Missouri who had been caught while trying to escape. He was armed with a knife and killed his master, a planter named Seneca Diggs. When Anderson was located in Toronto, the United States sought his extradition on a charge of murder, entirely possible under the Webster-Ashburton Treaty of 1842. The fugitive was arrested and the Canadians protested.

Throughout the provinces there were meetings, demonstrations, and even an attempt to rescue Anderson. The Canadians raised an interesting question. Was not Anderson striking in self-defense against his master, who had committed a crime more horrendous than murder in robbing a man of his lifetime of freedom? Many impassioned speakers, King one of them, declared that Canada had no right to condemn a man to death—which would be certain for Anderson if he were returned—until this question was answered.

The Anderson case caused diplomatic difficulties between the United States and Canada, between the United States and Britain, and between Canada and her mother country. It was debated in the Privy Council and in the British Parliament, and Lord Brougham declared flatly that Britain would not be party to return of any fugitive slaves to the United States. While the problem occupied the capitals of three countries, a cooperative judge in Toronto freed Anderson on a technicality and he disappeared. All of the diplomats were relieved.

In Chatham a protest meeting at which King was the principal speaker was held in the Town Hall on December 31, 1861. There were three hundred there, including Edwin Larwill. After his speech, King offered a resolution to be transmitted to all courts, the public, and the press: "*Resolved*, that it is the duty of every Canadian freeman to protest most strongly against the rendition to the United States of the fugitive Anderson."

Before he could continue, Larwill struck. One of his friends, H. B. Woods, offered an amendment, "That in the opinion of this meeting the case for the prisoner may with safety and propriety be left to the disposal of the courts."

Such a reasonable amendment might have passed and the meeting become without point if not for Larwill's intemperance. He quickly seconded the amendment and launched into a speech. In the words of the *Chatham Planet:*

> Mr. Larwill apparently stepped forward, to the astonishment of the entire audience, and upheld the institution and perpetuation of slavery, said it was a divine institution, sanctioned by the laws of God, the laws of men, the laws of nature and the laws of nations. The amendment was put to the meeting and, though supported by a considerable number, it was declared to be lost and the original motion carried by a clear majority.

Meanwhile, events in the United States surged toward their dramatic climax, and all of King's plans hung in the balance between the Secessionists and the new president, Abraham Lincoln.

Lincoln's first inaugural address forecast the future. He took no action on the seizure of Fort Sumter but did declare that the Union would be preserved by violence if "it be forced upon the national authority." When King read this in the *Toronto Globe,* he knew it spelled the end of the African Aid Society even before it had been born. Soon after, he recorded:

> In the spring of 1861 I had several young men prepared to go out as pioneers of the colonies. While I was corresponding with the Society in London about sending the young men out, the southern states seceded and war was declared. I then wrote to the Society in London that the sword had been drawn from the scabbard and would not be returned until liberty was proclaimed for the captives. The market for slaves as far as the U.S. was concerned would come to an end with the war. The young men who intended to go out to Africa to colonize the West Coast were prepared to go south to fight for liberty as soon as the opportunity would be given them to enter the northern army.

☆

PART SIX: THE LAST EFFORT

XVI : THE AMERICAN DREAM

THE NEXT TWO YEARS were to be tortured ones for the people of Buxton. King named "the latter part of 1862 and the spring of 1863" as "their darkest period."

They shared with the half-million free Negroes of the northern states not only the dread of a southern victory, as the Confederate armies won battle after battle, but a host of other doubts. President Lincoln himself was responsible for one of the most pressing. Even if the tide of battle turned, would this fratricidal war end slavery? Both Frederick Douglass and King assured them that it would. Then what about Lincoln's words at his first inaugural address?

"I have no purpose directly or indirectly to interfere with the institution of slavery in the states where it exists."

And when the *Toronto Globe*, which reported the Civil War as fully as the American newspapers, had the news that slaves finding their way to the Union armies were being returned to their masters, Lincoln's words were underlined. When, in May 1861, General Fremont declared the slaves of Missouri free, Lincoln rescinded that order. A year later, General Hunter proclaimed emancipation in all the still-unconquered states under his command—South Carolina, Georgia, and Florida—and again President Lincoln canceled the order.

To Buxton, these decisions were proof that the Civil War was not being fought to free the slaves. It was a white man's war having nothing to do with slavery. If it were otherwise, wouldn't President Lincoln allow the Negroes to fight for their own freedom? They were waiting for word, in Canada as well as the United States, and each time Negro leaders in the States begged for an opportunity to fight, they were rejected.

Even the preliminary proclamation of emancipation of September 1862 only confused. Many of the Buxton settlers had escaped from the border states of Kentucky, Missouri, Maryland, and Delaware which were not included. If the Emancipation Proclamation was to be issued on January 1, 1863, as Lincoln had promised, was it for the duration of the war only, a military expedient and not really abolition? Besides, if a nation could not endure half slave and half free, how could the South be so divided?

The despair of the 1850's, dissipated by Fort Sumter, returned to Buxton, and it is quite understandable. If such devoted friends as William Lloyd Garrison and Wendell Phillips—for thirty years dedicated companions—if they could fall out over that same question of Lincoln's intent, the people of Buxton were justified in their doubts. Their futures were directly involved. They all had "folks" down there where the battles were raging. They could describe the terrain, could follow the armies of both sides over hills and streams they themselves had crossed. Somebody in Buxton came from every battle area and could adorn the newspaper stories and wonder what had happened to mother, brother, father, wife, or children who lived right where men died.

There was an overriding question for all of them, for all

Canadian fugitives, one they had been asking themselves ever since the first shot was fired. If the war was to end in freedom for all blacks, would they go back "home"?

The South was still home to them. In a hundred interviews by Benjamin Drew in 1854, and an almost equal number by Dr. Samuel Gridley Howe in 1863, the majority expressed their nostalgia for the scenes of their slavery. In songs, spirituals, and poetry, the Negro has always expressed almost a maudlin love of the Southland. With the Canadian kind of freedom they knew, the "Negro Paradise" General Grant spoke about was entirely possible. James Weldon Johnson's poem expressed the roots of his people's attachment to their homeland:

> For never let the thought arise
> That we are here on sufferance bare;
> Outcasts, asylumed 'neath these skies,
> And aliens without part or share.
> "This land is ours by right of birth,
> This land is ours by right of toil;
> We helped to turn its virgin earth,
> Our sweat is in its fruitful soil.

Of course they would go back "home" if they could live as they did in Canada, as free as any white, the law backed up by enforcement, proper marriage, and the sight of their families securely with them, able to practice the Christianity they had been taught, and the horizons of education opened to them. There were skeptics, of course, and they were chiefly the fugitives from the "free" states who had lived under the Black Codes. They had experienced the perfidy of being part free. Those fresh from slavery, however, yearned to "go home." For nearly two years they waited and worried.

Then came the magic month of August 1863, and, like a Lake Erie snow squall, the pall of despair was suddenly gone. Two things happened in Buxton that month—Abe Lincoln proved that he intended full emancipation for the slaves by sending Dr. Howe to them to find out what had happened to the Canadian Negroes, so that plans could be made for the day of freedom for four million slaves. And it was in that month that Lincoln called for Negro troops.

A friend in Detroit notified King that a Captain Ward had opened a recruiting office for the First Michigan Colored Infantry. That same night, August 12, King called an emergency meeting, and only those who had to take care of the children failed to attend. At that meeting, the man who had warned them against the possibility of a "lawless, desperate act," now gave them a fiery recruiting speech.

"Those who would be free must strike the blow," he told them. They had the choice. They could stay right in Buxton and, when they went over to Chatham on market days, could mingle with the draft-dodgers from both the Union and Confederate armies who had found refuge there. They could remain comfortable and safe and be on the side of the mobs of whites who, just the month before, had stormed through the streets of New York, killing Negroes and burning their homes because they opposed the draft to fight for the black man. He sounded only one warning. Any who went to fight must first see that their families and their land would be secure. All the young men from a single family should not go. Nor should a man leave nobody at home but a wife and small children, too small to work the land.

The same night, forty young men stepped forward and proved to King that they were free to sign up. Thirty more needed time to arrange for their families. The first contingent left for Detroit two days later, and they were welcomed by Captain Ward. Nowhere in the United States were there Negroes who had been trained in the fundamentals of drill and army combat. These young men formed most of the Buxton company in the Twenty-fourth Kent Regiment of Militia.

Abraham W. Shadd, at about 18
He was one of the Buxton members of the 24th Kent Militia
who joined Union forces at Detroit in August 1863.
Later he served in the 104th U.S. Colored Troops
with the rank of captain as aide and chief clerk
to its commander, Major Martin R. Delany.

North Buxton (Ontario) Museum

King was proudest of Solomon, the boy he had bought for $150 in 1848 so that he would not be taken from his mother in Louisiana. Captain Ward found him so bright and personable that he made him recruiting sergeant while the First Michigan was being mustered.

"He was now in his twentieth year," King wrote, "tall, squarely built, light quadroon and quite military in his bearing when dressed in the regimentals."

Solomon recruited throughout Canada West and also made forays into Kentucky to find men for his regiment. He went South with them and fought through all their battles. After the war, he married and settled in South Carolina.

The First Michigan Colored Infantry joined the Ninth Corps at Annapolis, Maryland, and fought eleven major engagements in North Carolina, Florida, South Carolina, and Georgia. Only half of them returned to Detroit to be mustered out on October 17, 1865. The rest had been killed or died of yellow fever. Though they were Canadian citizens, twenty-two of the Buxton soldiers received pensions from the United States for the rest of their lives.

The second event of August 1863 was the arrival of Dr. Howe with the secretary of the Freedmens Enquiry Commission, J. M. W. Yerrington. Dr. Howe was to report for the Commission on the Canadian Negroes and offer recommendations to Secretary of War Stanton for handling the overwhelming problem posed by emancipation of four million slaves. Though he had toured most of the concentrations of Negroes in Canada, and interviewed most of Canada's leading spokesmen, only King's lengthy comment, taken down by Yerrington, was to be appended to the report that became part of the Congressional debate on the Fourteenth Amendment.

The very presence of this huge and still handsome man

of sixty-two was assurance to Buxton that the slave would be freed. They knew this man as a veteran Abolitionist from Boston, an unrelenting foe of slavery, the man who had freed Dick Sims. They knew him better than school children do today, for John Greenleaf Whittier's florid poem "The Hero," comparing him with Sir Philip Sidney and Chevalier de Bayard as a knight-errant, is not read much. However, his wife's name is better known, since all school children sing Julia Ward Howe's *Battle Hymn of the Republic*.

Dr. Howe was the Byronic figure who both tended the wounded as surgeon and fought the Turks in Greece in 1824, and who later in life went back to the Aegean to fight for Cretan independence. But he was much more than an adventurer. Dr. Howe had an infinite compassion for the disadvantaged and founded the first school for the blind, the famous Perkins Institute, pioneered in lip-reading for the deaf, care of the feeble-minded, the insane, and for prison reforms. He published an antislavery newspaper for two years, was head of the Boston Vigilance Committee that attempted to steal Anthony Burns in 1854, and was one of the "Secret Six" who fled to Canada to escape prosecution for supporting John Brown in Kansas and at Harper's Ferry.

Dr. Howe's report was to be a most valuable weapon for Senator Charles Sumner in the Congressional debate on the Fourteenth Amendment. Perhaps the preface contains as important an observation as any of his conclusions.

> It is commonly said that the Canadian refugees are "picked men;" that the very fact of their escape from slavery is proof of their superiority, and therefore, however well they may succeed in taking care of themselves, it does not prove that ordinary Negroes can do the same . . . No! The refugees in Canada earn a living and gather property; they marry and respect women; they build churches, and send their children to schools; they improve in manners and morals

not because they are "picked men" but simply because they are *free men.*

Although he was opposed to all "colonies" of Negroes as a form of segregation, he commented quite favorably on Buxton. But he left to King the task of reporting fully on his settlement and appended it to his report.

After approving the physical aspects of the settlement and the farms and barns, Dr. Howe comments:

> There are signs of industry and thrift and comfort, everywhere; signs of intemperance, of idleness, of want, nowhere. There is no tavern and no groggery; but there is a chapel and a school-house . . . Most interesting of all are the inhabitants. Twenty years ago, most of them were slaves who owned nothing, not even their children. Now they own themselves; they own their houses and farms; and they have their wives and children about them. They are enfranchised citizens of a government which protects their rights. They have the great essentials of human happiness, "something to love, something to do, and something to hope for" and if they are not happy, it is their own fault.

He then cited Isaac Riley as an example and, in language as florid as Whittier's, describes his escape and settlement in Canada. He does not name Riley, but the circumstances are identical and so was the settler's boastful gesture at the conclusion of Dr. Howe's visit. Riley deplored Dr. Howe's hired rig and offered his own to the visitors. "He said, with pardonable vanity, 'I can send you in a wagon of *my own* (Dr. Howe's emphasis) and behind a pair of *my own* horses, who will take you to Chatham in less time than you can get there with your team.' "

Events have since proved that some of the conclusions reported by Dr. Howe to Secretary of War Stanton and the Congress were quite wrong, such as a predicted decrease in the Negro population due to "the inferior fertility of the

Isaac Riley, First Arrival at Buxton

mulatto breed," and that "natural laws which govern movements of peoples toward the tropical regions" would send the Negroes from the North to the South. Quite the reverse has taken place in recent years. Still to be tested, however, is Dr. Howe's summary:

> Finally, the lesson taught by this and other emigrations is that the Negro does best when let alone, and that we must beware of all attempts to prolong his servitude, even under the pretext of taking care of him. The white man has tried taking care of the Negro, by slavery, by apprenticeship, by colonization, and has failed disastrously in all; now let the Negro try to take care of himself. For, as all the blood and tears of our people in this revolutionary struggle will be held as cheap, if they re-establish our Union in universal freedom, so all the suffering and misery which this people may suffer in their efforts for self-guidance and support will be held cheap, if they bring about *emancipation from the control of the whites.*

So, while they differed in premises, Dr. Howe and King were in total agreement as to the goal—"emancipation from the control of the whites." King's theory of "self-emancipation" was just that.

His own section of the Freedmens Enquiry Commission report contains, in addition to facts already discussed, some pertinent comments on the characteristics of the Buxton settlers.

> The whole of my plan was this: to provide these people with a home and their children with an education; and, with these two things, I felt confident every blessing would come . . . I had an anti-alienation clause inserted in the deeds so that these people could not transfer their land to a white man until they had been here for ten years. That has kept them a compact body, so that the political power they have got will protect them. Prejudice has melted before that political

power and now the people are respected and elected to office —pathmasters, school trustees and (township) trustees . . . From the day I came here to this, there has not been a drunken coloured man in this settlement . . . With regard to the climate, I find that when the coloured people are clothed the same as Canadians, it has no more influence on them than on whites . . .

We have had one or two cases of petty larceny, and one of manslaughter. The class we have here has been very free from pilfering; it has been an exception to the generality of the race; I will tell you one fault they have; when they borrow an article from me, they never return it. I cannot say they have stolen it, but they neglect to return it. . . .

King did not neglect, however, to emphasize his confidence in his people's economic ability and integrity, plus an obvious pride in their accomplishments:

At the present time (1863), two thousand acres are deeded in fee simple, one-third of which has been paid for, principal and interest. The whole block contains nine thousand acres. The population of the settlement is about one thousand—men, women and children. I have made them self-supporting in all material matters and they are more than half supporting in their schools at the present moment. They have established two schools in the northern part of the settlement, of which they pay all the expenses, and as soon as I can get them to pay for the land, I shall make this school (the central) self-supporting. . . . I expect to settle the whole thing up in eighteen months. I have no doubt in regard to their paying every cent on their land.

King's recommendations also amount to the same as made by Dr. Howe "if freedom is established in the United States." With freedom, give the Negroes land, he advises unequivocally:

I consider that this settlement has done as well as any white settlement would have done under the same circumstances; and I am prepared to prove that a coloured community can be made industrious and self-supporting, if they are properly treated. I have no doubt that the coloured people of your country, as soon as the war is over, if they are put on farms in the South, will become self-supporting. A finer class of laborers cannot be found in the world for raising cotton. Only introduce Northern capital, or Southern capital, give them full remuneration, and in a short time you will find them an industrious, respectable, self-supporting community.

In speaking of "community" King used an all-embracing term for the entire Negro population of the South, not in the restricted sense of settlements. But since neither Howe's nor King's recommendations have ever been adopted, they remain theory.

When the news came through in March 1865 that President Lincoln had signed an act establishing a Bureau of Refugees, Freedmen, and Abandoned Lands, it was also accompanied by all the rumors. The plantations were to be broken up. Every former slave was to have "forty acres and a mule." The Freedmen's Bureau would put the emancipated slaves on the abandoned or confiscated land and the land hunger of the Negroes would be assuaged.

There was a basis of fact in these rumors. General Oliver Otis Howard, the founder and Commissioner of the Freedmen's Bureau does substantiate, in his autobiography, the intent of the original Act. Initially, the land was to be leased to the emancipated Negroes for a period of three years and a charge of six percent of its valuation as a rental, with the right to purchase at the expiration of that time. But that was Lincoln's intent, far from President Johnson's.

A movement initiated in Buxton and spread throughout Kent County. In the summer of 1865, a large delegation of Negro settlers waited upon King and presented him with another dream. They wanted to pool their resources and buy land in the South "and form a colony there, similar to the Elgin Settlement, employ free labor and raise cotton and sugar. . . ."

"They wished me to go with them, as the Elgin Settlement would no longer be required as an asylum for fugitives; coloured men were now free everywhere and my work in the Elgin Settlement was now nearly done."

They did not know that emancipation and freedom were not synonymous. Nor could they know that "forty acres and a mule" was a cruel fiction, or that President Johnson's form of Reconstruction was to differ totally from Lincoln's. Thaddeus Stevens in the House of Representatives and Charles Sumner in the Senate had not yet stormed against Johnson's policies to the extent of impeachment proceedings. The Buxton people could not know these things yet, nor the actual conditions in the South.

The plan presented to King was a practical one. After selling their holdings in Kent County, each of the men could produce between $1,000 and $1,200 in cash as down payments on land in the South. They had decided that each would buy between four and five hundred acres of cotton and sugar land abutting each other. They would duplicate Buxton on a huge tract, its schools, churches, and industries, as well as its common shipping and marketing. They would govern themselves as they did in Canada. Their community would be a beacon to all the freedmen of the United States, as the Elgin Settlement was to the fugitives in Canada.

Fortunately for them, King followed his usual course and asked for time to think about it. As far as he himself was concerned, it required little thought. It was a new challenge, a huge one. He knew the South and white southerners and he knew the slaves. The problems differed little from those he had encountered right here in Kent County, but he knew it could succeed against all opposition because a "City of God" was possible in any clime, in any economy, and among all people. He called another meeting.

There were difficulties, he pointed out. If all the settlers who had expressed their readiness to return South were to do so, a minimum of twenty thousand acres would be required. It would have to be found in one tract if they were to have their own community, their own churches and schools. He doubted that the news from the South could be totally reliable, and believed that "the country was still in a very unsettled state." He doubted too whether "planters who had lost their land by rebellion" would permit peaceful settlement. Finally, where would they find, in one block, the desirable cotton and sugar land they would need? It would have to be somewhere in the Black Belt.

He therefore proposed that he go to Washington, to the Freedmen's Bureau which had charge of the public lands, and determine the practical aspects of the plan, then report back to them. There was total agreement and King set to work in his practiced way.

Knowing that he was acting as a British subject for British subjects, he wrote to Secretary of State William H. Seward, and, late in September 1865, he received a reply from his secretary, William McDougal, welcoming him to Washington to discuss the plan. From friends in Detroit, he obtained letters of introduction to General Howard of the Freedmen's Bureau.

King ran into situations in Washington during October and November 1865 that were part and parcel of the present. It was then that Reconstruction—as applied to the Negro—failed, even before it had begun. During that summer President Andrew Johnson had usurped the powers of Congress, then recessed, to proclaim the amnesty of May 29, the offer of pardons to the Confederates who would swear allegiance, and the recognition of the governments of the rebel states which would adopt the Thirteenth Amendment ending slavery. He also appointed their governors to convene legislatures whose membership was to be elected by those whites who had voted before secession.

Just three weeks before King's arrival, Senator Charles Sumner had launched the opposition to Johnson at a speech in Boston:

> When last I addressed my fellow citizens, at the close of the late presidential canvass . . . I said to friends near me, "This is my last anti-slavery speech." I so thought at the time; for I anticipated the speedy downfall of the rebellion, carrying with it slavery. I was mistaken. Neither the rebellion nor slavery is yet ended. The rebellion has been disarmed; but that is all. Slavery has been abolished in name; but that is all . . . The work of liberation is not yet completed. Nor can it be, until the equal rights of every person once claimed as a slave are placed under the safeguard of irreversible guarantee.
>
> It is essential . . . that all men should be hailed as equal before the law; and this enfranchisement must be both civil and political. Unless this is done, the condition of the freedman will be deplorable. Exposed to every brutality, he will not be heard as a witness against his oppressor. Compelled to pay taxes, he will be excluded from all representation in the government. Without this security, emancipation is illusory. . . .

This speech, delivered at the Massachusetts Republican State Convention on September 14, was the Congressional declaration of war against Johnson, and King listened to its reverberations from the day of his arrival in the capital.

There were complications at first. Secretary of State Seward "received me courteously" but, after listening to him for a while, told King that he could not take any action for him without first obtaining some formal communication from the British ambassador. King was a British subject and diplomatic etiquette demanded it.

Fortunately, the British ambassador was Lord Bruce, a younger brother of Lord Elgin's, who was intimately informed about Buxton. King spent an hour with him and Lord Bruce confirmed the discussions he had heard.

"His Lordship told me that matters were still in a very unsettled state, the abandoned lands were being restored to rebels who were pardoned by Johnson, then President, giving the rebels both their land and their pardon."

Lord Bruce not only gave King the grim facts but advised him to tell his people to remain in Canada, at least until there was some order established.

But King had to find out for himself. He went back to Seward with the proper letter from the British ambassador and was given an introduction to General Howard.

In that interview, King's disillusionment was completed. The gentle and benign Howard, whose success with the Freedmen's Bureau during its brief existence was to assure its death at the hands of Johnson and the southerners, was even more discouraging than Lord Bruce. He told King flatly that twenty thousand acres in one block was not obtainable, nor could he guarantee that they could be retained, if found. Also, "Negroes would not be safe to settle on any of these lands in the present state of public feeling." King summarized General Howard's statements:

> In short, a state of lawlessness reigned through the slave states that was only kept in check by the strong military force kept in each state since the close of the war. The states in rebellion had to be reconstructed and a civil government

appointed and a national policy adopted with regard to the coloured race that had been set free before there could be any security for life and property in the southern states.

General Howard was being bluntly truthful. At the time of King's visit, the Freedmen's Bureau had theoretical control over 768,590 acres of land either abandoned or confiscated and for the settlement of refugees, both white and black. But he could guarantee no tenure even to the lands already leased or bought and under cultivation. His courageous fight against Johnson in the disposition of these lands was to lead to his court-martial, a victim of the larger storm raging over Reconstruction in all its aspects. All he could report to King was his own frustration. In his autobiography, General Howard discloses his own sorrow. "My heart ached for our beneficiaries, but I became comparatively helpless to offer them any permanent possession."

King returned to Buxton with the broken remnants of another dream. He did not spare the people. He called a public meeting and told them every discouraging and disheartening thing he had heard regarding both land and emancipation. But, while he advised against the establishment of a "New Buxton" in the South, he also charged them with a mission.

As soon as it was safe, he told them, there would be "a large field of usefulness" for them. If they could not return to the South as colonists "those now educated in the settlement could go and give instruction to their brethren in ignorance . . . they could go as individuals and make themselves useful."

King himself prompted the exodus from Buxton with this recommendation to his disappointed people. It was in December 1865, that the young people began to go south, and within a year there were mostly schoolchildren and their parents left in the settlement.

The young people left with King's blessing, for in no other place, not even in Africa, was the need for their missionary effort more urgent. He did not relinquish the dream of a "City of God" in the South. Though he warned the settlers against it, he prayed for the conditions which would make it possible some day.

King felt the tragedy of those Reconstruction years as keenly as any Negro. With each report in the *Toronto Globe* of another Presidential veto of civil rights legislation, with each letter from the Buxton boys down South, with the bitter sight of President Johnson's sabotage of the Port Royal experiment in South Carolina and its withering away by 1866, King suffered every frustration of the times. Port Royal had been an attempt, by Negroes who believed they had a right to "forty acres and a mule," to establish themselves on the land when it was captured early in the Civil War. That colony had virtually disappeared within five years.

Port Royal was declared officially extinct in January 1866, when Johnson restored most of the lands to the former owners. But the Southern historical theme that Negroes are incapable of meeting responsibility, which has persisted ever since, was based on Port Royal as a failure in Negro settlement rather than its imposed destruction. King quickly reacted to that propaganda theme. Among his many letters to the newspapers of all Canada West was one in February 1866.

> This settlement is a standing protest against the charges brought against the Negro, of idleness and incapacity to manage his own business. Just at this critical period in the reconstruction of the slave states, and the settlement of other questions connected with the freedom of the slave, it is well that we have at least one community of freed men, of whom it can be said that they are self-supporting and industrious. While enjoying the rights of freemen, they are well-behaved, and exercise their civil rights with as much judgment as any

> other settlers coming into the province. Today, the thermometer stands at five degrees below zero, with snow a foot deep, and yet there is not an able-bodied man in the settlement who is not in the woods with axe and crosscut saw making staves for the foreign market, and taking saw logs to the mill. . . . The settlement never has been in a more prosperous condition than it is this year.

But when even Charles Sumner's thunderous protests were dismissed in Washington, any example cited by an obscure clergyman in the wilderness of Canada West was futile. Officially, Reconstruction ended with abolition of the Freedmen's Bureau on June 30, 1872.

But a seed had been planted by the Freedmen's Bureau. Against all odds, it had established 2,677 day and night schools, with 3,000 teachers and 149,581 students. It had founded four institutions of higher education, Fisk, Howard, Hampton Institute, and St. Augustine Normal School. Most fundamentally, it had secured in the American mind one truism not yet dislodged, that education for the Negro is not merely a right but as fundamental a necessity as food. Not all the historians of the South or their Congressmen have been able to filibuster acceptance of that need out of the American attitude.

So there was a continuing and a vital necessity for Buxton and for King, not an end to his usefulness as he had declared to the settlers in 1865 before leaving for Washington. The schools of the South had desperate need for his young men and women.

☆

XVII : BUXTON'S FINEST CROP

No single community in either the United States or Canada contributed so much to the emancipated Negroes as the sons and daughters of Buxton. Until 1890, when the Black Codes were general in the South, approximately two thousand Negro graduates of the Buxton schools, the Chatham Collegiate Institute, Knox and Trinity Colleges (the latter becoming the University of Toronto) went South as educational, agricultural, political, and religious missionaries.

Some filled minor roles required by the Freedmen's Bureau in the new schools, hospitals, and land settlement, and remained on duty after its destruction. Others rose to national prominence. A recapitulation made in 1871 showed that within five years of the first exodus to the South, Buxton had sent seven hundred young men and women there. Among them were: four doctors, two army surgeons, two ministers, five educators in the new Fisk and Howard Universities for Negroes, sixteen school teachers, five lawyers, one U.S. Congressman, one State Senator, one Speaker of a State Legislature, one Internal Revenue Assessor, and one Circuit Court Judge.

By 1876, when Reconstruction was nullified and restoration almost completed, King had adapted his training program for the African Aid Society to the needs of the South, and even the adult class graduates were supplying missionaries. But among them all there was a handful who had not waited for an end of hostilities, chiefly from King's first class of classical scholars. Both Anderson R. Abbott and Jerome Riley, who had received their licenses to practice medicine in 1861, were among the original doctors to found the Freedmen's Hospital in Washington, D.C., in 1863, the first public hospital for Negroes in the United States. A "graduate" of the adult school, Thomas W. Stringer, went to Mississippi in the fall of 1865. Perhaps James Rapier was the first to reach the "deep" South, however, in December 1864.

James Thomas Rapier was one of the valiant handful of Negro legislators who have been drummed out of American history by the post-bellum historians. Yet he was the first, either black or white, to rise up in Congress and face the opposition to a Civil Rights Bill with the fundamental question of that day and today. The act of secession, he said, was "following to its legitimate conclusion the doctrine of states-rights (which of itself is secession)."

But the war had made clear that "national rights are paramount to states-rights, and that liberty and equality before the law should be coextensive with the jurisdiction of the stars and stripes."

Rapier was with the Union army as a civilian at the battle of Nashville in December 1864, and remained there while Tennessee was being cleared of Confederate troops. At General Schofield's request, he helped organize the first civil measures to be taken in Andrew Johnson's home state. He was one of the leaders of the Nashville Colored Convention in 1865, and wrote that body's appeal which was to achieve Negro suffrage and peace in that state, at least for a time. It was entitled *Address to the White Citizens of Tennessee.*

When Alabama was placed under military rule, Rapier was able to reach his father's plantation near Florence, which became a refuge for hundreds of utterly helpless blacks, driven from their slave homes by the battles or their masters. But Rapier was not allowed to remain on his plantation. He was one of the handful of educated and articulate Negroes in all the state.

He was a prominent delegate to Alabama's Constitutional Convention of 1867, one of eighteen Negroes. His legal training in Toronto made him a keen legislator, and his classical training at Buxton a forceful, incisive orator.

He pleaded against vengeance on the rebels and for adherence only to the country's Constitution. He warned the Convention against indiscriminate disfranchisement of rebels as a punishment, knowing full well that the precedent could be turned against Negroes as well as whites. He asked for a State Constitution which would disfranchise only "those persons who are now disfranchised by certain Acts of Congress."

Rapier's rationality was accompanied by a power of biting ridicule in battling the forty-six planters and others of the old South among the delegates. He is reported in the *Selma Daily Messenger* as tangling at the Convention with Henry C. Semple of Montgomery, on the question of common carriers in the state and their use by Negroes.

> He wanted the gentleman from Montgomery to understand that he did not consider himself honored by sitting in a car beside him because he was a white man simply, but only because of his intelligence. He had dined with Lords in England in his lifetime. Out of respect for their constituents the delegates ought to vote for the Amendment [for equal rights on trains].

It was while serving Alabama in many capacities that Rapier realized that the fight for emancipation could only be decided in Washington. He was elected to the Forty-third Congress where he served from 1873 to 1875, after which the whites were supreme in Alabama and the Negroes lost the vote. Meanwhile, he kept in touch with King, and one of the few remaining letters reveals his feelings. It is dated July 7, 1870.

MY DEAR FRIEND:

After a long silence on my part without any good cause, I take advantage of the present opportunity to address you

> this letter knowing full well, you have always taken a lively interest in me, and not only in myself, but all the boys who attended the old log schoolhouse and church. Whether I have profited by the education I received there or not, is not for me to practice. John Riley was preaching to a large congregation in Louisville, Kentucky; his brother Jerome was practicing medicine in the hospital in Washington. I hope to visit Canada this fall on private business, when I hope to see you. Remember me to the friends in Buxton.

Rapier made his greatest contributions in the House of Representatives during the struggle for the Civil Rights Act of 1875, which was to be negated by the Supreme Court in 1883 and, until 1964, the last attempt by Congress to implement the Fourteenth Amendment.

His speeches would often drip acid. Once, during the debate in the House, an opponent suggested that Rapier should consider the social consequences of the Civil Rights Bill. His reply:

> I am told that I must respect the prejudices of others . . . no one respects reasonable and intelligent prejudice more than I . . . But how can I have respect for the prejudices that prompt a man to turn up his nose at the males of a certain race, while at the same time he has a fondness for the females of the same race to the extent of cohabitation?

As to the infinite number of contradictions found in the attitudes toward Negroes, Rapier often delighted in taunting his fellow-Congressmen.

> Here a drunken white man is not (only) equal to a drunken Negro . . . but superior to the most orderly and sober one; here an ignorant white man is not only the equal of an unlettered Negro, but is superior to the most cultivated.

Again, regarding the common carrier clause in the Civil Rights Bill:

> Just think that the law recognizes my right to secure to me any accommodations whatever while traveling here to discharge my duties as a representative of a large and wealthy constituency. Here I am the peer of the proudest, but on a steamboat or car I am not equal to the most degraded. Is this not anomalous and ridiculous? . . . I affirm, without fear of contradiction, that any white exconvict . . . may start with me today to Montgomery, that all the way down he will be treated as a gentleman while I will be treated as a convict.

Perhaps Rapier's greatest contribution to that bitter debate was his unswerving reiteration that only Congress had the authority to enforce the Fourteenth Amendment. "Congress is the law-making power of the General Government whose duty is to see that there be no unjust and odious discriminations made between its citizens." That, he added, was the reason "I come to the National, instead of going to the local Legislatures for relief."

That James Rapier was a most worthy product of King's "Christian Education" is shown not only by his legal and oratorical brilliance. At one name-calling session he also showed his uncompromising pride.

> Mr. Speaker, nothing short of a complete acknowledgment of my manhood will satisfy me. I have no compromises to make and shall unwillingly accept any . . . I cannot willingly accept anything less than my full measure of rights as a man, because I am unwilling to present myself as a candidate for the brand of inferiority, which be as plain and lasting as the mark of Cain. If I am to be thus branded, the country must do it against my solemn protest.

Rapier was the conscience of the House of Representatives during the long battle for the Civil Rights Act of 1875. He once more struck to the heart of the controversy, in a speech on June 9, 1874, and his arguments then could just as well have been presented on the floor of the House in 1966 when another Civil Rights measure was politically doomed. At his conclusion, Rapier declared:

> Sir, it matters not how much men may differ upon the question of State and National rights; there is one class of rights, however, that we may all agree upon, namely, individual rights. But when I press my claims, I am then asked "Is it good policy?" My answer is "Policy is out of the question; it has nothing to do with it; that you can have no policy in dealing with your citizens; that there must be one law for all; that in this case justice is the only standard to be used, and you can no more divide justice than you can divide deity."

In many ways, Dr. Anderson R. Abbott's career resembled that of Dr. Martin Delany. He was not only a highly praised surgeon and physician, but also an orator, teacher, and writer. Among his writings was a delightful poem to his future wife, Mary Ann Casey, which found its way into print in the *Toronto Globe*. She said "Yes" after its publication.

THE DECLARATION

Oh Mary dear, I come not here
With blandishment to woo thee,
I know the secret of your heart,
I know full well you love me.

I see in your soft bright eye
What your lips concealeth,
I hear it in that smothered sigh
Your chaste breast upheaveth.

With courage then, I've come at last,
To tell you how I love thee,
Knowing full well you'll not refuse,
You cannot do without me.

'Tis death to me, my Mary dear,
If you reject my love plea;
You know that love, and knowing it
You would not long survive me.

Oh! then my darling do not pout,
That coldness is all put on.
Just say the word— Yes sweetest,
Go and fetch the parson.

Toronto, Nov. 1869 A.

Abbott's mentor in medicine was the first great Canadian Negro physician, Dr. Alexander T. Augusta, the same "Dr. Augusta" praised to Dr. Howe by the President of Trinity College, and a fugitive born in Norfolk, Virginia. He was practicing medicine in Toronto when the Emancipation Proclamation encouraged him to write to Secretary of War Stanton, offering his services as a surgeon. To his surprise, he was immediately called to Washington for examination. There he found opposition from the Army Surgeon-General, and to obtain his examination, was forced to get special orders from Stanton. Anderson Abbott, in his own manuscript on his experiences during the Civil War, relates the following regarding that examination, as told to him by a member of the Examining Board:

> He says that Dr. Cronyn, who was president of the examining board, having occasion to go into the Surgeon-General Hammond's office a short time after Augusta had passed, was asked by the General: "I say Cronyn, how did you come to let that nigger pass?" Dr. Cronyn replied: "The fact is, General, that nigger knew more than I did and I could not help myself."

Augusta was first commissioned as a major of Cavalry

and surgeon of the Seventh United States Colored Troops at Camp Barker in Washington. It was this tent hospital to which Dr. Abbott came on July 26, 1863, and soon was followed by Jerome Riley. The three Canadian Negroes were part of the founding staff of the Freedmen's Hospital. Dr. Augusta was transferred first to Camp Birney and then to Savannah, Georgia, to establish a freedmen's hospital there. He was mustered out as a lieutenant-colonel.

Anderson Abbott was a captain in rank and was Surgeon-in-Charge on Dr. Augusta's transfer. But before the latter left Washington, the two had some singular adventures. It was Dr. Augusta who initiated the eventual ending of discrimination on District of Columbia street cars. He had been summoned as an important witness in a court-martial, but a conductor on the Pennsylvania Ave. cars threw him off. As a result, he was late for the proceedings and the judge advocate demanded an explanation in writing before holding him in contempt. Dr. Augusta obliged, but also sent a copy to Senator Charles Sumner who immediately read it in the Senate and presented his bill to end such discrimination.

The two were also the first Negroes, other than diplomatic representatives from Haiti, to attend a public levee in the White House. This was in the winter of 1863 and Dr. Abbott's account of it is confirmed by the news item that appeared in the *Washington Star* in its story of the occasion. "During the evening Dr. Augusta, the colored Surgeon of the District of Columbia Colored Regiment, dressed in his major's uniform, also Asst. Surgeon Dr. Abbott, colored of the same regiment, called upon the President and was kindly received by him."

They had none of the difficulties encountered by Frederick Douglass over a year later, at the ball celebrating the second inauguration. Dr. Abbott relates:

Dr. Anderson Abbott

As a graduate, as an Army surgeon, and as a physician in Chatham.

Toronto Public Libraries

> Mr. Lincoln on seeing Augusta advanced eagerly a few paces forward, grasped his hand, and, as he held the doctor's hand Robert Lincoln, who had been standing beside his mother about six paces off, came up to the President and asked a question very hastily, the purport of which I took to be—"Are you going to allow this innovation?"—referring doubtless to our presence there. The President replied promptly "Why not?" Nothing more was said and Robert Lincoln returned to his mother's side, while the President turned again to the doctor who gave his hand a hearty shake, and then I was introduced and the President shook hands with me also, and we passed on to a position in front of Mrs. Lincoln and was again introduced to that lady.

They were ushered into the East Room and "there we were destined to undergo an ordeal. . . ."

> The moment we entered the room, which was crowded and brilliantly lit up, we became the cynosure of all eyes. I never experienced such a sensation before as I did when we entered the room. We could not have been more surprised ourselves or created more surprise if we had been dropped down through a sky-light. I suppose it was because it was the first time in the history of the U.S. when a colored man had appeared at one of these Levees. What made us more conspicuous of course was our uniforms. Colored men in the uniforms of U.S. military officers of high rank had never been seen before. I felt as though I should have liked to crawl into a hole. But, as we had decided to break the record, we held our ground.

Dr. Abbott returned to Canada after mustering out in July 1866, but Dr. Jerome Riley went on to Pine Bluffs, Arkansas, where he practiced medicine and was the County Coroner there. Dr. Abbott was to become the first Negro as Kent County Coroner in 1874. When he settled in Chatham, Dr. Abbott was immediately elected to the boards of the

Chatham Collegiate Institute and the Wilberforce Educational Institute, in company with his former teacher. He served with King for the next ten years. He was also elected President of the Kent County Medical Society in 1878.

Dr. Abbott was not only honored by his colleagues. He was elected the first President of the Chatham Literary and Debating Society and edited the church paper for the Chatham BME Church. When he moved to Dundas in 1881, he was appointed and elected, by whites chiefly, to responsible posts in both educational and church affairs of the city. In Toronto he was welcomed into the Grand Army of the Republic Post and became aide-de-camp to the Commanding Officer of the Department of New York in 1889. In GAR ranks Anderson Abbott achieved the highest prestige, not only in Canada but in the United States, ever awarded a Negro.

When the great Negro surgeon who founded Provident Hospital (for Negroes) in Chicago, Dr. Daniel H. Williams, was called to Washington, D.C., to reorganize Freedmen's Hospital, he appointed Dr. Anderson Abbott the Surgeon-in-Chief at Provident while he was away. Later, Dr. Abbott was on the staffs of the Illinois Colleges of Medicine and Dentistry.

Wherever he lived, Anderson Abbott was an outstanding citizen. In Canada, where Negro participation in civic life was (and is) so much greater, his abilities as an educator and orator were recognized. In both countries, the medical profession accepted him as another of many able Negro surgeons. He returned to Canada several times, to die there in 1913, because of the greater freedom to be found as a Negro.

In another state, Mississippi, another Buxton man assumed leadership of his people during its blackest years. Thomas W. Stringer was a grown man and a family man when he took up land on the 12th Concession. It was fully paid for by 1856, so he must have been an able farmer.

Stringer was a fugitive from the Fugitive Slave Law, having lived in Ohio as a boy after escape from Mississippi with his family. In Ohio, he was a most active layman in the African Methodist Episcopal Church. He was one of the founders of the British Methodist Episcopal Church in Buxton, and was so able as its elder that he was assigned organizational duties throughout Canada West by the Church.

When he went south, at the end of 1865, it was in behalf of the AME Church in the United States. He established the church at Vicksburg and again was so successful that he was appointed general superintendent of all the AME churches in the state. The first conference ever held by that Church in Mississippi took place in Vicksburg in 1868. Two years later, Stringer had founded thirty-five churches with nearly five thousand communicants.

He accomplished equally remarkable strides in development of Negro Masonry in Mississippi. It assumed a social and economic significance in the lives of the besieged Negroes of that state that can never be calculated. Inherent in membership, of course, was mutual aid, but in addition the Lodges supplied medical and emergency aid to the impoverished Negroes. Perhaps their greatest contribution to Mississippi morale during all the difficult years was a program that may appear somewhat insignificant today.

All through slavery Negroes had never been able to hold ceremonial funerals or rest in marked graves except when the master allowed them. The fundamentalist depth of the Negro religious tendencies demanded some recognition of the rapture they felt in "going to Jesus." To perpetuate satisfaction of all these needs, Stringer organized the Fraternal Life Insurance Benefit in 1880 and it became the most successful cooperative Negro business venture in the Black Belt. By

1908 it had fourteen thousand members and owned outright a thousand acres of land along the Yazoo and Mississippi Railroad.

Thomas W. Stringer is credited by the records as the guiding hand in this Masonic growth. Beginning with the Stringer Lodge in Vicksburg in 1867, the Lodges grew in such number and membership during the next few years that the Vicksburg Lodge was named the Most Worshipful Stringer Grand Lodge in 1876.

Stringer was no orator, nor was his education legislative or legal. He had none of Rapier's classical scholarship either. King's adult classes were severely practical. But, as one historian states, "The man had a genius for organization." It was inevitable that he should apply his abilities in behalf of his race in the stormy political arena. Here at least one part of his experiences at Buxton, his membership in the Courts of Arbitration, were to be invaluable. He was named the most influential Negro delegate to Mississippi's famous "Black and Tan" Constitutional Convention in 1868 and "the most powerful political leader of his race in the state" for several years afterward.

The "Black and Tan" Convention of 1868 was either a "malodorous conglomeration of Solomons or sages," as its secretary Colonel (Confederate) J. J. Power declared, or a continued "Slavocracy Legislature," as a northern commentator called it. Whichever authority chosen, it was not a constitutional convention at all, for of all the requirements listed by the first Reconstruction Act of March 2, the only concession to the Negroes was to rights on public conveyances. Stringer led a demand for public education applicable to Negroes and legalization of intermarriage between white and black, but was unsuccessful in both. Immediately afterward an all-white convention was organized in Jackson and it adopted the following:

> That the nefarious design of the Republican Party in Congress to place the white men of the southern states under the governmental control of their late slaves, and degrading the Caucasian race as the inferior of the African Negro, is a crime against the civilization of the age, which has only to be mentioned to be scorned by all intelligent men, and we therefore call upon the people of Mississippi to vindicate alike the superiority of their race to the Negro and their political power, and to maintain constitutional liberty.

The Black and Tan Convention was the third in the state to reject the Fourteenth Amendment flatly. Mississippi was the pioneer state of the South in the disfranchisement of Negroes through the vagrancy and "grandfather" clauses, literacy tests, poll taxes, and other laws. It was also to lead all thirteen southern states in the number of recorded lynchings between 1882 and 1950.

Many of the Buxton girls went south too, encouraged by King, to fill the urgent need for teachers all over the South, in the Freedmen's Bureau schools and those founded by private donors through the Christian Commission, American Missionary Association, American Tract Society, and the churches. By 1866 these groups had contributed approximately $12,000,000 for the establishment of schools for the Negroes. But their efforts were hampered more by lack of teachers than money.

As recently as 1882, Buxton girls were going south to teach. King encouraged the girls to attend Chatham Collegiate Institute, and many of them boarded in his home while receiving their teacher training there. One was Harriet Rhue Hatchett, who, at the age of seventeen, graduated from CCI and went south to teach near Licking River, Kentucky, for ten years. She taught the Negro children of her mother's childhood friends, and also former slaves. Her mother, Serena

DR. ALFRED SHADD (*standing*) AND HIS BROTHERS
On the left is William who farmed the land settled by his grandfather, Abraham Shadd; on the right is Charles who became a teacher.

North Buxton (Ontario) Museum

Lewis, had escaped from there herself in 1853. At the Underground Railroad Station in Marshall, Michigan, the following year, she met another fugitive heading for Canada. It was Harriet's father, William Isaac Rhue, who had escaped from the Eastern Shore of Maryland. They were married and had fourteen children. William Rhue settled on the 6th Concession where he farmed two hundred acres some sixty years. Harriet taught both her father and mother to read.

Harriet continued to play the piano after Mrs. King had her "spell." King gave her the freedom of St. Andrews Church, where she played for the choir and began writing hymns. In Chatham, she had more opportunity to study music.

Harriet Rhue returned from Kentucky to Buxton when that state's "Black Code" proved unbearable. In the choir of the First Baptist Church of Buxton she met Millard Hatchett, whose beautiful tenor voice was exceptional. They married and Harriet returned to writing hymns.

In 1913, her first hymn was published. It was "The Sacred Spot," and was adopted by the Canadian Army of World War I as its official marching hymn. In 1918, "Jesus, Tender Shepherd of My Soul" was published, and in 1936, "In the Land Beyond the Sky." All three may still be found in hymnals.

Among the many Buxton boys and girls who remained in Canada was Alfred S. Shadd who first taught at Buxton and then went on to medicine. He settled in Saskatchewan, where he practiced in the Carrot River Valley for some years. He became interested in cattle and began experimentation in breeding cattle adapted to conditions there. There is a memorial in his honor for contributing so much to the province in this area.

In Kinistino, where there was no schoolteacher, Dr.

Shadd taught school. When he felt that an opposition newspaper was needed in the valley, he published the *Melfort Journal* and wrote its editorials. When the Conservative Party needed a provincial candidate and none of greater stature was available, Dr. Shadd ran for office and was beaten by a narrow margin. He died in Winnipeg in 1915, one of Saskatchewan's most prominent citizens.

Aside from Dr. Shadd, Abraham D. Shadd of the 11th Concession and the Buxton schools fathered two lawyers and three schoolteachers.

The family was typical. William King's formula resulted in the production of men and women who, despite the disadvantage of their color, have contributed to many communities in at least two countries.

☆

PART SEVEN: THE LAST BATTLE

XVIII : POLITICS AND PEACE

WILLIAM KING did not relinquish the dream of a "Buxton of the South" until 1871, when the last Confederate state had been readmitted to the Union and promptly set about evading Reconstruction. When his students wrote back from the South that the Ku Klux Klan and the Knights of the White Camellia were the actual police authorities, he gave up. He had one consolation, though. He had lived to see an end to the slave trade from Africa to the United States.

Ironically, both Buxton and King were never so prosperous as during the war years and Reconstruction. There was a market for everything the settlers could raise or make from the land. In the year 1866 alone, approximately 500,000 feet of prime lumber was sent down the Center Road tramway, for transshipment to high prices at all Lakes ports. There was a marked increase in cash crops such as grains and tobacco, for by then the first phase of the drainage system had been completed and each family had more tillable land.

Neither the schools nor the church had any remaining financial problems. The schools had been incorporated into the common school system but, in addition, the settlers were contributing an average of one thousand dollars annually in order to continue King's classical curriculum. New schools of their own brick were built in Buxton from the tax funds paid for common schools.

The Buxton Mission too was more prosperous than ever, for it received an income of three hundred dollars annually from the £50 that was voted by the Irish Presbyterian General Assembly in 1859, after King and William Howard Day appeared before them. In addition, St. Andrews had a devoted congregation. Their average number during the 1860's, despite the exodus to the South, was 250, and the number of children in the Sabbath School averaged 118.

When the new St. Andrews Church and Manse had been completed in 1868, the final report of the Buxton Building Fund handed in by its treasurer showed that the Church had cost $2,751.50 and that there was a balance of $3,114.75. This was approximately the sum intended for new schools, but the shift of Buxton's day schools to the common school system had made that unnecessary. In 1870 the General Assembly voted its appreciation to King once more and approved the recommendation of the Home Mission Committee that the balance of the Building Fund be invested, and the income granted to King for life in appreciation of his financial sacrifices of the prior twenty years.

Now King's own financial problems were resolved. His income was adequate for his modest scale of living. He received $150 a year from the Buxton congregation, and the Maidstone congregation petitioned the Synod for his services on alternate Sundays, for which he received an additional $150 annually. Finally, several of the mortgages he himself had financed for the settlers and for the sawmill were repaid.

For the seven years of Reconstruction King enjoyed his ministerial duties, and he had whole days in his study at the Clayton House for his personal communion.

There were still secular problems such as the continued expansion of the drainage system and the Raleigh Township Council meetings at which he had to represent the settlement.

King was busy with church affairs such as the formation of the Presbytery of Chatham, in 1869, at which he presided. He also became involved in the long negotiation leading to union between the Free Church and the United Presbyterian Church.

Self-government in the settlement and a brand-new church, new schools and competent teachers spelled William King's final achievement of his life's purpose. After 1873, he was to be rid of the "secular affairs" against which he had protested and pleaded for so many years. After 1880, when Rev. John Cairns arrived, fresh from Knox College, to become St. Andrews' second minister, King was relieved of the cares of the congregation and could devote himself to his first love, the role of missionary among the people.

He was to enjoy this function for the rest of his active life, and all that he recorded in those peaceful years reflects his happy communion with his people and his God. King appears to have adjusted to Jemima's continued illness and his last secular battle was fought in 1872.

During that year, King and his old comrade, Archie McKellar, were pawns in a typical Canadian political struggle. As ever, it involved the Tories vs. Reform Party. The actual target was the McDonald-Cartier coalition government formed with the Confederation in 1867. The ammunition used by the Tories was a series of five "scandals" charging misdeeds and defalcations by Reform Party leaders in land, railroad, and other transactions. One of these charges of corruption was labeled the "Elgin Association Frauds." Archie McKellar was the primary object of attack because he was Commissioner of Crown Lands in the McDonald cabinet. King was a secondary target because his influence over the Negro vote invariably saw it cast for Reform Party candidates. Both were accused of embezzling Elgin Association funds, but the amounts cited varied considerably, from four thousand dollars to sixty-eight thousand dollars. Before it had run its course, the "scandal" also involved two of King's nephews, and even William Howard Day.

McKellar's fight was in Parliament, and when it ended, with standard political bed-fellowship, he was still Crown Commissioner and still a highly respected member of the government, esteemed by both Tories and his own party members.

King's war was in the newspapers. Rufus Stephenson, M.P., from Kent County, Tory and owner of the *Chatham Planet*, was in charge of the "Elgin Association Frauds" for his party. His material appeared in his own paper and also in the new *Toronto Mail*, a newspaper established by the Tories for political use against the Reform Party *Toronto Globe*.

The *Toronto Mail* opened the eight-month campaign on August 15, 1872, and grew nastier as the editions went by. As an example, when the *Toronto Globe* reported in all detail the twenty-three-year report to Parliament made by the Elgin Association secretary, Thomas Henning, and its treasurer, Rev. William Reid, there was only one item paid to Rev. William King in all those years. It stated: "Paid traveling expenses of Rev. Wm. King . . . $550.53." This averaged twenty-four dollars a year. Otherwise, the financial condition of the Association was in fine shape.

The *Toronto Mail* blithely disregarded the report to Parliament. Ten days later it printed its own financial statement as follows:

By cash, Remuneration of Messrs. McKellar and King, for noble services rendered on behalf of the coloured freedmen of Buxton, in Great Britain and Canada; also, for postage; likewise, stationery, firewood and incidental expenses; eke (sic) mileage to and from Buxton and Chatham; likewise prayers on account of Southern Rebellion; also other minor expenses which need not be detailed in connection with a work so glorious as that of Emancipation, but which were legitimately incurred, inasmuch as Mr. King is a clergyman and Mr. McKellar a member of the great Reform Party . . . $68,644.74.

During the early months of the political war, King kept silent. His own conscience and the regard of his associates was unchanged. At the height of the outcry, he was elected to the high honor of Moderator of the General Assembly of the Presbyterian Church of Canada. When word reached England that King was under attack, the stockholders were indignant. Earl Spencer, who had become Viceroy of Ireland, wrote from Dublin: "I renounce all claim to £250 which I paid to the Elgin Association for the settlement at Buxton, Canada West."

Only when the *Toronto Globe* demanded a statement, in January 1873, did King reply, and he unleashed three packed columns of attack quite as vitriolic as those in the *Mail* against him. He wrote:

> The money which the *Mail* charges me with embezzling has been accounted for ten years ago to the General Assembly of the Canadian Presbyterian Church to which the Buxton Mission belongs. On rendering my account to that venerable body, I received publicly the thanks of the General Assembly for the faithful and efficient manner in which I had discharged the duty of the Mission.

Then, after describing his mission to the British Isles, he asks, "What part had Mr. McKellar in that mission? None whatever." He defended his friend at length and explained why he had had him speak at the Edinburgh meeting. "I wished him to identify himself with a cause that was popular in Edinburgh, as he had identified himself with the same when it was unpopular in Chatham."

> I have hitherto treated these calumnies with silent contempt, for there are men like the member from Kent, of such low instincts and grovelling desires, that they see in no scheme for benevolence for the good of our fellow-man anything but money, and they imagine that all who engage in such work are actuated only by mercenary motives . . . The cause of the coloured people in Chatham and vicinity has been very unpopular, but it is now rising in public favor. When they had nothing to give, but few respected them; but now, when the Elgin Settlement can give 200 votes, that is worth something. The member from Kent might be seen before the last election, going through the settlement, hat in hand, begging votes, and taking the coloured man into his warmest embrace, and dandling their babies on his knee. Why this change? The settlers had votes and he wished to obtain them, to give him a vote in the Dominion Parliament. Rufus Stephenson knew full well that a vote at Ottawa, given in favor of a corrupt and sinking Administration, *was money*.

By March 1873, it apparently was time to go into real scandal, the "Pacific" railroad frauds beside which the Elgin Association affair was reduced to petit larceny. But the last salvo in the *Toronto Mail* on March 29, 1873, leaves a mystery.

The newspaper, in a lengthy editorial, repeated the familiar charges and continued:

> Moreover, Mr. King has a nephew, named King Bruce, who labours under the hallucination that his uncle, on one or two occasions, swindled him. He was book-keeper at the

saw-mill and was also well acquainted with the workings of the Association. When he saw our expose of its affairs he, with the instinct of a true King, thought he might make money out of it. The uncle had made money by swindling, the nephew would make money by exposing his uncle.

Then followed two letters ostensibly signed by King Bruce, son of King's sister Elizabeth, who had moved into Buxton in 1857, and then to Toronto in 1871. They offered to sell to the *Mail* for one hundred dollars, "but not less," information concerning the Elgin Association. "The facts would be relative to amounts of moneys received, history of the Buxton Mill, history of some land sales, and other matters bearing upon the affairs and information relating to the Buxton Mission."

Whether or not these letters actually were received is not known, nor is it known whether the *Mail* bought the "information." That was the last printed word on the whole scandal. Nor does King mention King Bruce or is he referred to in all the lengthy Parliamentary record.

The whole affair does not seem to have influenced the people of Canada West a single bit. They still revered the man and gave dramatic proof of their regard that same Fall.

On July 7, 1873, King and his wife boarded the train in Chatham for New York and overseas to the British Isles. There were two purposes in the trip, the major one a last effort to help Jemima King back to normalcy. The hope was that a visit to the homeland again might bring her out of what appeared to be a schizophrenic retirement from the world. While her father was dead, Jemima had relatives in Liverpool.

The second was to have no purpose—a vacation—the first purely self-serving action taken by William King since he had landed in Philadelphia forty years before.

Leaving Mrs. King in Liverpool, King went on to London. He did not preach or even search out a worthy cause. He was a most traditional tourist. In fact, his own listing of the tours he made in London does not depart from the customary itinerary of today, except perhaps the omission of the side excursions to the night life of Soho. He saw the Parliament buildings, the Bank of London, the government buildings, St. Paul's, Westminster Abbey, the British Museum, the Zoological Gardens, and watched the changing of the guards at Buckingham Palace. But perhaps he would not have been in character without finding, in Whitechapel, a Home for Nameless and Destitute Boys as well as the standard tourist props.

From London he wrote home to Buxton that he was rejoining Mrs. King in Liverpool and that they were to sail home on the SS *Hungarian* on a scheduled sailing date.

The word was first received at the *Toronto Globe* and its flag was flown at half mast. It was telegraphed to Chatham and sent by fast horse to Buxton.

The SS *Hungarian* had sunk at sea without a single survivor.

All through Buxton Settlement, the men were called in from the fields and the families went to all three churches. In Chatham, the stores along King Street began to close and they opened the following morning to hang mourning black on the store fronts. Mayor R. O. Smith had proclaimed a day of mourning for Rev. King. As the news speeded through the farms and villages, the Negroes particularly banded together in sorrow and wore their Sunday clothing for church.

But before the day was over, it was turned into one of jubilation. Archie McKellar had telegraphed from Toronto. The Kings had not been aboard the scheduled passage at all. When he had reached Liverpool, King was sick with a minor stomach ailment. He was put to bed by a physician and missed the ill-fated sailing. The Negroes returned to their churches, this time to offer their prayers of thanksgiving.

Three weeks later the Kings were greeted at the Chatham railroad station late at night. There was a huge torchlight procession and "Welcome Home" placards on the store fronts. There were happy speeches and even in the taverns, despite King's uncompromising temperance speeches, there was joy with every drink.

Happiest of all was the company of the Twenty-fourth Kent Infantry, in full uniform, their dark faces reflecting their happiness in the glare of the torchlight. They were the proud escort back to the Kings' home in Buxton.

☆

XIX : PASTOR WITHOUT PORTFOLIO

Officially, William King ended his ministry at St. Andrews Church in 1880, but actually he never left it. In no way did it alter his patriarchate, except that he did not preach so often at Buxton.

He continued his missionary calls throughout the settlement, his visits with Robin Phares. There was no lapse in his rigid examination of every new teacher and class in the schools. He was still re-elected President of the Buxton Branch of the Upper Canada Bible Society, which he had founded on October 29, 1860. He was to remain its first and only president until 1891, when his physical condition began to match his age.

Until then, he was hale and vigorous, as busy as he had always been, but without the problems he had lived with for so many years. The pressures were gone, and by now the only shadow on his days was the haunting presence of Jemima in her bedroom of the Clayton House. The trip to England had done nothing to bring her back to the world, and now in the last years before her dcath, she showed no interest in anything, not even the piano.

But William King was surrounded by love. It was everywhere in the settlement and met him at the gates of the homes as he made his calls. That was why he was also a collective responsibility as the years went on. The old settlers who had been at school during those years recalled the worry.

King made his calls on a big horse named Ajax who never hurried, just ambled along. They began to notice that often, when King passed them on Ajax and they called out a greeting, he did not answer. This was most unusual because he always had the heartiest of responses. Soon they discovered that he often fell asleep on the horse.

What if he fell off while asleep? They called a meeting without notifying King, and the sole topic on the agenda was the danger to him in riding Ajax. It was decided to present him with a petition that hereafter he ride in his carriage while he made his rounds. He had always respected the democratic decisions made at their meetings and he might accept this one.

He did, and that caused another problem. Whenever he drove into Chatham, he insisted on taking the short cut through the Duck Pond Swamp which had never been totally drained. He could be mired or could tip over. Should a sudden storm come out of Lake Erie, he would be exposed and stranded.

A spy system was established. Whenever King announced his intention of driving to Chatham, somebody in the Clayton House would hurry to the school and notify the schoolteacher. A boy would be assigned to follow King but to hide in the woods. They feared his anger if he knew he was being guarded.

William Newby, who died in 1966 at the age of 90, after seventy years as Buxton's cobbler and elder in the British Methodist Episcopal church, once was caught by King right in the swamp.

> First he asked me why I wasn't in school. I couldn't tell him the truth, that we were watching out for him. And I couldn't lie to him. You didn't lie to Reverend King. So I guess I just didn't say anything. He got so angry. He told me to go right back to school and report to the teacher. He said when he got back from Chatham he'd tell my teacher too. And he did. After that, they always sent some other boy after him.

King had received many honors in his lifetime, but in

the evening of that life there was one that he prized most of all. It was a scroll and a silver water pitcher and drinking cup that he was given by all the residents of Buxton on May 3, 1880, to mark his retirement from the active ministry. Both were at his bedside when he died fifteen years later.

It was a Thursday night, and he spent part of the day as he had for thirty years when in Buxton, preparing for the weekly Bible Class. But that evening, as he crossed the grass to the church he saw the carriages and the crowds. Large as it was, the new St. Andrews Church was overflowing. They had come from miles around and from other cities to give him the surprise. Both the Baptist and the British Methodist Episcopal congregations were there. The children were there.

Led by the new Rev. Cairns, they prayed for him and sang for him. Then a delegation read the scroll they had written in the finest penmanship on rag paper:

Rev. and Dear Sir:

We the undersigned inhabitants of this settlement, deem this, the eve of your departure from us, a fitting occasion to express our due appreciation of the many favors you have shown us for the past thirty years, not only in your capacity as a Christian minister, but also as a true friend of our race—favors so many and so great that we can neither enumerate nor adequately express them in words.

When we were under the iron arm of oppression in the United States of America, when the national laws of that great Republic disregarded those rights wherewith we were endowed by nature, when, with a few honorable exceptions, the minds of her people were in an unfit state to receive the grand truth uttered by our Lord, "Thou shalt love thy neighbor as thyself," you came forward in the ranks of that exceptional few, midst persecutions and obstructions many and vexatious on both sides of the great lakes, and defended our cause. By unremitting, indefatigable and persevering efforts you surmounted every obstacle that stood in your way.

Desirous to make good use of the privilege granted by Her Gracious Majesty the Queen who offered us an asylum in Canada, you founded this settlement for the express purpose of alleviating our sorrows and ameliorating our helpless condition, and today this tract of country which we found in a state of primeval antiquity—seemingly unfit for the habitation of man—is, under your patronage and kind counsel, converted into a fruitful land, contributing supplies not only to our homes, but also to distant lands, and affording habitations of comfort to us and our children as well as hundreds of the human family. The monuments of the progress of this settlement occupy her soil; and will remain to commemorate your noble acts, so that unborn generations shall rise to bless your name. Your illustrious deeds have endeared you to us, and proved to the world that, with equal advantages, the coloured race is as all other races of mankind. We hope that at some future day, the grand design of carrying the gospel to our brethren in Africa through our instrumentality, which you worked out years ago, will be worked out by us.

Our sons who have been educated under your kind care, your watchful eye and your Christian teaching, are now filling positions which do honor to the coloured race. You have never relaxed any of the vigor with which you commenced this good work; you still continue to assist our young men who desire to excel in education, and Mrs. King never failed to second all your efforts for our good. We cannot express in words the great loss we are about to sustain by your removal from our midst. To us, it would have been a source of unutterable delight if you could have spent the evening of your days amongst us. Never, while memory holds her seat, shall we cease to think of the good you have done to our race. As a Christian minister, regardless of our creeds, you never neglected to point us to the Lamb of God that taketh away "the evils of the world," and you were always willing in that capacity to help us in time of adversity.

He was too filled with emotion to reply at length and every word he said was taken down and preserved. He not only thanked them but did not fail to preach too.

> I have lived to see slavery abolished in the West Indies, United States and Brazil, and Africa opened in the interim to commerce, civilization and missionary effort. A bright future lies before your race; but remember to improve that future. You must be educated, industrious, and moral, and I do believe that when Ethiopia stretches forth her hands to God, her own sons and daughters will be the honoured instruments in carrying religion and civilization to their benighted countrymen.

As he backed away from the pulpit a lone voice took up the lines of his favorite hymn *In Immanuel's Land*—"The sands of time are sinking; the dawn of heaven breaks . . . ," and all joined in.

The rest was quiet triumph, years filled with reverence from his own and the new generations. For a time, he considered moving to either London or Toronto since he was called upon so much more, now that he was free, by the Presbytery and the Synod. But there was always the question of how he was to take care of Jemima. In Buxton, he could make his trips to preach all over Kent, and even travel to the other cities of Canada on church business, without the least worry about her care. By now, Mollie was gone and her children grown up. Joseph Simon took care of his land, and Mrs. Simon of Jemima. She was better off at Clayton House.

By the end of 1880, the winter trips into Chatham for the monthly meetings of the Kent County High School Board were becoming too strenuous. He resigned, and on February 2, 1881, at their regular monthly meeting of the Board of Trustees, the following resolution was passed:

> WHEREAS, the Rev. Wm. King has ceased to be a member of this Board, be it
>
> *Resolved,* That the High School Board of the County of Kent desires to record their very high appreciation of the faithful manner in which Mr. King has discharged his duties as a member of the Board and as secretary thereof during the long period of twenty-eight years, and beg to express the hope that the many qualifications of mind and heart that have been productive of so much prosperity to the High School and that have always won the respect and cordial esteem of his colleagues on the Board may long meet the fullest appreciation in the locality to which he is about to remove.

However, he did not move, not until the summer after Jemima's death in November 1887. One reason was the new family he was acquiring. The Clayton House was no longer a sprawling temple of silence where at one end he lived in the isolation of his study, and at the other Jemima lived in her own withdrawn world. In between them came youth and laughter as his nieces and nephews, grandnieces and grandnephews took possession. It became the kind of home he could remember in Ulster, with all his brothers and sisters providing the noisy normalcy of children in a house.

By then King had only two sisters left, Mary Kane and Catherine Donahue, both living on the King homestead in Delta. James had died the year before, and John in 1865. Jane and Elizabeth were long gone, but eight of Elizabeth's nine children survived and one of them, Mary Bruce, began the invasion.

Mary came to visit her uncle from Delta in 1856 and she stayed in the Clayton House—and stayed and stayed. The reason became apparent when she insisted on helping in the school where a young divinity student from Knox College, John Straith, was in charge for six months. He was an exceptionally able teacher and King had hopes of keeping him. But John Straith and Mary Bruce had other plans. When he returned to Knox College, to finish his studies and be ordained, she returned to Delta. In the summer of 1857, there was a wedding reception in the Clayton House, and King lost both his teacher and his niece. Rev. John Straith had a congregation in Hamilton, and there he remained for the rest of his life while he and Mary had ten children. In those early years, the best King could do was bring Peter Straith, John's brother, into the settlement.

But in later years, all of the Straith children joined the Bruce children and Catherine Donahue's children in the Clayton House. There was always a batch of them visiting "Uncle" King, and as they married, their children were brought to the Clayton House too. Ann Kane, Mary and Annie Straith were to take care of King in his last years. Henry Kane settled on the 14th Concession in 1872, and soon his children joined the others in the Clayton House.

Even after he moved to Chatham in July 1888, the children followed "Uncle" King. When Jemima died, King leased the remainder of his one hundred acres, after he had turned over five acres to the church and school, to Joseph Simon with an option to purchase. He himself bought two lots at 49 West St. in Chatham, at one thousand dollars each, and enlarged the house on one of them to accommodate the children. That too was a happy house. Annie Straith (Jamieson) wrote:

> Thus with Mary, Harry, Catherine and their comrades coming and going, music and laughter enlivened the house. But it was "Uncle" King who appeared ever the happiest one of all when listening to their songs or joining in their mirth. He liked the society of young people. If success crowned their efforts he was glad with them, and if not, with a wise shake of his head and a twinkle in his eye, he reminded them of

Lord Beaconfield's beatitude. "Blessed are they that expect nothing, for they shall not be disappointed."

The Chatham years were happy ones in spite of his declining health. When the doctor would not allow him to drive to Buxton for his rounds, he was busy either with international correspondence or visitors. His mail came from every state in the Union and from all the Canadian provinces, for the Buxton boys and girls had scattered throughout the continent. To the very end he continued correspondence with Dr. Richard M. Johnson, who was to serve forty years as a Presbyterian medical missionary in Africa.

To the very last, he was intensely interested in the world around him. Until 1893, he was to preach often at the First Presbyterian Church in Chatham, and his text each time related to the objectives of his lifetime, all incorporated in a "City of God." In May 1889, he was delighted to read a report in the *Christian Leader* that the Chalmers Memorial Church in West Port now had a congregation of 1,435. He had helped in the fund-raising for the new church, in both the United States and Canada, and was overjoyed. He wrote immediately to the pastor:

> My object in writing to you is to ask you to send me a report of the Mission. I understand that such a report was published . . . The Sabbath School began in 1844 with about twenty-five scholars. When I left in 1846 there were 300 on the roll. The few who attended the Church were only collected on the Sabbath by constant visiting during the week. The people, from neglect, had sunk down to the lowest state of moral degradation. I had seen slavery in its worst form in the cotton and sugar growing states of America, and I confess I had seen nothing so bad as the scenes of wretchedness I met when visiting in West Port. In many plantations, in calm summer evenings, when the day's labour was done, I have heard the voice of prayer and praise from many a

> negro cabin. Such scenes I never met with when visiting in West Port.
>
> I rejoice to hear what God has done, and the blessing which has attended the labour of His servants. West Port Church was begun with much earnest prayer and strong faith in the power of the Gospel, and today it has been amply rewarded by a large and flourishing Congregation gathered from a degraded people.

William King's last official work for his church was to travel to Toronto in 1893, when he attended the Pan-Presbyterian Council held there. Its sessions were as much occupied with honoring the "elder statesman" of the Presbyterian Church in Canada as with business.

King's last journey before he was bedridden was in June 1893, when he attended the King family reunion on the old homestead in Delta, Ohio. He was the last survivor of the original family and the guest of honor attended by eighty of his brothers' and sisters' children, grandchildren, and great-grandchildren.

In a speech from the steps of the King home, he told these descendants of the pioneers of the year 1834 and the Six Mile Woods of the abiding faith of such men and women who raised the first log cabin where he stood. It was that faith that he was to take as his text in the last sermon King ever preached, on Sunday, June 11, in Delta Presbyterian Church. It was almost to a day forty-six years after he, the first Presbyterian minister to preach in northwestern Ohio, had delivered the first sermon in the King barn.

His text was from John 3: 4: "Jesus answered and said unto him, Verily, verily, I say unto thee. Except a man be born again, he cannot see the kingdom of God."

William King was survived by only one friend of the early struggles. When Robin Phares was told that "Massa" King was dead, he did not understand. Nor did he understand the executor, John B. Richardson of Valetta, when he stopped at his cabin to tell Robin the terms of Rev. King's will. The first consideration given any inheritors was the assurance that the fifty acres on the 10th Concession would remain Robin's for his lifetime.

Death came peacefully on January 5, 1895, at the age of 83.

No evaluation of William King can be separated from his work. The *Chatham Banner* devoted its front page and most of an inside page to such an evaluation under the black-bordered lines, "A MIGHTY MAN HAS FALLEN," and yet only a eulogy resulted for "One of the truly great men of the age . . . whose name will go down to the ages as one who loved his fellow man."

A similar expression was made by representatives of all the Negroes of Kent County who met on the night of January 10, 1895, in the home of Chatham Alderman Henry Weaver. They adopted a resolution which contains the prediction that "Generations of the future, looking back in perspective upon the work accomplished and for that reason, perhaps, better enabled than we of today to grasp its full significance, must enshrine his name and memory in their hearts, earnestly striving to be true to the principles he so strikingly exemplified in his own pure, christian, philanthropic life. . . ."

But his name did not "go down the ages," nor has his "work accomplished" been looked at in or out of "perspective." Only a comparative handful of Negroes and whites, either living in Kent County today or Buxton descendants in Canada and the United States, are even familiar with his name.

His accomplishments cannot be evaluated numerically. The answer is not in statistics. Nor can it be found in the vol-

William King at 80

umes written by sociologists, anthropologists, geneticists, or psychologists concerned with "the Negro problem." The truth lies in the contrasts, and they exist. King himself was able to realize his own deeds the year before he died. From the pen of the boy he had taught and in whom he had expressed so much pride came a report of the Buxton Settlement as it and Kent County was in 1894. It was written by Dr. Anderson R. Abbott.

> A large number of white settlers now occupy the land, but that makes no difference. The two classes work together on each other's farms, go to the same churches, their children attend the same schools, the teachers are white and coloured, and the pupils fraternize without any friction whatever. The teacher of the North Buxton School, Alfred Shadd, is an Afro-Canadian. He holds a second-class certificate from the normal school, Toronto, and has been a successful teacher for a number of years. One third of his pupils are white. There are three hundred pupils in the schools. The various offices of the municipality, such as councillors, school trustees, path masters, constables and justices of the peace are fairly distributed among both classes. The coloured farmers who now occupy the land are of the best class. Very few of them had any means at first; their only resources were their courage and determination to succeed . . . When they appear in the Chatham market side by side with their white neighbors, as vendors, there is nothing to distinguish but their colour.

Much had been accomplished in the forty-five years since August 10, 1849, when William King stood on the balcony of the Royal Exchange Hotel in Chatham and declared that he would never surrender. The seed he had sown that day has borne fruit through all of Canada, as his missionaries from the Buxton school have spread east and west.

Meanwhile, below the "Line" what had happened? The answer was given in that very same year, 1894, when the grandson of William King's mentor at Coleraine Academy, James Bryce, issued a new edition of *The American Commonwealth.*

> And it must, I fear, be added that in some parts of the South a white man would run little more risk of being hanged for the murder of a Negro than a Mussulman in Turkey for the murder of a Christian . . . No prospect is open to them, whatever wealth or culture they may acquire, of finding an entrance into white society, and they are made to feel in a thousand ways that they belong to a caste condemned to perpetual inferiority . . . The peculiar feature of the race problem as it presents itself in the United States is, that the negroes are in many districts one-third or even one-half of the population, are forced to live in the closest local contiguity with the whites, and are for the purposes of industry indispensable to the latter, yet are so sharply cut off from the whites by colour and all that colour means, that not merely a mingling of blood, but any social approximation, is regarded with horror, and perpetual severance is deemed a law of nature.

The contrast between Canada and the United States still exists. Perhaps it might not if somewhere south of the "Line" there had been a Buxton Settlement to show the way. What then would William King advise today?

Look to the North Star.

☆

INDEX